Women
of Wisdom &
Knowledge

Women of Wisdom & Knowledge

Talks Selected from the BYU Women's Conferences
Edited by Marie Cornwall and Susan Howe

Sheila Olsen • Kate L. Kirkham • Elouise Bell

Francine R. Bennion • Marilyn Arnold • Julia Mavimbela

Tim B. Heaton • Stephen G. Wood • Richard C. Ferre

Carol Cornwall Madsen • Anna Tueller • Catherine Corman Parry

Keith Norman • Ann Finlayson • Eugene England

Marlene W. Owens • Norma B. Ashton • Emma Lou Thayne

Susan Howe • Louise Plummer • Elaine L. Jack

Marian S. Bergin • Allen E. Bergin • Marie Cornwall

Kathleen Bennion Barrett

Deseret Book Company
Salt Lake City, Utah

Library of Congress Cataloging-in-Publication Data

Women of wisdom and knowledge : talks selected from the BYU Women's
    Conferences / edited by Marie Cornwall and Susan Howe.
       p. cm.
    ISBN 0-87579-310-X
    1. Women, Mormon—Religious life—Congresses. I. Cornwall,
Marie, 1949–   . II. Howe, Susan, 1949–   III. Brigham Young
University. IV. BYU Women's Conference.
BX8641.W66   1990
289.3'32'082—dc20   89-49431
                                                                CIP

Printed in the United States of America

10   9   8   7   6   5   4   3   2

Contents

Contents

Contents

Acknowledgments

This book is the fourth volume of selections from the annual Brigham Young University Women's Conference. It follows *Woman to Woman, A Heritage of Faith,* and *As Women of Faith.* None of these volumes would be possible without the support of the BYU administration and faculty, and the many women and men who plan, organize, and participate in the conference.

Selections in this volume were presented in 1988 and 1989. While it is impossible to acknowledge all who contributed to the planning of these two conferences, thanks must be given to Mary E. Stovall, chair of the 1988 conference and director of the BYU Women's Research Institute at that time, and to Carol Lee Hawkins, chair of the 1989 conference.

We also want to thank the staff of the Women's Research Institute who helped create this volume. Karen Frazier spent many hours in the library checking quotations and citations, Tosha Strickland provided the computer skills needed to produce the manuscript, and Edith Pratt kept the institute functioning while everyone else focused on the book.

Finally, we thank the several authors who were willing to prepare their conference presentations for publication.

Marie Cornwall and
Susan Howe

Introduction

*Let's not talk about women's "role,"
but instead let us talk about the importance of parenting, community
service, scholarship, and leadership.
Let's talk about who women are and
what their experience is.*

— MARIE CORNWALL

Introduction

*N*ot long ago I sat at a banquet table with members of The Church of Jesus Christ of Latter-day Saints whom I did not know. The topic of conversation turned to women and their experience in the Church. Two questions were raised that night that I would like to address.

First, why do women come together for women's conferences when men don't come together for men's conferences? My answer to that question is, simply, because women want to. Women want to meet together to talk about their lives and how to respond to the challenges and problems they face. I don't think we need to justify our interest in women's conferences; they are simply something we enjoy. When it becomes important to men to have the opportunity to meet together to talk about their common experiences, the challenges of fatherhood, the role of men in society, or just to be with fathers and brothers and friends, they will organize and hold men's conferences. In the meantime, Brigham Young University will continue to invite members of the Church, both women and men, to the BYU Women's Conference.

The second question is a little more difficult to answer. One man, a bishop, who was concerned about the experience of women in his ward but puzzled by their many different responses to the Church, asked, "What is it that Mormon women want?" That question cannot really be answered by me or by anyone else because women are individuals. Their lives and circumstances are different; their needs and desires are different. But perhaps that by itself is the answer. My preference

Marie Cornwall is an assistant professor of sociology and the director of the Women's Research Institute at Brigham Young University. She received her doctor of philosophy degree from the University of Minnesota. Her research has focused on faith development in adolescents and adults.

is to be recognized as an individual—not as a member of a category. I would rather be known as someone who loves dogs and kids and hikes in the mountains than as a single Mormon woman, a sociologist, or a BYU faculty member. The former description is much more central to who I am than the latter.

By the same token, I grow tired of our constant attention to the "role of women in society." It is the singular *role* that bothers me. If I could draw, I would create a cartoon. In the first frame I would picture women in a demonstration kitchen much like the kitchens we have in the Home Economics Department at BYU. The instructor has just demonstrated how to roll a little piece of dough. She has placed it carefully in the center of her table. In the next frame we see the same roll several minutes later. It has grown in size to where it appears to be just right for baking. Then in the next frame, the instructor and other women in the kitchen look with amazed faces at the same roll, which has risen far more than it normally should. And in the final frame we see the women fleeing before an overgrown, enormous roll, which is about to devour them. That is the "role" of woman.

Actually, it is my understanding that rolls come by the dozen, and if you buy a whole dozen at a time, you get a better bargain. Not only that, but in any given dozen you can find wheat, rye, or sourdough rolls, crescent rolls or parkerhouse rolls. And if you really want to get complex, these days you can buy twelve-grain rolls, and if you buy a baker's dozen, you actually get thirteen rolls instead of twelve. So let's not talk about women's "role," but instead let us talk about the importance of parenting, community service, scholarship, and leadership. Let's talk about who women are and what their experience is. And then we won't need to worry about what it is that women want, because we will be better able to accommodate the individual woman who is Relief Society president or wife or social worker or scientist or mother or PTA president.

As I think about the diversity of women's lives, I recall a conversation I had last fall with a woman in Cache Valley, Utah, where I had been asked to speak at a conference for the single sisters of the stake. She was to introduce me. As I told her a little about my experiences, she shook her head and with a quiet sigh said, "I've got to do something with my life." Later I asked her to tell me a little about herself. She said that she had cared for her younger brothers and sisters after the death of her parents and that she currently worked at Thiokol. I asked what she did there. She was employed as a technician, helping to test equipment to be used in the space program. I said to her, "It sounds to me like you are involved in the space program. You're making the dreams of tomorrow possible, and you say you have to do something with your life? What exactly did you have in mind?"

Shortly thereafter, I talked briefly with my cousin Diane, who had just turned forty. That is an event soon to come for me, and we were discussing her experience. She told me she had cried all morning. When I asked why, she replied, "Because I haven't done anything."

"But, Diane," I said, "You are the mother of eight children, and you feel you haven't done anything?"

"Anyone can have children," she replied.

"That's not true, Diane," I said. "Would you like me to give you a list of the women I know who can't have children, or can't have as many as they wish?"

Sisters, let's stop having these conversations. Let's stop saying to each other, "Your life is better than mine." In Doctrine and Covenants 19:25, the Lord declares, "I command thee that thou shalt not covet thy neighbor's wife; nor seek thy neighbor's life." I have always thought these commands referred to adultery or murder, but think about the way that second statement is phrased in the context of the first. Do you *covet* your neighbor's life?

People frequently tell me that my life seems so exciting and interesting. It is, sometimes, but if my private struggles were as readily apparent as are my public accomplishments, I doubt that anyone would want to trade places with me. Sisters, do not covet your neighbor's life. You may want what appear to be her special blessings and opportunities; but life is a package deal, and it is not likely that you would be so covetous of her difficulties if you really understood them.

There is another question I would like to address. It is what I call the gender question. The gender question takes many forms, but generally it asks, "What is the experience of women in this area?" or "How would we understand things differently if we compared the experience of women with the experience of men?" Why do we need scholarly research that asks the gender question?

Let us begin with history. For a number of years Jill Mulvay Derr, Carol Cornwall Madsen, Maureen Ursenbach Beecher, and others have worked to create a history of the women of the Church. Did you know, for example, that for many years it was deemed the responsibility of LDS pioneer women to care for and to heal the sick? They accomplished this task by educating one another about effective medicines and herbs and by administering to and praying for the sick. My own great-grandmother was told in a patriarchal blessing, "Thy mind shall expand, wisdom shall be given thee, and thou shalt counsel in righteousness among thy sex and in thy habitation. Thou shalt be enabled through prayer and faith to heal the sick of thy family and hold the adversary at bay that health and peace may reign in thy dwelling."[1] What a great heritage we have. Do you know the history of Mormon women? Do you make sure your sons and daughters learn about the accomplishments of grandmothers as well as grandfathers? My Grandmother McAllister made fine quilts and grew the most beautiful roses in all of Mill Creek. My Grandmother Cornwall raised chickens and sold the eggs to support two sons and two daughters in the mission field. If we do not seek out and discover the history of women, we have only remembered half the story. Do we want future generations of women to have only half the story, to wonder as we do now about Nephi's sisters, about the women who followed Alma to the Waters of Mormon?

We must be assured that when the history of South Africa is written, that the story of Julia Mavimbela is told—a story about an unassuming woman who taught the children to plant seeds, to begin to build again in a country where difficulty and strife had already destroyed too many lives. And when the story of the Church in South Africa is written, we must be assured that the story of Julia Mavimbela is told — a story about a woman who dedicated her life to bringing the restored gospel of Jesus Christ to the people of Soweto.

What about the gender question when studying film or poetry or literary criticism? Do male writers portray women and women's lives accurately? Do male critics judge women too harshly and misunderstand the intent of their work? Do we stand by and allow male critics to judge the poetry of Emily Dickinson with observations such as "the woman poet as a type . . . makes flights into nature rather too easily and upon errands which do not have metaphysical importance enough to justify so radical a strategy"?[2] Don't men and women learn more about our own humanity when they read the writings of both men and women and come to understand both the common and the unique approaches of diverse authors?

And what about the gender question in psychology? Psychologists have begun to realize that theories of individual development are based primarily on the experience of men, not on the experience of women. Let me demonstrate what we learn when we ask the gender question when studying human development. A description of healthy teenaged boys with well-developed identities suggests they are "oriented toward personal success and greater self-differentiation. . . . Active, growing youths who are exploring a variety of possibilities, . . . [they] express the spirit of what they would like 'to be' . . . rather than what they want 'to have'. . . . [They have a] recognition and tolerance of variation among people . . . [which] allow[s] themselves to grow in their own direction."[3]

The tendency has been to ask why girls don't seem to be so self-sufficient, autonomous, and independent. But listen to the same psychologist describe healthy teenaged girls with well-developed identities: "they are the most articulate and the least self-conscious; . . . these are serious girls . . . who take themselves seriously. . . . They are engaged in a process of valuing themselves for the kind of people they are. They are . . . attempting to discover who they are and who they want to be

7

in relation to the significant others in their lives. . . . Their girl friends matter to them as people. . . . Friends are to listen to you, to share things with, and . . . to be partners in identity testing."[4]

The psychologists who did this study concluded "the single most predominant and recurrent difference found between girls and boys at this age is that girls have a far greater interpersonal focus, while the boys' identity rests more directly on their development of autonomy. . . . Interpersonal ties serve not only as a vehicle for exploration of the girl's emerging sexual nature but also as a means of defining her individuality and goals."[5]

When one asks the gender question in psychology, one soon discovers that there are a variety of ways in which people develop and that the uniqueness of female development is a wonder to behold, not something that needs to be remolded so that it is consistent with male-defined models of how individuals should develop.

When sociologists recently asked the gender question, they found very interesting differences between the relationships boys form and the relationships girls form. In a large-scale study of the social networks of girls and boys in seventh through tenth grades, researchers found that four out of every ten girls surveyed selected a same-sex friend as the most significant other in their life. By comparison, only two of every ten boys did so. Boys reported about the same level of intimacy with mothers, fathers, and same-sex friends, while girls reported much higher levels of intimacy with their same-sex friend than with mother and father.[6] How can scholars ever come to understand the complexity of social institutions without asking the gender question?

If asking the gender question provides us with additional insights in the academic world, how much more important it is that we ask the gender question in our religious communities. Perhaps we will understand what Mormon women want when we better understand how the experiences of women and men differ in the Church.

The diversity of the BYU Women's Conferences is represented in the selections we have included in this volume. Women and men come to the women's conference with many questions for which they are seeking answers. But answers do not always come easily, because the questions are often complex. This modern world presents women with many options, and the choices are often difficult. Fortunately, the answers and the choices do not have to be the same for all women. But that means finding the answers and making the right choices are even more difficult for any one person.

The theme of the 1989 BYU Women's Conference, taken from Isaiah 33:6, was, "Wisdom and knowledge shall be the stability of thy times." Seeking wisdom and knowledge requires that we fearlessly ask searching and challenging questions and that we not be afraid of the answers we might discover. The selections we have included in this volume represent some of the important ideas expressed during the 1988 and 1989 conferences. It is likely that they will not provide simple or clearcut answers, but they will certainly provide insights and perspectives that will guide you in your own search for wisdom and knowledge.

Notes

1. A blessing given by John Smith, patriarch, upon the head of Charlotte Cornwall, daughter of John and Sarah Carter, born in Hampstead, Berkshire, England, June 21, 1840. Blessing no. 376, Salt Lake City, Oct. 27, 1882.
2. John Crowe Ransom, quoted in Alicia Suskin Ostriker, *Stealing the Language: The Emergence of Women's Poetry in America* (Boston: Beacon Press, 1986), p. 5.
3. Ruthellen Josselson, Ellen Greenberger, and Daniel McConochie, "Phenomenological Aspects of Psychosocial Maturity in Adolescence. Part I. Boys," *Journal of Youth and Adolescence,* vol. 6, no. 1 (1977), pp. 41–42.
4. Ruthellen Josselson, Ellen Greenberger, and Daniel McConochie, "Phenomenological Aspects of Psychosocial Maturity in Adolescence. Part II. Girls," *Journal of Youth and Adolescence,* vol. 6, no. 2 (1977), p. 159.
5. Ibid., p. 162.
6. Dale A. Blyth and Frederick S. Foster-Clark, "Gender Differences in Perceived Intimacy with Different Members of Adolescents' Social Networks," *Sex Roles,* vol. 17, nos. 11/12 (1987), pp. 689–718.

Women's Lives

Today, some women become confused — and even feel guilty — if their life pattern is not like that of the majority. Yet there is no royal road to exaltation. Many divergent paths lead back to Heavenly Father's kingdom. Whatever our circumstances, we must learn the lessons of life.

— NORMA B. ASHTON

The Touch

NORMA B. ASHTON

We are so much like violins
Frames, with sensitive strings
The touch of the hand
That holds the bow
Determines the music it brings.[1]
　　　　—Edna Machesny

*I*n this large audience are sisters who have many, many kinds of challenges. There are widows, divorcees, women who are unmarried and married women who have been unable to have children. Some women are married to husbands who have strayed, who are inactive or are so involved with their professions that the family sees too little of them; some women are working with rebellious children, and others with handicapped children. And there may even be a few women who have almost perfect mates and super children. Probably there are some who suffer from a low self-image, and yet others who are comfortable with who they are and what they can do.

We all have sensitive strings, like the violin, but oh, how different is the touch of our hands holding the bow, and what

Norma B. Ashton, homemaker and civic leader, was graduated magna cum laude from the University of Utah with a bachelor of science degree in education. For several years she served on the Relief Society General Board and has held many leadership and teaching positions in stake and ward Relief Society and Young Women organizations. Her community activities include PTA, Pink Lady volunteer, and community drives chairman. At present she is a member of the Intermountain Health Care board of trustees and is vice-chairman of the Cottonwood Hospital board of trustees. She has traveled worldwide with her husband, Marvin J. Ashton. They have four children and eighteen grandchildren.

13

different music comes into our lives. Wouldn't it be boring if we all played the same melody? Would there be opportunities to grow, to develop individual talents and character if each of us experienced the same challenges? Confucius said, "Seek not every quality in one individual."

Often we have heard: "For all have not every gift given unto them; for there are many gifts, and to every man is given a gift by the Spirit of God. To some is given one, and to some is given another, that all may be profited thereby." (D&C 46:11–12.) All of us have been given blessings and gifts. The programs of the Church offer innumerable opportunities to develop our talents. William George Jordan once said, "Man has two creators: his god and himself."[2] With the package of blessings and gifts life hands each of us, we have the opportunity to meet challenges and shape our own destiny, knowing full well that divine help is waiting if we will but ask.

Some words from Joseph Smith give us specifications to follow: "Happiness is the object and design of our existence, and will be the end thereof, if we pursue the path that leads to it; and this path is virtue, uprightness, faithfulness, holiness, and keeping the commandments of God."[3] Yet we are also told, "In the world ye shall have tribulations." (John 16:33.) So if happiness is the design of our existence, yet—as we can all testify—we shall have tribulations, how do we walk through the maze of life?

Lowell Bennion has said, "Be not defeated twice, once by circumstances and once by oneself."[4] In other words, don't yield to the temptation to feel sorry for yourself or to blame yourself for the circumstances in which you find yourself.

Self-condemnation has a paralyzing potion in it. We stagnate when we agonize over what we might have been or what we might have done. Patti Perfect[5] has had a lot of publicity and has fallen out of grace lately. She is the woman who seems to be able to do everything well but then has a nervous breakdown brought on by guilt and her fears that she isn't doing enough. In *East of Eden* John Steinbeck wrote of one of the characters that when she knew she didn't have to be perfect,

14

she could be good.[6] Sisters, we can be good without being perfect.

I am concerned about the damage that guilt can bring into women's lives. So many voices call. So many demands are made. When we can't answer all the calls or finish all the projects, how can we avoid that monster guilt? This little couplet written by Gaile Cook gives sage advice:

> I'll be content if I can just learn
> Which bridges to cross and which to burn.

I can't tell you which to burn. Only you can set your priorities. You have the right and the gift of personal revelation to help you make those decisions. But, I plead, when you have to decide between two right choices, between two worthy activities, wipe guilt feelings totally away.

You can't be two places at once, so if you decide to conduct a PTA meeting because you are the president and have to miss a leadership meeting, don't feel guilty when someone at church says, "Where were you last night?" Or maybe your husband unexpectedly asks you to go on a short trip with him, and you have a bushel of apricots that should be bottled. Can you give the fruit away and not feel guilty later when a neighbor calls you over to see her shining rows of newly canned fruit? When you choose between two rights, leave guilt feelings for Satan to use on someone else.

Know that you don't have to be perfect. Contrary to opinion, we are not expected to achieve perfection in this life but rather to make steady progress towards it. We are masochists, sometimes. For example, I overeat one time and think, That's it. I've blown it. No reason to stay on the diet now. Sometimes we withdraw too readily from other challenges as well. If we have been impatient with our children or if we arrive late to church, during Relief Society we feel we'll never be able to measure up to everything we're told to do. So, in effect, we give up, because in the back of our minds we think, I can't do all of this so I'm a failure. Again, such a thought pattern is a clever and successful tool of the adversary. We must keep trying but be able to forgive ourselves when we can't do it all and then get on with life.

In Romans 14:22 the Apostle Paul makes this wise statement: "Hast thou faith? have it to thyself before God. Happy is he that condemneth not himself in that thing which he alloweth." After the fact, we can't give too much heed to what might have been. Such regrets can actually get in the way of what still can be. We want to learn from the past, but we don't want to carry it around like a monkey on our backs. We must make do with the present and look forward.

In the *Church News* of February 6, 1988, there was a story about Sister Lenore Kimball Nitsch, who is paralyzed from her waist down. For forty-five years she has been the chief receptionist at Welfare Square. She has greeted the leaders of many countries, heads of universities, and government officials. Elder Glen L. Rudd said of her, "There is something deeply spiritual about her that radiates over the telephone and when people meet her in person. People from all over the world have visited Welfare Square; they have felt from her everything the Church represents. You don't meet her without receiving a spiritual lift. She is a star."[7]

Yet Sister Nitsch has known many kinds of trauma. At birth she had spina bifida and was not expected to live. She did not attend school because of her disability; her older sister taught her to read. Her formal education began at age twenty. Her only Church experience came during her frequent stays in the Primary Children's Hospital.

When she came to Salt Lake City to attend the marriage of her sister, she was determined to be independent and refused to go home to California. She began job hunting. Disabled and uneducated, she was turned down time and time again. Someone in the employment offices finally said, "If she has determination enough to keep coming, I'll find something for her or die trying." Soon she was called for an interview at Welfare Square and hired. So for forty-five years she has brought her radiant spirituality to her job. She taught Sunday School for twenty-five years, wrote ten road shows, and cared for a sick sister. She sustained herself with pride and dignity. She nourished herself and then nourished others with her faith.[8]

We learn from Sister Nitsch about another needful trait. She lived by the counsel from James 2:14: "What doth it profit, my brethren, though a man say he hath faith, and have not works? can faith save him?" As we nourish ourselves in faith, we must also anxiously work at growing and learning.

Regardless of the circumstances in which we find ourselves, the way we face life is in our own hands. Bobby Jones, one of the great golfers of all time, was asked to what he attributed his greatness. He answered, "I have learned to hit the ball where it lies." His advice seems simple. But sometimes it is difficult to start from where we are and go on from there. Some of us may spend so much time wishing that our golf ball were on a nice smooth patch of grass instead of out in the rough behind a tree that we forget to finish the game.

As best you can, work at solving your problems, and if you have chosen between two rights, don't beat yourself over the head. C. Kay Allen has written, "One of the hard facts of life is that self-esteem comes from your ability to solve problems, not from sympathy, not from realizing that life has handed you a raw deal, and not from blaming your parents or teachers or employer. If you can't solve problems and deal with conflict, your self-esteem is going to stay low."[9]

How can we solve our problems? I'm sure there are as many methods as there are challenges in life. Each of us has different obstacles. We learn in Romans 14:22, "Happy is he that condemneth not himself in that thing which he alloweth." Condemnation of self prevents us from moving forward.

As I was visiting with a friend who is divorced, I asked her what advice she might have for others in a similar situation. "First," she said, "never give up. There is a light at the end of the tunnel. This too will pass. If you look for it, there is always a glimmer of hope. There is no divorce without hurt. Your earning power is limited. Widows get a lot of sympathy, but divorcees don't get much attention." A bishopric member helped her, and she found some support from singles' groups, but her greatest help came from a source available to all of us. She said, "I came to realize that I was entitled to answers from God about my problems if I were in tune. I prayed a lot. You don't know how much I prayed. When I started asking, I realized I was getting help with my problems." Her advice is applicable to most of our challenges in life. There are good times and bad times. Sometimes the path of life is easy, and at other times all obstacles hedge up our way, but we can all pray.

Patience is another helpful ingredient. Paul advised us, "And let us run with patience the race that is set before us." (Hebrews 12:1.) When the American hostages came home after 444 days of awful captivity in Iran, I remember what Bruce Langland, the spokesman for the captives, said when he was asked how he was able to endure it all. He told how a friend had slipped a tiny piece of paper into his hand. On it these words were written: "Patience is a bitter cup from which only the strong can drink." He kept these words firmly entrenched in his mind, and they helped him through those dark days. He knew he had to have patience to be strong.

As God helps us and as we help ourselves, the obstacles that come into our lives can be overcome. Optimism, prayer, and patience are important ingredients. My husband has helped many people with these words: "No one is a failure until he stops trying. The direction in which one is headed is what is important." Dr. Brent Barlow has these words printed on his business card: "What we are is more important than what we have been. And what we can become is more important than what we are."[10] As women in the Church, we have vital roles to fill. Motherhood can never be diminished. Generations to come will be influenced by mothers who nurture, teach, and produce honest, good, faithful sons and daughters. Many in the world today tend to look down at mothers and suggest that only those not smart or motivated enough to work stay home. But that's just not true. It is a clever ploy of the adversary to try to persuade women that their God-given role is somehow lesser or unimportant. Yet motherhood takes so many twists and turns these days. Very few women go through life with only the traditional parental challenges of colic, teen rebellion, and a few fender benders.

There is no "typical" living situation. No one lives a "normal" life, even though we all think there is such a thing and then compare our lives against this imaginary normalcy we have created in our minds. But our own lives always come up short, because we're comparing our actual experiences with a utopia that doesn't exist. I hope that we as women will stop comparing our lives to an imaginary perfection.

Single parents are becoming more prevalent, and their challenges more demanding. But from time immemorial great people have come from single-parent homes. Children can develop hope, courage, and faith if their mother displays those qualities herself. She becomes a role model, teaching by example to help her children progress. Testimonies are gained by various means. What matters is that spiritual growth goes on and on during life, regardless of the path life takes.

Today, some women become confused—and even feel guilty—if their life pattern is not like that of the majority. Yet there is no royal road to exaltation. Many divergent paths lead back to Heavenly Father's kingdom. Whatever our circumstances, we must learn the lessons of life. Our challenge is to learn and not be defeated by the package life hands us or by our attitude about that package. Remember Lowell Bennion's words, "Be not defeated twice, once by circumstances and once by oneself." Isaiah promises, "They that wait upon the Lord shall renew their strength." (Isaiah 40:31.)

I cried out for help as I prepared to come before you. I felt so inadequate. I haven't been divorced or widowed. I have a faithful husband, and I have experienced motherhood. I asked many questions, read a lot, and prayed often. One day as I was struggling, I felt as if Heavenly Father were saying, "You may not know what many sisters face. Nor do they know altogether what others have to face, but I know. Don't let them forget that their Heavenly Father knows." What can be more comforting than to realize that our Father knows and will help? Yet we have all found out that He helps the most after we have helped ourselves all we can.

I have often quoted Sister Camilla Kimball's words delivered at the Paris Area Conference:

"I would hope that every girl and woman here has the desire and ambition to qualify in two vocations — that of homemaking and that of preparing to earn a living outside the home, if and when the occasion requires. An unmarried woman is always happier if she has a vocation in which she can be socially of service and financially independent. . . . Any married woman may become a widow without warning. Property may vanish as readily as a husband may die. Thus, any woman may be under the necessity of earning her own living and helping to support dependent children. If she has been trained for the duties and the emergencies of life which may come to her, she will be much happier and have a greater sense of security."[11]

Not only do we need temporal preparation but we also need spiritual strength. There are no priesthood role models in many homes. Stories of spiritual power exercised by women of faith filter through Church history, are expressed in missionary testimonies, and are retold over the back fence. Our faith is nourished as we learn to fortify ourselves with the basic principles of the gospel of Jesus Christ.

I learned an important lesson in reading President Ezra Taft Benson's biography, by Sheri Dew. She reported an incident concerning his great-grandparents. Pamelia was interested in the Church and got her husband E. T. Benson to go with her to sacrament meeting. A dispute arose between two individuals who were administering the sacrament. Harsh words were spoken. Pamelia was worried about the effects the dispute would have on her companion. She asked him what he thought of it all. "He replied that he couldn't imagine the actions of its members altering the truth of Mormonism."[12] To me that philosophy is one we should all internalize. The truths of the gospel of Jesus Christ can never be altered by the actions of imperfect people. When the truths our Savior teaches become firmly entrenched in our very soul, we will become women of unshakable faith and not lose our testimonies as we observe human weaknesses in those around us.

What different specifications we all have for our life's journey! And though our goals seem similar (to gain exaltation), the Builder uses very different blueprints to help us build our mansions on high.

Jeannie McAllister is a single Latter-day Saint woman who has a deep conviction of eternal marriage and family. She has wondered how she fits in. In a chapter of the book *A Singular Life* she describes her struggle to understand and deal with her circumstances. She says that the words of Viktor E. Frankl helped her realize that "Why am I in this situation?" is the wrong question to ask. "Speaking of the horrors of life in a concentration camp, Frankl says: 'We had to learn . . . that it did not really matter what we expected from life, but rather what life expected from us. We needed to stop asking about the meaning of life, and instead to think of ourselves as those who were being questioned by life—daily and hourly.' (*Man's Search for Meaning: An Introduction to Logotherapy* [New York: Pocketbooks, 1963], p. 122.)"

Sister McAllister goes on to say: "As a single woman, whenever I have replaced the question 'Why is this experience happening to me?' with the question 'What does this situation require of me?' I have discovered specific actions, the doing of which has prevented my derailment and kept me pushing along the path, even in darkness. Unmet expectations may be bitter, but I want to be better for my experiences. . . . Asking 'What does this situation require of me?' helps me see that I can make choices. I can control my life, even if that control extends only as far as my perceptions and attitudes."[13]

When we feel fatigue and discouragement, we still have the promise that God can make weak things become strong.

Belle Spafford, former general president of the Relief Society, gave comfort and guidance to another single sister with these words:

"The only thing that is important in this life is that you endeavor to make your contributions of the highest quality. If you will do that, you will fulfill your destiny, and you will realize the blessings of eternity. . . . This is a new day and a new age where we need strong, available, capable, righteous women to carry our womanhood so that extremists will not run away with it."[14]

From another very talented and accomplished friend, Sheri Dew, I was given this insight: "I think it is interesting that in our society we tend to categorize each other primarily according to marital status, when that is only *one* distinguishing factor. Regardless of which group we fall into, we tend to think we have the hardest set of circumstances with which to deal. We may tell ourselves that no one else can really understand how difficult life is for us—that no one who lives in one of the other 'categories' can possibly have as hard a 'row to hoe' as we do. But, in fact, we all have challenges, we all face disappointments, we all feel sorrow and pain.

"The real challenge, I think, is to not focus so intensely on marital status and thereby divide us into little groups but to learn as women how many things we have in common. When all is said and done, what we must do is work to sink our spiritual roots deep—deep enough that when the winds of life blow (as they most certainly will) we'll be prepared to face them and to give the kind of nurturing strength our sex is known for. I know that I much prefer to be thought of as an LDS woman rather than as a single LDS woman."[15]

These words of advice are applicable to all of us. The young mother who feels that the days of diapers and dishes will never end, the single woman trying to find her niche, the middle-aged woman with wrinkles and arthritis starting to appear, and the older woman who wonders where she fits in, all need to ask, "What does this situation require of me?" Then we can choose a course of action and pray for strength and faith to find joy promised to us wherever we find ourselves on the path of life. When we accept our own situations, we can give a helping hand to those around us.

President David O. McKay wrote, "Our lives are wrapped up with the lives of others and we are the happiest when we contribute to their happiness."[16] Christ admonishes us, "When thou art converted, strengthen thy brethren." (Luke 22:32.) We are challenged to strengthen ourselves in the faith and then strengthen others.

I suspect that those two admonitions run concurrently. It seems to me that whoever helps a sister grows stronger herself, whoever teaches a lesson is a greater learner than her students, whoever gives service to another is the recipient of increased love. Nevertheless, we do need to be aware that with us always are those who need a helping hand, who need to feel noticed and accepted and loved.

One winter Sabbath my husband and I were attending a stake conference. As often happens, a member of the stake presidency took Elder Ashton in to greet the Primary children, who were meeting separately. He spoke to them briefly, patted the heads of a few children sitting close to him, and left to join the main body of the conference. As the two men were walking down the hall, they heard the running of small feet and a voice calling, "Elder Ashton." Marv stopped, waited for a little boy to catch up to him, and asked, "What can I do for you?" Looking up with hurt in his eyes, the young lad said, "You didn't pat my head." Marv gave the young man an extra pat or two, ruffled his blond hair a bit, and was rewarded as the Primary child smiled and ran back to his class. Only a pat on the head, but just what this child needed. He was assured that he was as important as those on the front row.

It seems to me that one of our important roles as daughters of God is to be givers of pats. The touch of a hand, a word of appreciation, or an expression of love — as small as these things seem to be, they can help people reach their potential. Our little day-to-day acts of love and positive encouragement water spiritual seeds and help them grow in all of us. By showing our love to others, we give them added hope that they are loved by Christ. And if we show our love for the word of God, perhaps others will experiment with the Word and believe enough to plant the seed of faith in their lives.

It is true that we are encouraged to plant our own seeds of faith in fertile soil and keep them well watered and nourished, but none of us does that task completely alone. In addition to the women and men of the scriptures, great women and men in our lives have pulled some of the weeds from around our seeds and handed us watering cans to revive wilting plants. As sisters in God's kingdom we can, and are obligated to, nourish each other in the faith.

This assignment needn't be overwhelming. I'm reminded of a couple we met who had lived most of their lives on the East Coast. Missionaries had given them the lessons a few times but had never been able to baptize them. When our paths crossed, they were living in Idaho and had just come into the Church. As we heard their story, we asked what changed their minds about baptism. "The quiet living of the gospel by our next-door neighbors," they replied. "We wanted what they had."

The wife had a deep love for music and musical talent she hadn't developed since her school years. Her first assignment was to direct the music for Relief Society, and she was thrilled about her calling. I stopped to think how some of us react to a call. Have you ever said, "Oh no—not that job." Sometimes it takes a person with a new perspective to help us realize that Church calls are more than "just a job." God helps us develop our talents, which strengthen not only ourselves but others as we share our God-given gifts and take part in the programs the Church offers.

Throughout the world, excited sisters two by two or older couples with a sparkle in their eyes are stalwarts in the mission fields. How mission presidents plead, "Send us more couples." Most live in circumstances much less comfortable than they had at home, but they are sharing talents developed through a lifetime of living the gospel. They nourish the faith of all whose lives they touch. They are eager to tell us of their wonderful experiences. They share their talents, as President Spencer W. Kimball counseled: "Our great need, and our great calling, is to bring to the people of this world the candle of understanding to light their way out of obscurity and darkness and into the joy, peace, and truths of the gospel."[17] Our missionaries are bringing that candle to many all over the world.

Examples of courage and faith strengthen all of us. A few weeks ago we sat at a luncheon with a couple who were on their way to the Gilbert Islands to fill their second mission. Their dedication and enthusiasm were very evident, even

24

though they knew of the "less than comfortable" living conditions they would find there. Only as we parted did we learn that just a week and a half earlier they had lost a son to leukemia. Tears glistened in the father's eyes as he told us about this outstanding young man. My faith was strengthened by their courage.

If we can live gospel principles with quiet dignity, we can be an influence for good among all people. Sister Belle Spafford, after at first being shunned by the National Council of Women, went on to serve as their president for two terms. She said, "In my experience in working with non–Latter-day Saint women, in the main women of good conscience but living by man-defined rather than God-revealed truths, I have countless times had to call upon all the courage I possessed in order to stand firm for what I knew to be right. In doing so, I have never once lost a friend — temporarily perhaps, but never permanently."[18] She respected the beliefs and points of view of her associates in that organization, but in no wise adopted them if they ran counter to what she believed. Yet she became one of the most highly esteemed members. They created new jobs to keep her on their executive board.

Edward Markham's poem "A Creed" describes the results of nourishing those around us:

> There is a destiny that makes us brothers.
> None goes his way alone.
> All that we send into the lives of others
> Comes back into our own.[19]

Alan Loy McGinnes says it this way: "Self-confidence, like happiness, is slippery when we reach out to grasp it for its own sake. Usually it comes as a by-product. We lose ourselves in service or work, friendship or love, and suddenly one day we realize we are confident and happy."[20]

As Seneca wrote: "Soil, no matter how rich, could not be productive without cultivation, and neither could our minds." And neither can our faith. Day by day, week by week, month by month, we must nourish our faith and the faith of those with whom we associate. It is in this process of learning how to sink our spiritual roots deep and anchor them in the Savior and His message — and then in helping those within our sphere of influence to do likewise — that all women share common ground. We have many programs in which we may take part. We may think we are helping the bishop or even the Lord, but every time we participate, we are the ones who benefit.

Challenges are ever present. But always when we have done our best, the helping hand of the Lord is reaching out for us to grasp. How grateful I am to live in this time when the gospel is here on earth to point us in the right direction.

Regardless of where we are in the special world of women, we can handle our problems with wisdom and dignity by combining faith and works. Alma reconfirms this point with this counsel: "Whosoever shall put their trust in God shall be supported in their trials, and their troubles, and their afflictions, and shall be lifted up in the last day." (Alma 36:3.)

To recall the poem with which I began:

> We are so much like violins
> Frames, with sensitive strings
> The touch of the hand
> That holds the bow
> Determines the music it brings.

May the notes each of us plays be written on the staff of the gospel of Jesus Christ. In the eyes of God, nobody is a nobody. Each of us possesses gifts that make her distinct. We can recognize these qualities and develop them by working diligently, by using the opportunities offered by the Church, and by exercising patience and faith.

The gospel of Jesus Christ is true and is our guiding light.

Notes

1. Edna Machesny, "Different Strokes," *Good Housekeeping,* Feb. 1988, p. 206.
2. William George Jordan, *The Kingship of Self-Control* (New York: Fleming H. Revell Co., 1899), p. 7.

3. Joseph Smith, *History of the Church*, ed. B.H. Roberts, 2d ed. rev. (Salt Lake City: Deseret Book Co., 1949), 5:134–35.

4. Lowell L. Bennion, *Jesus the Master* (Salt Lake City: Deseret Book Co., 1980), p. 11.

5. Margaret B. Black and Midge W. Nielson, "Patti Perfect," *Exponent II*, vol. 10, no. 2 (Winter 1984), p. 13.

6. John Steinbeck, *East of Eden* (New York: Bantam Books, 1955), p. 670.

7. Quoted in John Hart, "45 Years at Welfare Square: She Greeted Presidents, Rulers," *Church News*, Feb. 6, 1988, p. 6.

8. Ibid., pp. 6–12.

9. C. Kay Allen, "Where Self-Esteem Starts," *Ensign*, Feb. 1979, p. 61.

10. Brent Barlow, "Focus on What You Can Become," *Deseret News*, 31 Dec. 1987–1 Jan. 1988, p. 2c.

11. Camilla Kimball, "A Woman's Preparation," *Ensign*, Mar. 1977, p. 59.

12. Sheri L. Dew, *Ezra Taft Benson, a Biography* (Salt Lake City: Deseret Book, 1987), p. 4.

13. Jeannie McAllister, "What Does This Situation Require?" in *A Singular Life: Perspectives on Being Single by Sixteen Latter-day Saint Women*, ed. Carol L. Clark and Blythe Darlyn Thatcher (Salt Lake City: Deseret Book Co., 1987), pp. 2–3.

14. Quoted in Cheryl Ballard, "Bright Stars," in *A Singular Life*, ed. Clark and Thatcher, p. 29.

15. Personal interview, Feb. 1988.

16. David O. McKay, in Conference Report, Sept–Oct. 1950, p. 112.

17. Spencer W. Kimball, "Are We Doing All We Can?" *Ensign*, Feb. 1983, p. 5.

18. Belle S. Spafford, "Horizons as They Affect the Latter-day Youth," address given at the Institute of Religion, Weber State College, Feb. 2, 1973, p. 15.

19. As quoted in David O. McKay, *Pathways to Happiness* (Salt Lake City: Bookcraft, 1957), p. 272.

20. Alan Loy McGinnis, *Confidence: How to Succeed At Being Yourself* (Minneapolis: Augsburg, 1987).

Waiting in Stillness

ANNA TUELLER

*E*leven years ago this week, I turned twenty-two and faced a crisis of such magnitude that even now I cower at the memory. I was graduating from Brigham Young University in two weeks, and I was unmarried. I notice that you laugh. I suppose that after eleven years, I can almost laugh with you, but it was with no sense of humor or perspective that I faced that particular unknown, and on fast Sunday in April 1978, I left my student apartment determined to find a secluded spot where I could plead, pound, batter at the doors of heaven until I received some guidance. I went to the Joseph Smith Building and wandered for a long time in its labyrinthian hallways. I read recently that the university will be replacing that building because its design is so confusing, but at least for me that day it served as a fitting symbol of my fear, perplexity, and uncertainty. I found an unoccupied room and for several hours pleaded, wept, and prayed, "Tell me what to do. Show me thy will. Make the fear go away. Please make it all better. Send me a man." Somehow, in spite of all my contradictory instructions, I felt the presence of the Spirit very clearly. In fact, its manifestation that day was very tangible. I was enfolded by strong, loving arms and heard or felt a voice that said, "It's going to be okay, Anna." I left that room comforted, energized, and motivated. I sailed through the last two weeks of my college career. In fact, I was notified within days of that bleak Sunday morning that I had received a fellowship for graduate school that would pay all my tuition and living expenses until I completed a Ph.D. During those two weeks, I

Anna Tueller, a high school English teacher, received her bachelor of arts degree from Brigham Young University and her master of arts degree from the University of Virginia. She has taught English for five years in Morocco and Utah, and is now head of the Meridian School, a private school in Provo, Utah.

was also asked to speak at the graduation convocation. The despair of that early Sunday morning disappeared easily and quickly in the midst of these laurels, and I was cocky and confident about my future.

In fact, I remember vividly the day after that graduation ceremony when I went to have all four of my wisdom teeth pulled. (It was what I had asked my parents to give me as a graduation gift.) I would like to attribute my delusions of grandeur that day to the laughing gas that the dentist administered — I couldn't possibly have been that naive — but as I sat in the chair, I confess that I saw the complete blueprint of my life: four years to a Ph.D., fame and fortune through my brilliant and scholarly research, tenure at a prestigious university, years of ease in the ivory tower, secure retirement. Indeed, I thought, it is going to be okay. Do I even need to rehearse the details of my well-deserved comeuppance, after describing the pride that went before the fall? Perhaps it is enough to say that my favorite poem during my graduate years at the University of Virginia was one by Robert Frost, the relevant lines of which are

> No memory of having starred
> Atones for later disregard
> Or keeps the end from being hard.[1]

The voice that whispered, "It's going to be okay," was not, as I had supposed, giving me a road map for my life. It comforted me, motivated me, energized me, and cleared the fog enough so that I could get on with the business of my life, but it was the business of my life, and it was for me to struggle and for me to decide and for me to wrestle with the decision to leave graduate school and to teach high school and to move to Washington, D.C., and then to move to Morocco and then to Boston and then back to Utah and now to . . . well, I keep on wrestling. And it is my salvation that I have to work out with fear and trembling. And during the passage of these eleven years, I have learned some things, I believe, about how the Spirit does not operate in our lives.

29

I have already suggested that the Spirit does not provide detailed instructions of paths to pursue. No matter how many times I read my patriarchal blessing, it does not contain directions to each and every destination, and, believe me, I have searched mine endlessly with all the expertise of an English teacher who can read something into nothing. Will you laugh at me when I confess my latest folly? The paragraph in my patriarchal blessing that promises me an eternal marriage with a righteous husband follows a paragraph that says that children will reach out to me and that I will teach and lead them. You can perhaps imagine how enthusiastically I accepted the calling to be Primary president two years ago; imagine, in turn, my chagrin when I was released from that same calling, only to discover that smooth, elegant transitions aren't any more sacred in patriarchal blessings than they are in my students' papers. Once again, I wanted a road map. I wanted the veil to be lifted, and I wanted to see my life set out before me, clearly defined, neatly arranged, and with no loose ends. How easily I forget that our corporeal existence includes separation from God, that the veil is an inherent part of the plan we joyously accepted, and that, in fact, without this veil to obscure the path back to Him, we would be living a model of existence remarkably similar to one we deemed unacceptable and rejected. If we knew step by step, day by day, there would be no need for faith, no opportunity for growth, no chance for eternal life.

So the Spirit working in our lives is not a road map. Neither is it the host of *Let's Make a Deal*. We do not stand in front of three doors trying to second-guess a divine Master of Ceremonies. We will not be spending eternity with the gaggle of geese that we chose behind Door Number Three instead of with the dream vacation that we did not choose behind Door Number Two. Despite the outlandishness of that example, I think we often conceptualize the Spirit in this way. My younger sister Betsy, who has been home from her mission for about a year, recently repeated a conversation she had with several of her missionary companions. They were talking about marriage and their hopes and fears for the future. Betsy mentioned that she had two older, unmarried sisters, and one of her companions said, "Oh, but you don't need to worry about that; you went on a mission." Betsy is now engaged and will be married on May 12. Did I at some point stand in front of those three doors, choose the wrong one, and now live with my own, particular white elephant? I often feel that way about my life. I have many times microscopically examined my life, looking for that wrong turn that led to what too often appears to be a dead end. But I think I am wrong when I feel that way. In fact, I think it is destructive, dangerous, and damning. First, it ignores the spiritual confirmations that I have sought and received at each junction along the way. Second, it ignores the many promises that assure us that all things work together for good for those who love the Lord. Third, it negates the reality of repentance. I think, however, we are often tempted to try to make deals with the Spirit: "I will read my scriptures, do my genealogy, say my prayers, visit the sick, yea, even go to homemaking meeting and visit teach, and then, then, then I will get rich, get married, get well, get answers." The spirit doesn't deal; it simply waits for us to be able to pray, "Be it unto me according to thy will," not as I so often pray, "Be it unto me according to my will."

So how does the Spirit operate in our lives if it doesn't make deals or hand out road maps? (For I am convinced that we live in a world that is imbued with its power.) If it will not force us back to God, how do we feel its presence? I believe the Spirit cautions, confirms, cajoles, comforts, and cares. (And I am very proud of those alliterations.) How often I have felt the cautions. I call them "stupids of thought." For years I thought Doctrine and Covenants 9 really said "stupid" instead of "stupor," and recently I have decided that it should even if it doesn't. I feel those stupids of thought when the wrongness of a decision is demonstrated by my own lethargy and torpor, when my very inability to get out of my bed and throw away the junk food and the junk novel hints that perhaps movement in the direction I am considering would be wrong. Those moments are in direct contrast to those times when the Spirit confirms, when I have thought my path out in my own mind, earnestly sought for an answer, and reached a decision. On

31

those occasions, lo and behold, I manage to arise from my bed, even make the bed, leave behind the chocolate chip cookie binge, and act. The miracle of that energy and renewal after the sloth, despair, and despondency, I have come to believe, is the Spirit confirming the rightness of the decision. And the Spirit cajoles, teasing our minds, bringing ideas, hints, nudges, incessantly, unceasingly until we no longer ignore and begin to entertain the notion, when an idea just won't leave us alone until we take it seriously. And the Spirit comforts. In fact, above all else, I believe the Spirit is a Comforter. How often the Spirit is there healing the broken-hearted, giving rest to the weary, pushing us up one more mountain until we hit a valley, granting us a lull in the storm until we are ready to face it again with our usual gutsiness and tenacity, dispensing comfort and assurance that all is well, that it is going to be okay. And the Spirit cares, letting us know through a rain-washed spring day, through a speckled sunset, or through the gesture of a grateful student that we matter in this big, silent universe, that we are not alone, that if the journey seems long, it is not forever.

Often along this journey, the Spirit simply convinces us to wait, to be still. I teach a ninth-grade world literature class, and we often discuss journeys in that class. We trace archetypal journeys, those stories found so often in folktales and fairy-tales across the globe, stories of heroes who go out into the world and face dragons and temptations and trials, rescue princesses, descend into the depths of hell to get the silver chalice, and return to the world triumphantly to marry the princess and live happily ever after. I always start this class with *The Odyssey,* and I use Ulysses as the archetypal male hero who has all the exciting trials and adventures in his years of wandering and who then returns home to Ithaca victorious. When I began to teach this course five years ago, I also pointed out the inherent sexism of Western literature because while Ulysses is off adventuring, Penelope is home wasting time waiting until he returns. But my feelings about Penelope have undergone a radical change, and she is now a heroine of mine. Penelope is plagued with many suitors (poor, poor Penelope) who insist that Ulysses is dead and that she consider their proposals. They torment her so and become so rowdy and belligerent that she finally agrees to choose among them, but only after she has finished an elaborate tapestry. She diligently works on the tapestry all day, only to spend all night unraveling that same tapestry. I no longer believe that Penelope was wasting time; she was simply heeding the voice that whispered in the nighttime that her husband was alive and that she must wait. How often I make plans all day, only to unravel them in the silence of the night. How often I have plotted and planned, written resumes, filled out applications, made lists of people to contact, only to undo the plans because in the stillness of the night I have sensed that it is time to wait. Certainly, I believe that we will all have times in our life when we will be Ulysses, whom Tennyson describes as a man who seeks and strives and finds and never yields; we will have times when we flee the Lotus-eaters, combat Cyclops, and fight at the very gates of hell, and we will do all those things heroically, valiantly, strengthened by the Spirit. But there are other times when we are meant to wait, to be patient, to endure, to wonder, to question, to doubt. During those times, too, the Spirit is there, whispering peace, assuring us that it is going to be okay. I know this is true. I promise that it is going to be okay, that if we wait in stillness, we will hear the still, small voice.

Note

1. Robert Frost, "Provide, Provide," *The Poetry of Robert Frost,* ed. Edward Connery Lathem (New York: Holt, Rinehart, and Winston, 1969), p. 307.

Stability in These Times

*O*ur times have been termed "the days of miracle and wonder"[1]: the Concorde crossing the ocean in four hours, artificial organs extending life, communication encircling the globe instantly, vast networks of information storage and retrieval. Such innovations have made the impossible possible. At the same time, they have made our lives more complex: we face a tremendously accelerated pace of life; medical technology has forced us to ask when life should be extended; the constant bombardment of information requires that we process more and often conflicting data. And the complexity goes on and on. Our world is not the same place today that it was last year or even yesterday.

What a change the last two years — or two months — have brought into my life. I never imagined that I would be speaking at a women's conference or that I would be asked to serve in the Young Women General Presidency.

I am a very ordinary woman who has spent much of my life dealing with the day-to-day complications and joys of being a wife and a mother of four sons. Complications like keeping enough milk in the refrigerator; joys like having an even number of socks come out of the dryer. Complications in managing a home with busy high school students and a husband who is

Elaine L. Jack grew up in Cardston, Alberta, Canada, and attended the University of Utah, where she majored in English. It was there she met her husband, Joseph E. Jack. She has served as a ward Young Women president and counselor, as Laurel advisor, and in various Relief Society positions. For eleven years she served as a member of the Relief Society General Board and has served more recently as the second counselor in the Young Women General Presidency. She and her husband lived in New York, Boston, and Sitka, Alaska, before making Utah their home. They are the parents of four sons.

bishop; joys in seeing my sons prepared to serve missions, prepared for life.

In the middle of the mothering phase of my life, however, I was not thinking about issues or forming philosophies. I was just dealing with one day at a time. Many of you are in that stage now. But there is life after sixty. The aging process may bring wrinkles and rigidity, but it also brings time to contemplate. As I get older, I can see how the world has opened up because of many innovations. But it is sometimes hard for me to make the personal changes necessary to take full advantage of them. In my own daily life I am constantly assaulted by so much that is new. I wrote this talk on a typewriter with penciled corrections. I have seen my secretary make the same changes in seconds on a computer. I can see how easy using a computer is, but I still like a pencil. I am hardly used to the idea that a letter can be faxed over the telephone, and it is still embarrassing to be told by a car, "Your brake is on!" even when that information gets me out of a snowdrift.

I am sure you have areas where you are resistant to change, too. I hear similar echoes in our society. The bywords of this time are coping, stress, future shock, megatrends, the lonely crowd. These bywords are daily reminders of our insecurity as we are confronted with change. Why do we resist change? What will give us the confidence necessary to accept change and incorporate that which is good? *Stability.*

As I define stability, it is not inflexibility or resistance to positive change. It does not mean fewer choices or avoiding challenges. Stability is constancy of character or purpose, tenacity, steadfastness, reliability, and dependability. It is a grounding, a rooting, or anchor. Unfortunately, stability seems rarer and rarer as life goes faster and faster. One of the great joys of living now is the opportunity to create stability in our own lives. It can be a happy challenge. I'll share today five anchors that help stabilize my life. They are testimony, relationships with others, charity, progression, and maturity.

Testimony

My testimony developed from an early age. I was blessed to grow up two doors away from my grandparents, who were guided throughout their life by impressions that I know came from simple, righteous living and complete faith. Their belief in the tenets of the gospel was so internalized that it was the foremost consideration in all circumstances, whether in giving a healing blessing to a sick child, abandoning insurance selling to become custodian at the temple, or searching for the names of Scottish ancestors. Grandpa's impressions even prompted my grandparents to move a thousand miles to a new country, Canada. Grandpa wrote in his journal, "I prayed for guidance concerning my future. Then one spring morning in March of the following year, from a pamphlet which came in my mail, I read of a settlement in Raymond, Canada, and turning to my wife said, 'Mary Ann, I feel impressed to move to Raymond, Canada.' My wife felt as I did that the impression was from the right spirit."[2]

Such faith is my heritage, a firm foundation. Like my grandparents, I, too, believe in a God who strengthens me, helps me, and causes me to stand, upheld by His righteous, omnipotent hand. This belief is the basis of my life.

Stability is the fruit of internalizing the gospel, of listening, praying, searching, lifting up our voices to attain wisdom from the Lord. In Proverbs 2:2–5, we read: "Incline thine ear unto wisdom, and apply thine heart to understanding; . . . if thou seekest her as silver, and searchest for her as for hid treasures; then shalt thou understand the fear of the Lord, and find the knowledge of God."

As I listen, pray, and search, I increasingly identify with the theme which Young Women throughout the world recite every week. They say, "We are daughters of our Heavenly Father, who loves us." I have adopted this theme as part of the credo of my life. I personalize it and often recite to myself, "I am a daughter of my Heavenly Father, who loves me, and I love him. I will stand as a witness for God at all times and in all things and in all places." I feel grateful that from my own girlhood I learned who I was and that God's love transcends change. Such knowledge brings stability.

Even though I have a heritage of gospel belief, I have made the choice to develop a testimony. Testimony is a result of choice, not of circumstances. The wonderful thing about life is that despite the injustices of this world, each of us still has the choice to believe. I can see great injustices — homeless children, innocent victims of war or ignorance, people alone and unloved — and they trouble my soul. Because I have a testimony, I must accept the responsibility for helping others. This responsibility goes with my choice to follow the living prophet and to embrace currently revealed and emphasized truth.

Some people equate stability with ease. They are not the same. A friend of mine recently said to me, "Women who have stable, happy lives are made to feel almost scorned." She had met several women for lunch. One of them was having serious problems with a son; another was suffering with her husband because their business was failing. These women said to my friend, "What do you know of trouble? I wish all I had to worry about were Christmas stockings for my grandchildren." She said she felt almost guilty to admit in a group where so many problems were being discussed that her children were happy and not considering divorce and that her grandchildren were healthy. But perhaps trials or even a lack of trials has been individualized for our own personal growth. Elder Neal A. Maxwell termed our experiences "customized challenges." We hear often that the Lord gives trials to those He loves, that those who have trials are stronger than those who have none, implying that only those with trials are worthy. I believe that the Lord loves us as individuals, and, whether or not we have great trials, we can make good choices that will build our testimonies.

We must actively seek a testimony. Elder William R. Bradford suggested prioritizing as we seek when he said, "Many things are only interesting and enticing, while other things are important."[3] Jacob tells us, "Remember that ye are free to act for yourselves." (2 Nephi 10:23.) At some point in life, each woman must make a decision and say, "I will do *this* with my life." And then circumstances don't determine our actions or drive us away from the truth. In all seasons of life, testimony is a conscious choice. I have chosen to develop my testimony, and this choice gives everything else in my life meaning.

Relationships with Others

Friends are very valuable to me. One of my favorite ways to spend an evening is to invite six diverse but compatible friends to my home for dinner and a lively visit. Cultivating a variety of friends, including those in my immediate and extended family, has brought me stability. I love my friends and family. I feel that "ye are they whom my Father hath given me; ye are my friends." (D&C 84:63.)

I delight in developing new friends while doing things I enjoy. I like to cook. I like to have parties. I feel at home in my kitchen. One of the skills I have mastered is to be able to get the potatoes and vegetables done at the same time as the meat without the gravy getting cold. When I was first called to the Young Women's organization, there was so much I didn't know. My escape then was to bake chocolate chip cookies because that was one thing I did know. I baked a lot of chocolate chip cookies! I don't have to bake as many now because I am beginning to feel at home in my office as well as in my kitchen.

The point is that I have had so much enjoyment over the years in developing friends at the same time I've enjoyed my kitchen and home. I love the stimulation of developing friendships with many types of people, and I value what they teach me.

Friends multiply my store of knowledge in the most pleasant ways. I can hardly wait to see an attorney friend when I have read about a legal issue and have questions. I solve many of the world's problems with my friend Donna when we walk together most mornings. My son, a biochemist, sent me a book entitled *DNA For Beginners*[4] so we could converse intelligently about his work. It is illustrated with cartoons, and I'm still only to page 83.

I have three friends who are outstanding scriptorians, who open up my mind and pour in their understanding. There is so much I want to learn, and with friends I am free to ask questions and to be nurtured in an encouraging way. I can provide the setting for this in my home or in the park or in a car on the way to the symphony. It doesn't take a big home or an expensive menu or lavish centerpiece. I have had some wonderful conversations over curdly soup and rolls that have burned on the bottom and are doughy in the middle. I have had a fascinating discussion about a trip to the bird refuge with my grandson over a peanut butter and jelly sandwich.

I could not live in isolation. I respond to family and friends. They encourage me; they buoy me up; they make me feel worthwhile. Friends are gifts from the Lord that bring stability to my life.

Charity

Friendships are enhanced through exercising charity—another of my anchors. All life is enriched through charity. The high status of charity is extolled by Paul in 1 Corinthians 13. No quality is as enduring or comforting as charity. Charity *never* faileth. Charity is a constant—dependable, reliable, stable.

I have learned over the years that charitable people have all the real fun, too. They are the people others are drawn to. They expend their energies in positive ways that bring light and energy to others and themselves. That could be a description of one of my associates in the Young Women office. In the past week I have seen her give a treasured shell to encourage an unhappy employee. I watched her rejoice with a handicapped former student who proudly reported getting A's and B's at the community college. I am aware of her deep concern and constant caring for aged parents—even though it is by long distance. Nearly every Church employee knows her, and, I suspect, makes many more than the necessary trips to our office to bask in the light she radiates.

It is a marvel to me that charity can be exercised in the smallest ways. From Mother Teresa: "We must not drift away from the humble works, because these are the works nobody will do. It is never too small. We are so small we look at things in a small way. But God, being Almighty, sees everything great. Therefore, even if you write a letter for a blind man or you just go and sit and listen, or you take the mail for him, or you

39

visit somebody or bring a flower to somebody — small things — or wash clothes for somebody, or clean the house. Very humble work, that is where you and I must be. For there are many people who can do big things. But there are very few people who will do the small things."[5]

What a profoundly simple lesson Mother Teresa teaches us.

We find stability as we take small opportunities to serve and to get support from others. I was comforted by a hand-delivered note from my Relief Society president when she knew I was nervous over an important assignment. Knowing I love flowers, the children of a thoughtful neighbor bring me blossoms from their garden every single week during the summer. The first bouquet of forsythia and tulips arrived last week. On the other hand, I felt the joy of serving when I tended a newborn baby so her parents could attend a sunrise Easter service. As we serve, we tacitly make clear, "You are okay, and I am here." I remember feeling the overwhelming goodness and support of others when our first son went on his mission. He received contributions and acknowledgments from such unexpected sources that it intensified my awareness of the love that was shown.

Charity is the context for all we do, for it is our major means of becoming Christlike. If charity is the pure love of Christ, then learning its laws is the way to know more about our Savior. No pursuit will bring more stability to our lives than that one.

Progression

I can feel good about myself if I can detect that in some way I am a better person today than I was a year ago. An awareness of progression, even if it is small in the eyes of the world, provides the stabilizing sense of worth I need. The challenging part is to separate real progression from that which only appears to be progression.

By whose criteria do we measure? The Church's? Society's? Progression is so individual that each of us must set an individual plan. For example, if our criteria is having a good husband and a large family, some women will feel they have lost out. If our criteria is academic, a mother of many small children can feel that she is not progressing because she is not continuing a formal education. An older woman can feel useless because she lacks a career opportunity; a couple, if they are not serving on a mission. Happily, progression is measured in many more subtle ways than counting numbers of children or degrees.

Several years ago we read about Molly Mormon and Patti Perfect and laughed—maybe a little painfully—because we all understood the stereotype. In these extremes we saw how easily we create barriers that stymie our individuality and our true progression.

Do you remember Aesop's fable of the lazy grasshopper and the prudent ants? During the summer the ants are busy gathering a store of food for the winter while the grasshopper, despite the ants' warning of a long, cold winter ahead, sings, dances, and plays his fiddle. At the women's conference in 1987, Louise Plummer gave "Thoughts of a Grasshopper," based on this fable. She said, "I always wondered if there was room in a family of ants . . . or . . . in a church of ants for a grasshopper. . . . [I] fear ants will not accept me unless I am just like them." And then she concludes that both grasshoppers, whose work may be bringing happiness to others, and ants, whose work is storing the food, are necessary. It is just that "grasshoppers work differently from ants."[6] Nourishing the body is necessary. Nourishing the soul is essential also. Our methods of doing either may vary.

Judged against someone else's standards, we are all losers. When we measure ourselves against arbitrary standards, we tend not to progress because we are focused on the wrong kinds of things. In such circumstances we might be compared to those Jews described in Jacob, whose blindness came from "looking beyond the mark." (Jacob 4:14.) Stability comes in my life when I focus on the things that are mine to do.

We discover what those things are by asking the right questions. One of my things is to make my home a welcome place, even when I spend a good deal of time away from it. Another is to fulfill my calling with Young Women so that I

41

will have no regrets when my release comes. Keeping a comfortable home is not all the Lord expects from me. President Ezra Taft Benson tells us the most important question we can ask is, "Lord, what wilt thou have me do?"[7] That is our gauge for progression.

Ponder the questions prophets have asked, as noted in the scriptures, and then relish the answers:

"How is it possible that ye can lay hold on every good thing?" (Moroni 7:20.) "By faith, . . . lay hold upon every good thing." (V. 25.)

"What think ye of Christ?" (Matthew 22:42.) "David . . . call[ed] him Lord." (V. 45.)

"What manner of men [or women] ought ye to be?" (3 Nephi 27:27.) "Even as I am." (V. 27.)

The answers I have found as I've asked about my own mission and path of progression have brought boundless stability to my life. They have given me a sense of purpose and vision, a nourishment of body and soul, which sustains me. Progress is an individual matter. Our achievement should be measured against our own past accomplishments. Progression brings stability because it brings goals and achievement. There is much more happiness in *becoming* something than in *getting* something.

Maturity

I found it delightfully refreshing to hear Barbara Bush, wife of the president of the United States, on nationwide television during the week of the inauguration, ask women to take a good look at her styled hair and her designer suit, because they probably wouldn't see them again. Women loved it because she was saying, "I don't have an artificial standard. I am comfortable with myself as I am, and I want you to know it." That's maturity—the ability to face yourself happily. Barbara Bush is a stable person. Maturity allows acceptance of self even when you are not all you would want to be.

We should never abandon the quest for a better self. Nor should we allow ourselves to become immobilized thinking we are nobody. One of Satan's greatest tools is to convince us to think that we are worth nothing or to deny our divine heritage. He would have us "be miserable like unto himself." (2 Nephi 2:27.) It is so refreshing to be able to say, "This is who I am, and I am happy to live with me."

Maturity allows us to accept who and where we are. This same maturity can give us the moral courage to make our actions consistent with our knowledge of right and wrong, that is, to be "doers of the word." I think a "doer of the word" is that person who has become integrated— sufficiently mature— to act on her beliefs, especially when they don't conform to the popular views of the day. James says it this way: "Be ye doers of the word, and not hearers only, deceiving your own selves. For if any be a hearer of the word, and not a doer, he is like unto a man beholding his natural face in a glass: for he beholdeth himself, and goeth his way, and straightway forget-teth what manner of man he was." (James 1:22–24.)

Mature people, regardless of age, are able to face them-selves and act in positive ways despite flaws they may see. We all have parts of our character we don't like. Mature people "press forward with a steadfastness in Christ, having a perfect brightness of hope, and a love of God and all men." (2 Nephi 31:20.) It is compelling to me that part of the same thirteenth chapter of 1 Corinthians that describes charity is a statement about maturity. Paul wrote at the end of his marvelous dis-cussion of charity: "When I was a child, I spake as a child, I understood as a child, I thought as a child: but when I became a man, I put away childish things." (Vv. 11–12.) As we put away childish things, as we mature spiritually, we understand what we see, we know who we are, and we act upon what we believe.

Stability is possible in these times. Through testimony, friendship, charity, progression, and maturity we can maintain lasting stability, which will endure despite the clatter of these changing times.

Notes

1. Paul Simon, "The Boy in the Bubble," *Graceland* (album) (Los Angeles: Warner Bros. Records, 1986).

2. Quoted in Lovina A. Low, *Biography of John Forbes Anderson, Sr.,* p. 16. Unpublished manuscript in my possession.

3. William R. Bradford, "Selfless Service," *Ensign,* Nov. 1987, p. 75.

4. Israel Rosenfield, et al., *DNA for Beginners* (London: Writers and Readers, 1983).

5. Mother Teresa of Calcutta, *Love: A Fruit Always in Season,* ed. Dorothy S. Hunt (San Francisco: Ignatius Press, 1987), p. 26.

6. Louise Plummer, "Thoughts of a Grasshopper," in *A Heritage of Faith,* ed. Mary E. Stovall and Carol Cornwall Madsen (Salt Lake City: Deseret Book, 1988), pp. 189, 190.

7. Ezra Taft Benson, *The Teachings of Ezra Taft Benson* (Salt Lake City: Bookcraft, 1988), p. 485.

Life, Death, the Known, and the Unknown

SHEILA OLSEN

Most of us here today do not fear life. But the women's rights movement has opened so many new doors for us that we may fear we will miss something if we fail to walk through those doors. Traditional women in today's modern world, even Latter-day Saint women, may fear that they aren't fulfilling themselves if they aren't reaching beyond their customary roles of wife and mother.

It is thrilling to look at the conference program and see so many competent, educated women available to share their insights with us. In the setting of this great university, their participation is particularly appropriate. At the same time, there are many women in this audience who, whether by circumstance or deliberate choice, do not have degrees or specific accomplishments to list by their names. After attending last year's conference, a friend of mine, the mother of eight, said she went home wondering what she had been doing with her life because she had no degrees to her credit.

Much could be said in response to my friend's comment, but I have three brief observations. First of all, I'm sure that if we were to question all here who have earned degrees, they would be the first to say that their education simply opened a window on all there was yet to learn. Life for every person, college degree or not, is an ongoing process of learning, pro-

Sheila Olsen, recipient of the first Brigham Young University Alumni Service to Family award, has maintained an active role in political, church, and community life while rearing ten children. She is listed in Who's Who in American Politics *and* Who's Who in the West. *Diagnosed as having multiple sclerosis in 1967, she was honored in 1989 by President George Bush as the National Multiple Sclerosis Society Mother of the Year. She was a member of the 1988 Electoral College, casting one of Idaho's four presidential votes. In addition to teaching a weekly scripture class, she is stake public communications director, and Relief Society teacher.*

gressing, and growing. A college education can serve wonderfully to launch and enhance the learning process, but to
mean something, learning must be a lifetime project. Second,
the greatest lessons are learned simply from living life. (Speaking as a mother of ten children, there have been times I have
learned more from living life than I wanted to know!) Finally,
it is possible to obtain a good education and find fulfillment
through individual effort. A library card and a thirst for learning
unlock treasures of knowledge. For more formal instruction,
the Brigham Young University Independent Study Program is
among the best in the nation.

I have also found that organizing and joining study groups
enhances self-education. One group of women decided to meet
weekly to study the scriptures, specifically the Book of Mormon.
When they came to the Isaiah chapters in 2 Nephi, they didn't
skip over them. These sisters made a concentrated study of
Isaiah, a study that lasted for weeks. Their teacher used five
source books, including two college institute manuals. Verse
by verse, they compared the King James Version to Dr. Avraham
Gileadi's translation of Isaiah. They discovered that 90 percent
of the book of Isaiah is written as poetry. They studied Isaiah's
brilliant use of chiastic parallelism, a complicated poetic form.
These sisters learned to love Isaiah. This month they have been
reading not only the text but all of the footnotes in the fifth
chapter of Alma, the second longest chapter in the Book of
Mormon. It has taken four weeks to cover twenty-eight verses.
One of the great blessings of my life is to be the teacher of
this class. It may interest you to know that seven members of
this group are in their fifties and sixties, six are in their sev-
enties, six are in their eighties, and one regular attender is
ninety-two years old. Certainly, their endeavors can be called
a lifetime of learning.

Advancing age brings to mind my second subject: death. I
don't know that we necessarily fear death. Rather, we just don't
think much about it. Like Robert Frost's swinger of birches,
we look toward heaven and cling to life here. In real terms,
we don't consider that death will come to us or our loved
ones, at least in the foreseeable future. I know I didn't plan

on becoming an early widow. My husband, Dennis, was eight years older than I. I knew chances were that I would be a widow before this life was over, but I had the time pegged for when I was eighty and he was eighty-eight. Instead, he was fifty-four and I was forty-six. The hereafter suddenly became a very real concept to me. The fact that I know my loved one continues with his life there makes it easier for me to continue with mine here.

Dennis's sudden death and his prominence in the community precipitated an outpouring of sympathy and support, all of which I deeply appreciated. The most beneficial help I received, however, was some practical, down-to-earth advice from a little pamphlet sent by the funeral home, "How to Be a Widow" by Janet Owens.[1] It contains specific suggestions and encouragement for living that sympathy alone can't match.

The advice I would give to any woman, especially those who are managing alone, is to *assume responsibility for your own emotional welfare.* People are well-meaning, and they do care, but they— friends and children included —are necessarily busy with their own lives and affairs. It is wonderful when friends are concerned and include us. I have an incomparable support system, for which I am very grateful. But in the final analysis, we alone are responsible for our own well-being, together with a loving Heavenly Father, and we alone must take charge of our own feelings of self-worth. Along with that, we also have a responsibility to reach out in love and service to others. If a woman—or anyone—will do that, everything else seems to follow.

When I mention fear of the known, I am thinking of the things we know that are going on in the world today. We know that many are homeless and hungry. We know there is pornography and widespread obscenity. We know drug and alcohol abuse is rampant. We know there is never enough money for education. We know that every two to four years we will be besieged by the conflicting claims and counterclaims of politicians who offer opposing solutions to society's ills. In addition, there are countless other problems that we don't even know we don't know.

47

The response to all of these issues by far too many women is to withdraw into the safe, familiar world of home and church and perhaps even the workplace. Here the unpleasant, difficult, vexing problems of the world need not be faced. We comfort ourselves that we have a church organization that so well meets the needs of its members. In the secure haven of home, we tell ourselves we need merely wait for the glorious promised time when all problems will be straightened out, and we certainly hope that time will come soon!

Long ago, in the midst of a war for freedom, Moroni desperately cried out, wondering how others could sit on their thrones "in a state of thoughtless stupor" (Alma 60:7) when their help was so critically needed. In like manner, how can we, LDS women who know revealed truth and who are trained from our Primary days in leadership and organizational skills, in good conscience sit on the sidelines and leave the pressing problems of the day to others?

I have seen what compassionate, competent Christian women can do to make a difference in the affairs of their states and communities. I have seen them serve in the community without neglecting home and church by using the principles of balance and efficiency and by carefully selecting their priorities. I have seen the development of sisterhood that crossed sectarian boundaries as women of various faiths worked together in an atmosphere of mutual respect.

I have seen the wholesome participation of Christian women in the political process. They work for better government without thought of credit or reward. (It is amazing how much good you can do when you don't care who gets the credit.) At election time, these women know who and what to believe because they have informed themselves about the candidates and the issues. I have seen the system improve because of their involvement. People tend to look down on politics and politicians, but the alternative is a state-controlled, closed society with no debate, no elections, no free choice. We need to understand that political parties are as good as the people who become a part of them, and we should become a part of the political process.

I would like to see women's conferences, this and others, devote workshops to the "thousand points of light" President Bush spoke of in referring to community volunteer organizations. I would like to see groups such as this one explore ways LDS women can effectively contribute to the life of their community, state, and nation. Key words would be balance, priorities, effectiveness, and mutual respect.

Life, death, the known, and lastly the unknown. The fact is, we don't know what life will bring. But we do know, through faith, that even as the Savior rose again, so we can rise from the unknown difficulties that may assail us. In an outstanding Easter sermon, Sister Beth Lords spoke of rising again from adversities. She cited possible afflictions: serious health problems, divorce, the loss of a spouse or child or parent through death, the loss of a job, financial difficulties, drug or alcohol abuse, sin or serious transgression, children who have strayed. "We each have our own Gethsemane," she said. "In times like this we think, 'This is the end of the world . . . I'm a loser . . . Why should this happen to me? . . . I'll never be the same.' There is a better way," she said. " 'I shall rise again' is a lesson for each of us. A man, woman, or child fails only when they fail to realize that they shall rise again."[2] The solution, then, to the unknown is the exercise of faith.

Please understand that for me the unknown could loom as uncertain and as ominous as for anyone here. A progressive, debilitating, incurable disease like multiple sclerosis provides a unique opportunity to test one's faith daily. I would like to tell you, from personal experience, that the tests of life are very real, *but they can be met.* And more than that, they can be met with joy and rejoicing in one's heart. I've known from my own life's experience that wisdom and understanding serve to enlarge our vision of life and death, that wisdom and understanding enable us to substitute faith for fear when facing the known and the unknown. In the simple words taken from a poem which has sustained me for years, "God give me faith; all else will follow course."[3]

Notes

1. Janet Owens, *How to Be a Widow* (Springfield, Illinois: OGR Service Corporation, 1971). The pamphlet can be obtained by writing the publisher at P.O. Box 3586, Springfield, IL 62708 or calling the toll-free number (800) 637-8030.
2. Beth Lords, talk given in sacrament meeting of the Twenty-Ninth ward, Ammon West Stake, Idaho Falls, Idaho, Mar. 26, 1989.
3. Anonymous, "My Prayer."

St. Hild, Abbess of Whitby

CATHERINE CORMAN PARRY

Our contemplation of women of faith often leads us to examine the lives of Latter-day Saint women in this century and the last or to look beyond them to women of the ancient world who are mentioned in scripture. As from their male counterparts, we seek from these women a pattern of faith and influence. One place where we tend not to look for such patterns, however, is in the lives of women in the Catholic Middle Ages. Although this period is an indispensable part of our Western cultural heritage, at first glance the time from the fall of enlightened Rome to the rebirth of classical values in the Renaissance seems to have little to offer women of our century. Our mistrust is even apparent in its alternate appellation, the Dark Ages. It takes little study, of course, to discover that the age was far from dark. As with any period covering so vast a stretch of time—in England the Middle Ages extend from A.D. 449 to 1500—some moments are lighter than others. For women in general, and religious women in particular, one of the brightest times can be found in Anglo-Saxon England during the seventh and eighth centuries.

What we call the Anglo-Saxon, or Old English, period of English history began in about A.D. 449, when tribes from the area of what is now Denmark arrived in Britain and began conquering the Celtic people who lived there. These tribes—mainly the Angles, Saxons, and Jutes—brought with them their rich Germanic culture and language. Before long the island became known as Angla-land and their language as Anglish. They lived in fairly large familial or tribal groups, each ruled

Catherine Corman Parry, a native of California, earned her master of arts and doctor of philosophy degrees at the University of California, Los Angeles. She presently resides in Provo, Utah, where she teaches Old and Middle English language and literature at Brigham Young University.

by a king who frequently vied for the land and booty of neighboring kingdoms. They were non-Christian peoples, worshiping the gods we generally associate with the north countries.

In the summer of A.D. 597, a Christian missionary named Augustine and his fellow missionaries landed in Kent, where they had some success converting members of the royal family. Eventually, a Christian princess from Kent married the pagan king of Northumbria, Edwin, on condition that she be allowed to practice her Christian faith and bring a bishop named Paulinus with her. It is about this time that the story of the remarkable woman who later became Saint Hild of Whitby, begins.

Hild was the daughter of King Edwin's nephew, born while he and his wife were in exile, fleeing the jealousy of a neighboring king. But the king of the region to which they fled offered even less friendship, eventually having Hild's father poisoned. Amidst this turmoil and violence the young Hild grew, a pagan Anglo-Saxon princess as yet unmoved by the Christian message. Thanks to the persistent preaching of Bishop Paulinus, however, and some violent but miraculous experiences, King Edwin and all his court finally received baptism on Easter Eve, April 11, 627. Among this group was the young Hild, then fourteen years old.

We know nothing of her life for the next twenty years, though one biographer assures us that from the moment of her baptism, "the obligations and happiness of this great spiritual dignity took up all her thoughts, and engrossed her whole soul."[1] When Hild was thirty-three years old, she desired to become a nun in order to spend the rest of her life serving God with contemplation and prayer. She planned to join an abbey in France where her sister was serving, but before she could do so, she was called back to Northumbria to serve in a small monastery. A year later she became abbess over a larger monastery, and some years after that was called to found the abbey at Whitby that became her life's work.

For us to assess Hild's achievements at Whitby, we need to understand something of the background against which she performed her work. We have seen even in a brief look at

Hild's biography that early Anglo-Saxon life was uncertain, violent, and often short. But despite this, or perhaps because of it, the Anglo-Saxons also prized beauty, particularly the beauty of word and image. We can see both this love of beauty and life's uncertainty in the words spoken by one of Edwin's councilors before the king's baptism. Urging Edwin to accept the new Christian faith, he says:

"The present life of man, O king, seems to me, in comparison of that time which is unknown to us, like to the swift flight of a sparrow through the room wherein you sit at supper in winter, with your commanders and ministers, and a good fire in the midst, whilst the storms of rain and snow prevail abroad; the sparrow, I say, flying in at one door, and immediately out at another, whilst he is within, is safe from the wintry storm; but after a short space of fair weather, he immediately vanishes out of your sight, into the dark winter from which he had emerged. So this life of man appears for a short space, but of what went before, or what is to follow, we are utterly ignorant. If, therefore, this new doctrine contains something more certain, it seems justly to deserve to be followed."[2]

In some sense the monasteries, or abbeys, of Anglo-Saxon England were these halls of light and warmth. Learning was valued, and a fair portion of the population in the seventh and eighth centuries was literate. But it still fell to the monasteries to copy and preserve the culture's religious and secular writings.

Nothing illustrates more clearly that this period was particularly interesting for women than does the role religious women played in the gathering and dissemination of learning. It was fairly common at this time for two monasteries, one for monks and one for nuns, to exist together, both of them under the direction of a woman—the abbess. Although she could perform no priestly functions, the position of the abbess—particularly over large double monasteries such as Whitby—was one of authority and influence. The abbess managed the abbey's considerable lands in addition to regulating the lives of the monks and nuns under her charge. She oversaw the collection and copying of manuscripts, a task not to be undervalued in an age when the printing press was not yet invented and books were precious. In some monasteries not only were women literate but they were even scribes, in later periods a privilege reserved only for men. We do not know if that was the case at Hild's monastery, but we do know that she took pains to encourage the spoken and the written word.

Our most dramatic evidence of this concerns a man named Caedmon, considered by some to be "the father of English poetry."[3] Caedmon was one of the lay brothers at Hild's abbey; he worked as a cowherd there but was not actually one of the monks. It was the custom during that period for a lap harp to be passed around the table after dinner, and each person would take a turn at composing an impromptu song, chanted to the accompaniment of the harp's strumming. Caedmon, with his less than average aptitude at poetic composition, usually excused himself from the table and spent the rest of the evening with the cows. One night he fell asleep and an angel appeared, saying, "Caedmon, sing to me." Though he resisted at first, the cowherd soon saw the futility of arguing with an angel and asked what he should sing. In response to the messenger's request, "Sing to me the Creation," Caedmon composed a brief but beautiful poem in the verse form of the day. When he awakened, he not only remembered that poem but had the ability to compose others. To his associates this transformation seemed nothing short of a miracle, and they promptly took him straight to the abbess. Hild, however, though herself a woman of great faith, was not one to accept blindly accounts of miracles and divine messengers. She tested Caedmon carefully by having her most learned monks read him stories from scripture (Caedmon was illiterate) and then allowing him overnight to compose poems from these stories. Each morning Caedmon returned with an eloquent, moving poem. Once she became convinced that his gift was genuine, Hild persuaded Caedmon to join the brothers of the monastery and nurtured his talent by having him both teach and receive instruction.

This event is remarkable not only for its miraculous circumstance but for what it reveals about Hild's foresight. Caedmon can be called "the father of English poetry" not because

he invented it but because he took the poetic forms and for-
mulae that had been used to express non-Christian, warrior
subjects and applied them to Christian themes. Hild quickly
perceived the potential of this method for spreading and establishing the new faith. A people accustomed to hearing poetry
of heroic deeds could accept verse in the familiar format that
instead extolled Christian heroes. In retrospect, it seems that
Hild's foresight was well-directed, for we are told that Caedmon
spent the rest of his life writing religious verse that not only
touched hearts but opened new directions for Anglo-Saxon
poetry.

Hild was also known for her influence and foresight in other
matters, so much so that kings and princes sought her advice.
An important council that changed the course of the Catholic
Church in Britain was held at Whitby, and Hild wielded her
influence to carry out its decisions. The controversy focused on
a few points of doctrine and practice in which the Celtic church
differed from the Roman. Hild at first sided with the older,
Celtic practices, but became convinced of the necessity for
Rome's authority and bowed to its direction. So complete was
her submission that she later sided with Rome against a former
ally who complained of having his diocese divided without his
permission. Hild seemed to realize the necessity of upholding
papal directives at a time when the new faith was expanding
and outlying regions resisted central church authority.

But although Hild's influence extended far beyond the con-
fines of her abbey, she was primarily an example to those
within. Under her rule, Whitby became known for the learning,
piety, and charity of its women and men. To encourage these
virtues, Hild followed the New Testament notions of shared
property, so that the monks and nuns held all things in common
and no one had private ownership of any object. Her success
can be measured to some extent by the lives of those she
governed: five of her monks eventually became bishops, and
one was even canonized as a saint. But strict though her rule
was, it was apparently loving, too, for one historian tells us that
all who knew her called her Mother. In fact, a few of those
under her charge knew no other home. The child who was

later to become St. Aelflaed, for instance, Hild's successor at Whitby, was given into the abbess's charge from infancy. Her father, an Anglo-Saxon king, had promised the baby to God in return for divine assistance against a heathen enemy. Hild took Aelflaed with her when she was called from the monastery where she was serving to Whitby, which became their permanent home.

Hild's final years were distressed by a serious illness, which took much of her strength and, eventually, her life. But throughout all the feverish attacks, she performed her duties and kept a cheerful attitude to impress upon those around her that one must serve God happily in sickness as well as in health. Hild died on November 17, 680, after spending exactly half of her sixty-six years in God's service.

But remarkable as Hild's life was, it was not unique. Other Anglo-Saxon women served similarly and exerted their pious and refined influence in various ways. The focus of the period, however, seems to be learning, as more often than not the early biographers praise a nun's piety or charity in tandem with her intelligence or diligence in study. In the following detail about one such woman, Leoba, we can not only see her interest in scholarship but also sense the male writer's approval of those values:

"For since she had been trained from infancy in the rudiments of grammar and the study of the other liberal arts, she tried by constant reflection to attain a perfect knowledge of divine things so that through the combination of her reading with her quick intelligence, by natural gifts and hard work, she became extremely learned. She read with attention all the books of the Old and New Testaments and learned by heart all the commandments of God. To these she added by way of completion the writings of the church Fathers, the decrees of the Councils and the whole of ecclesiastical law."[4]

It seems not so much that religious women of the period were encouraged to study and teach as that they were expected to do so. The Anglo-Saxon Germanic heritage probably contributed to this sense of equality between women and men engaged in religious work. The Germanic tribes considered women especially likely to be prescient—that is, susceptible to receiving prophecy and divine instruction—and frequently chose priestesses as well as priests.[5] This attitude may well have carried over into Christian times; if so, it would account for the absence of any paternal or condescending tone in the letters that survive from priests to nuns.

It is no doubt clear by now that Latter-day Saint women of the twentieth century have much in common with Anglo-Saxon religious women of the seventh and eighth. We, too, focus our lives on Christian values and seek an appropriate sphere of influence harmonious with a male priesthood. It may be useful for us, then, to observe in the lives of women such as Hild of Whitby a pattern of piety and learning that will allow us, too, to leave the world better than we found it. It may be useful as well to realize that nothing Hild actually wrote or said herself survives. Our entire knowledge of this remarkable woman's life comes from the lips and quills of those she influenced. Her legacy survives completely in the values and examples she gave to others.

Notes

1. Alban Butler, *Lives of the Fathers, Martyrs, and Other Principal Saints* (Baltimore: John Murphy and Co., 1866), p. 369.
2. Quoted in Bede, *Ecclesiastical History of the English Nation*, ed. David Knowles, trans. John Stevenson (London: J.M. Dent & Sons Ltd., 1954), p. 91.
3. *New Catholic Encyclopedia* (New York: McGraw- Hill, 1967), p. 891.
4. Christine Fell, *Women in Anglo-Saxon England* (London: Colonnade Books; British Museum Publications, 1984), p. 115.
5. Fred Robinson, "The Prescient Women in Old English Literature," in *Philologica Anglica: Essays Presented to Professor Yoshio Terasawa on the Occasion of His Sixtieth Birthday*, ed. Kinshiro Oshitari, et al. (Tokyo: Kenkyusha Ltd., 1988).

Women and Service

It can, it should, be a glorious thing to be a woman. It is important for women to be aware of their common lot. It is important for women to stand together and rise together to meet our common enemies—illiteracy, poverty, crime, disease, and stupid unjust laws that have made women feel so helpless as to be hopeless.

—Julia Mavimbela

I Speak from My Heart:
The Story of a Black South African Woman

JULIA MAVIMBELA

Introduction by Carol Cornwall Madsen

I have been uncertain where to begin in introducing this extraordinary woman who has come halfway around the world from her native South Africa to speak to us. I have decided to begin in the middle of her life, several years after the death of her husband, when she moved with her five children to a small home on a rocky parcel of land in Soweto, a township outside Johannesburg. There she reclaimed the rocky soil and planted a garden, continuing her lifetime dedication to organic gardening for food and remedial use. The garden attracted the children nearby, who began, under her tutelage, to plant their own gardens. In reclaiming these often tiny plots of land, making them beautiful as well as useful, the children learned nature's law, the law of return. I believe the law of return has been the guiding principle of Julia Mavimbela's life, for through initiative, determination, and remarkable vision, she has reclaimed not only unused land but scarred and impoverished lives, making them fruitful and productive.

With the help of her sister's earnings and her own, Julia acquired the education necessary to qualify her to be a teacher. She later became one of the first women principals in the Transvaal. In addition to her duties as principal and unbeknown to her superiors, she also taught a class of forty children who were too poor to attend the school. She conducted auctions and improvised other methods to raise money for her teachers when a severe depression cut off their paychecks. She organized the Homemakers Club, where mothers taught homemaking skills to one another, and in the wake of World War II started community Waste Not, Want Not clubs in which she instructed women how to recycle their clothes and use every scrap of food. She instigated a successful campaign to raise the literacy level of black women, organizing a group that now has 783 branches throughout the republic, teaching women to read and write. Julia is proud to say that because of these skills, "All the mothers today are becoming very special women in their way of life."

Her concern extended to the restless young boys she saw about her who lacked leadership and purposeful activities. She organized a club for them and, being a former physical education teacher, taught them sports. Through her leadership and coaching, the boys won numerous awards in youth competitions.

The 1976 riots in Soweto, which devastated the township and brought about harsh government restrictions, catalyzed Julia to further community action. At great risk she expanded her gardening project throughout Soweto, mobilizing her growing army of youthful gardeners to help repair the damage done by the riots, clearing rubble and planting trees, and helping others to provide scarce food by planting their own gardens. Again, through these acts of reclamation, came a healing lesson. "Where there is a bloodstain," Julia taught, "a beautiful flower must grow."

The riots impressed on Julia even more emphatically the need for women to unite to protect their common interest, the survival and future of their families. Thus she became a founding member and eventually copresident of Women for Peace, a multiracial organization that now numbers more than fifteen thousand women. With the strength of the organization behind her, she personally petitioned government ministers to intervene when young people were illegally detained or unnecessarily harassed by officials and deprived of their schooling. The peace this organization is working for is not just the absence of war and rioting but the peace that comes from living together as neighbors, bonded by a common land and a share in the bounties it affords. Through Women for Peace as well as the National Council of Women of South Africa, which she also headed for several years, Julia has worked in behalf of women and families throughout the republic. Her own words tell of her commitment:

"I give thanks to God that He has made me a woman. I give thanks to my creator that He has made me black; that he has fashioned me as I am, with hands, heart, head to serve my people. It can, it should be a glorious thing to be a woman. It is important for women to be aware of their common lot. It is important for women to stand together and rise together to meet our common enemies — illiteracy, poverty, crime, disease, and stupid unjust laws that have made women feel so helpless as to be hopeless."

In 1981 Julia encountered two Mormon missionaries and joined the Church within two months. From that time on she has been an unofficial assistant to the missionaries assigned to Soweto, many of whom assisted in bringing her and her companion, Sister Dolly Ndhlovu, to America. Fluent in several languages, she has translated for them and helped them gain entry into many homes. She is also Relief Society president in the Soweto Branch.

Ever the missionary, on one occasion, when the mission president brought some television equipment to her branch to show some Church videos, at least fifty curious children poured into the yard to see what was happening. Immediately Julia began teaching them "I Am a Child of God." They were eager to sing and learned it quickly. Then Julia asked them, "How many of you will go to your homes right now and teach this song to your families?" Every hand went up. She quickly added, "When you teach this song to your parents, tell them that we meet in church in this very room every Sunday morning at 9:00, and they are all invited to come and sing the song with us."

Despite urgent pleas to remain and a substantial increase in pay, Julia has just recently resigned a teaching post in order to serve as a self-appointed full-time missionary. "I feel my greatest work is yet to come," explained this youthful seventy-one-year-old woman to President R. J. Snow, the current mission president.

Whatever is yet ahead for Julia Mavimbela to do, she has already created a legacy of Christlike love, forgiveness, and service that invests the term Latter-day Saint *with genuine mean-*

ing. A hundred years ago another Mormon pioneer woman also brought imagination and courage to the challenges of her spiritually and physically impoverished frontier community: "As far as I am able," this pioneer woman wrote, "I will spread light into darkened chambers."

Throughout Julia's long life, and with the aid of the additional light of the gospel for the last eight years, Julia, like her spiritual sister before her, has spread life-giving light wherever she has found darkened chambers in the minds, the hearts, and the spirit of her people.

$\mathcal{J}$ come from a country of many, many languages — South Africa — especially my little area, which is called Soweto. As I greet you, I also bring you the greetings of all my brothers and sisters in South Africa and especially in Soweto. We love you. We learned the greatest love from you when your good sons and daughters came and won our hearts to the gospel, for which blessing we thank you.

I will tell you just how I came in touch with the Church. Because of the work I had been doing in Soweto, many people seemed to feel that if anything went wrong, I was the one to see about correcting it. I think that's what happened on the last day of September in 1981 when a group of Anglican women came to my home and asked me to help clean up the Dube Boys' Club, which was in terrible shape and which they were trying to bring back.

I was very reserved with these women, very stiff. I saw in their eyes that they had come to exploit me, to use me to promote their own causes. I refused them flat, but when they had left, something touched my heart. I had never snubbed anyone before, and I asked myself, out of all the women in Soweto, could they have just thought of my name? I felt I should humble myself and go to the boys' club.

So the following morning, without telling the Anglican women that I had changed my mind, I went to the club. As I came near I noticed two white boys (as I called them), greeted them, and asked them what they were doing. They said they were helping, and I asked, "Why? Where do you come from?"

"From America," they said, and that blew me down, for there is really no connection between America and my Soweto.

"Well," I said and walked into the office of the club. I had hardly entered when they were there on my heels.

"Will you please shake our hands?" they asked. "You have been so friendly. For the past three weeks, yours is the only hello that has uplifted us."

I was shy about talking with them. I said, "Come along, now, that is just how I greet people."

Next they proposed, "Can we come to your home?" This question was very challenging to me, because at that time in Soweto whoever admitted a white into his home was considered a traitor.

I took a breath and, just to appease them, said, "All right, but you must give me three days to go and clean my little house. I'm a woman who is always on the street, and cobwebs are hanging." I thought they might forget, but indeed, after those three days had passed, on the dot they were there at my door.

I let them in and had another shock when I read *Elder* on their name tags. Elder? I started to shiver. In my church, an elder was an untouchable, and I had just let two elders into my house. They gave a prayer and started with the lesson. I listened, but I want to tell you, my brothers and sisters, what they said carried no weight with me whatsoever. I said to myself, oh, they are just from another one of those groups that come to preach to us, and I dismissed them. Then they asked, "Can we come again next week, same day, same time?"

Something hit hard on my heart. I said, "Okay," and they were there again.

This time they came with two sisters, a group of four. And still, nothing they said touched me. The third week they looked on the wall at the wedding photo of my husband and me. They wanted to know where he was, and I told them that he had died. This time they kindled a spark of interest in me. They asked, "Did you know that you can have someone be baptized for him?" I want to tell you, my eyes opened wide because I had been taught that it was improper even to speak of someone who had died. The religions I knew totally rejected the dead, and to talk about them was heathenism and would lead to excommunication. Therefore, the missionaries were teaching me enlivening news. This time, they kindled a spark in me.

I answered, "It is strange for me to hear you whites talk about the dead as if they were alive. Will you come and explain this to me?" The next week, when they visited me, I was a settled woman, very attentive, most absorbing, willing to learn and understand. I could feel something turning in me, and from then on, I wished I could be with the missionaries almost every day.

As the lessons went on, more opened in my mind, in my heart. Soon I decided, "Come along, I'm ready for baptism." I chose a date, with no previous knowledge of what that date meant in my life or in the life of my family. I just said to myself, the 28th of November I'm getting baptized. When the missionaries came, they said, "No, Sister Julia, we are going to baptize you on the 23rd." But I said, "Please, the 28th." And later, that date became something of a testimony to me that genealogy is living because the date I chose was the date my father had died. As I was four years old at the time, I had not known much about it. I still knew nothing on the day of my baptism, but when I began to do genealogy, the two dates came together.

That was how I joined the Church. I feel that I became involved with the Church by being involved with the people.

My country is a country of many problems, some known to you. As one of South Africa's kings, King Goodwill Zwelithini of Zululand, has said, "When two widely divergent cultures meet at the tip of the African continent, it leads to a startling chapter in the history of the world, and attention is focused on the outcome." This same king, when asked about how he saw the future, said, "No problem at all if we can come together." That is the most important message I bring you: only when we come together can we understand one another.

At times some of the problems in my country make people think they can hardly open their doors or walk out in the streets and come back whole. There have been quite a few unpleasant times—1976, for example, which found Soweto most unhappy as a result of riots against changes in the educational system.* That was one of the most challenging times of my life—to see what we called schools going up in flames, what we called libraries being battered down, and, worse still, the waste of all that young talent when the educational programs ceased. All of what I would call our treasure was being destroyed. Later, strikes saw parents out of work, which made things worse for many families. I am grateful to the Lord that something was touched in me at that time. I developed a plan to try to help the young people, and my plan was to try to engage the hand to engage the mind.

With nothing to start with, I asked for the use of an abandoned churchyard that belonged to the Salvation Army. It was infested with rodents; it was covered with waste. I was allowed to use it, perhaps because it saved the owners from the endless summonses they would have received for failing to keep the

On June 16, 1976, a group of fifteen thousand Soweto high school students marched to the stadium of the Orlando West Junior Secondary School to protest a recent edict by school authorities that their arithmetic and social studies courses be taught in Afrikaans. (Although this was the immediate cause of the demonstration, other changes and limitations in the education system had led to student dissatisfaction and frustration.) The students were confronted by a police detachment that, failing to disperse them with tear gas, fired on them, killing two students and injuring several others. This action resulted in riots throughout Soweto and soon throughout South Africa. In the next few months protest marches, strikes, and demonstrations were met with harsh repression. The schools in Soweto were closed, and many schools and other public buildings were burned. Except for brief periods, schooling did not resume until 1978, so the students were left with neither educational opportunities nor any productive projects for a year and a half. Furthermore, many students were arrested for their part in the demonstrations and riots and held in jail for long periods of time.

property clean. I collected the little children, from four to ten years old, to go into that churchyard and start gardens.

I have always found pleasure in a garden. At times as a mother it isn't possible to get away from the family when some annoyance comes up. But if you can go into the garden, I can assure you, brothers and sisters, it's such a beautiful place. When you break up the soil, you feel your own heart melting, and by the time you have done a little work, often you forget what had disturbed you.

So I taught my little ones at that time, as we were dealing with the lumps of dirt, that these lumps could be overcome if we worked them with the knowledge that we were preparing to get something out of the soil. And when we began putting in the little plants, I would say to the children, "You see? Now the trouble you perhaps see at home, cover it with the soil, like we're doing with the plants. See what good things you can grow if you nurse this little patch." I could see us all begin to feel more peaceful, more at ease, though I, too, had been tense and frightened to speak of anything positive during the days of unrest when we were starting those gardens.

At times there was no water. We absolutely couldn't use water from the taps because of the high bills, so we had to use kitchen waste water. I took sand from the river and put it in tins, and then I would take the kitchen waste water and filter it through the sand into our little gardens. Even despite these efforts, sometimes we couldn't get enough water to cover the whole patch. And then I would say, "Come. Let's go home. Let's all pray. There is someone above us who sees what we are doing. We'll surely see something happen." At times, brothers and sisters, it was as if a telegram or telephone call went directly to the Lord. The next morning I would come to the patch, and there had been a good rain overnight. I can't tell you of the excitement I saw in those beautiful little faces, all convinced that surely there was someone interested in and caring for the work they were doing.

Then it came to me that I could use the gardens not only for cultivation but also for schools. When I bought a package of seeds, perhaps carrots, I would say, "Fine. Now you can see how to spell the word. From the picture you will get the answer of what word it is." Soon we brought little exercise books and pens and all sat down to write the word c-a-r-r-o-t, and then the children could learn the word *car*. There had been several scrap cars in the yard before we cleaned it, and I had insisted that one be left as a shelter for our seedbeds. I wrote the word *car* on it, so the children would see it whenever they worked. The word *rot* we associated with our compost heap. In this way, the children also learned the elements of the larger word *carrot*. Our school became very interesting, and at the end of the week we would dramatize what we had learned. This play carried many through their examinations.

Finally, as time went on, we found that the gardens were also attracting not only the younger children but also the youth who were hunted down like rabbits during the rioting or whenever things got out of control. So my little gardens became a sort of refuge home. If the police would pass and find the children busy with me, they would just walk on.

And, joy! As people watched us struggle with long stubborn weeds, they offered to help, and that was a beginning of family gardens. With almost no tools, we worked like ants. Where there had been dumping, we cleared, and we filled potholes and planted trees. I moved from corner to corner of Soweto. I was in demand almost around the republic, replacing the negative with the positive and with beneficial skills. With no school and no work for many, something had to be done. As Salvation Army yards were opened near Mofolo Park, we asked, "Can you allow us to clean and plant?" My great challenge of 1976 was referred to in *Soil Sense*, published the following year:

"Mrs. Mavimbela dreams and schemes to get the youth involved in making Soweto greener . . . to make them feel that their surroundings belong to them, that they are responsible for them and therefore will not destroy them. She wishes not only to repair the physical damage of the recent riots, but also the mental and moral damage, and her message to youth is, 'Where there was a blood stain, a beautiful flower must grow.' "

As you have heard, I am also involved in several organizations. Because of the unrest in 1976, Women for Peace was founded, which ultimately had fifteen thousand members of all races. The women in my country believe that we can come together to bring about change. Our men don't come together—I don't know why—but mostly women's organizations are the ones that work to bring about the understanding that is so desperately needed. We have made provisions to translate for the black sisters in these organizations who do not speak English or read it easily, so that they get the matter in their own mother tongue. These are some of the issues we are concerned about, to see that all women, educated or not, be taught to make the right choices for their families:

In the shops several types of powdered milk have been sold, some for whiteners or creamers. Many of these are dangerous to feed babies as replacements for mother's milk because they lack nutrition. We stood up to the shopkeepers, notifying them we felt they must make it clear in their stores what products are not good for babies. Their answer: they cooperated. We sent our members to investigate some areas and supervise others to be sure that this matter was carried out.

We have also worked for the passage of the Matrimonial Property Act. In my country a woman who is widowed may not operate her property unless her eldest son takes over. The son becomes responsible for the mother. We feel it is so silly that a son should stand in for his father. It makes the oldest son feel that all he has to do is sit and wait until daddy dies and then take over. He is encouraged not to be a working child but to wait to get whatever his mother and father have acquired. We have fought this situation and seen a matrimonial act pass, but it solves the problems only for our white sisters. Nevertheless, the law commission is at present investigating possible changes in the law relating to black marriages.

I bring up this example to show that not until you present your case will officials know what you need and where to start making changes. By making the problems known to the right people, you may get answers.

70

Many black women in South Africa live in "customary marriages," what you call common-law marriages. These marriages occur when two parents agree that they want to stay together, but their union has not been recognized by a formal ceremony. Customary unions can be registered in Natal, but not in the other provinces. Chief Mongosuthu (Gatsha) Buthelezi in Zululand, Natal, has taken the lead in liberating the black women to administer their estates when they are widows and also to sign their own travel documents. Nevertheless, we are still fighting for the women in the other provinces because we feel that all women should be the same before the law. Outside Natal, if the husband in a customary marriage dies, it is very difficult for the wife because she has no claim whatsoever on the estate. We confronted the minister of justice with this issue, and he agrees that the situation for these women is very unjust. He said he is distressed and will do something as soon as possible.

We looked into the pay of our teachers. To discuss this issue, I must again bring in that word that is the tale of South Africa—*apartheid.* Representing teachers of all colors—white, black, and brown—we went to the minister of education to request that the pay scale for teachers be improved. Soon white teachers were paid much better, and the pay for colored teachers was not so bad. It was the blacks, overburdened with work, who received just a small and unsatisfactory increase. And blacks are still struggling. But that partial defeat doesn't keep us from knocking on the door of the minister. When we make him uncomfortable, that's when we feel very happy as women.

Then I come to the question of black children who have been detained. That issue we have also attacked as women. We have spoken with leading officials, and they have given us hearing. And some have seen the injustice that has been dealt. We see improvement as the leaders have arranged the release of some of the children. But now these children are overaged; they may no longer be accepted into the schools. Women for Peace has found volunteer, unpaid teachers to help these children who are unable to return to the classroom because of

71

their age. A few who have continued their studies have taken their examinations, I think with success.

We go together, women of all races, to our leaders. We have broken the law by mixing races in our organizations, by making them above color lines, and we let the leaders know that. Despite the laws, they have accepted us. They know that what we stand for and what we bring them makes sense.

Our men, particularly our young men, don't have the patience we black women have. We believe in following the Bible when it says, "Let us reason together." If we cannot reason with our leaders, we might lose what we shouldn't lose.

I do feel, brothers and sisters, that little change will be accomplished until the women of the nation rise together and put their case to the leaders in one strong voice, not challenging with fists but making the men remember that they too have children, they too live with problems that affect their families. Mothers are the key to solving most problems. We must make the men remember when they are in their seats of office that they are not immune from the issues their families face. Life is the same for all. Economic sanctions from other countries may or may not contribute to the solution of my country's problems, but the power of change lies with us, the people within the country. We women will talk to our leaders, talk to them even if they close their doors on us.

We are not where we can say all is well. But we say all can be done, and we feel it will be done.

What I Have Learned
about Leadership through Leading

ANN FINLAYSON

I was selected for this panel because currently I am chair of the Pocatello, Idaho, District 25 School Board and my husband is the mayor of Pocatello. Both my husband's position and mine represented a midlife career change, his after years as a general contractor, mine a few years earlier, as an escape from the empty nest syndrome. (After three of our four children left home in one year, I called our oldest daughter to say, "I had better find something to do, or I am going to drive Nancy [the youngest] crazy!") Obviously, I intend to address leadership from a civic viewpoint and with very practical applications.

I suppose each of us has her own personal definition of leadership. Mine is simply seeing a need and doing something about it. This definition fits very well with the notion that leadership is service. Simply put, it is rising to the occasion. President Hinckley, in the April 1989 general conference, mentioned some of the serious problems of the world and then remarked that he was amazed at the number of people who rise up to help by the hundreds of thousands.[1]

It is of major importance to our nation, our communities, and really to our own lives that as Latter-day Saint women we be involved in community affairs. One important thing I have learned by working in my position and helping my husband in his is how very important interested and active citizens are. I intend sometime to compile a list of all the ways to serve I've become aware of by being invited to various group meet-

Ann Finlayson has served for eight years as a member of the Pocatello, Idaho, District 25 School Board. She has a degree in bacteriology from Washington State University. She has served in the presidencies and taught in Young Women, Primary, and Relief Society. She and her husband, Dick, who is currently mayor of Pocatello, have four children.

ings. There are groups that provide social services — for example, the Salvation Army, Girls' Homes and Boys' Homes, teen parenting groups, even a group of college students who plan outings for troubled or disadvantaged youth just to give them some fun and wholesome experiences. There are volunteers who help children to read, who work in adult literacy programs, who act as surrogate grandparents, who organize sales for public television, and who coordinate gift-giving at Christmas for nursing homes to assure that everyone gets not just a gift but a useful and appropriate gift. And the list goes on and on. There are those who work in the many areas necessary to our political process and those who work in programs for youth — Scouting and 4-H, for instance, to say nothing of those who work in our own extensive Church youth programs. It is difficult to imagine what our communities would be like without these people.

Through my experiences, I have learned that leadership results from any action you take to make things better: a phone call, a volunteer effort. So many times one or two school patrons (in my case) or citizens (in my husband's case) call to comment on a problem and perhaps offer a solution (I love people with solutions!), and their action results in improvements for everyone.

I have learned that following and leading are very similar and are intermixed. When one serves as a Primary teacher, she certainly follows the leadership of the Primary presidency, but she acts as the leader in her own class.

I have learned that public officials need to be treated with kindness and respect. Most are doing their best and are quite aware they do not have all the right answers. I am very concerned that we may find it difficult to get good people to serve in public places. The chair of a local boundary committee told me recently that she was expecting controversy over the decisions of her committee, but she was not prepared for how personal the comments would be. To help those on the firing line, it is important to support policies and leaders you favor. Believe me, a little positive reinforcement goes a long way toward countering the barrage of criticism that seems to be a part of public life.

I have learned the importance of asking questions and gathering information. To do so ties in with treating officials with respect. Media coverage is not necessarily correct on every issue; it may distort the situation and mislead the public. If you are upset about a certain action, call to ask why it was taken, and then express your opinion.

I have learned that leadership is facilitating and delegating, providing the environment for decision making and letting groups of people make decisions. It has been said, "If you want something done right, you have to do it yourself." That is not true; but it is true that if you want it done your way, then you must do it yourself. Your function as a good leader is to provide an accurate and good process for good decision making to take place.

I have learned that listening and doing your homework are important components of leadership. Doug Larson says, "Wisdom is the reward you get for a lifetime of listening when you'd have preferred to talk." Jesus was a good listener. President Spencer W. Kimball said, "Jesus was a listening leader. Because he loved others with a perfect love, he listened without being condescending. A great leader listens not only to others, but also to his conscience and to the promptings of God."[2] We all need to gather information for good decision making. Listening is an integral part of that gathering.

And last, I have learned that leadership is being involved to the extent that you are able. It is a one-step-at-a-time process and requires careful evaluation of what you are able to do at the present time. For our family and for me in particular, it worked well for our participation to grow along with the kids — Primary, Cub Scouts, Mutual, and Relief Society. Latter-day Saints don't often think what a marvelous leadership training ground the Church is, what a tremendous learning experience it is to work with wise, caring, and spiritual women and men in the presidencies of our organizations and then to assume some of those same responsibilities ourselves.

Along with our family's church responsibilities, we had

opportunities for leadership experiences through the schools—in PTA and on various committees. You can tailor these opportunities to your situation, taking into consideration the ages of your family members and your career obligations.

Being involved is very important, but not as important as caring for your children and getting established so that you have adequate resources to be able to contribute. There are seasons in our lives. Two mothers of young children have been on the school board during my tenure. Neither was able to complete her three-year term; the time and effort involved was too great at that time in their lives. Both were very effective, and I hope each will try the office again later.

Community involvement can fit into almost anyone's schedule. There is such a variety of ways to help, from year-long or longer commitments to short, one-time-only opportunities such as phone surveys, single-issue committees, or political assignments. We can take the opportunities that come our way and see where they lead. I have one good friend who began as a room mother in PTA and ended up as a state PTA officer, another who began helping in her political party and eventually became a councilwoman and mayor.

Women's leadership in the world community is vital. We all can and should contribute by beginning now. I promise that your involvement will be exciting, worthwhile, and rewarding. You can, as our Idaho state superintendent of education said in a recent talk, "Make lives better tomorrow because of the things you are doing today."[3]

Notes

1. Gordon B. Hinckley, "Let Love Be the Lodestar of Your Life," *Ensign*, May 1989, p. 65.
2. Spencer W. Kimball, "Jesus, the Perfect Leader," *Ensign*, Aug. 1979, p. 5.
3. Jerry Evans, quoted in *News and Reports*, vol. 17, no. 4 (March 1989), published by the Idaho State Department of Education.

Being about My Father's Business

MARLENE W. OWENS

On Temple Square, each Monday for ten years, I stood in front of the mural depicting the young boy Jesus in the temple. I told tourists that when Mary expressed her concern about not having known where Jesus was, he responded, "Wist ye not that I must be about my Father's business?" (Luke 2:49.) Despite the number of times I have talked about that scripture, I must confess that I am still uncertain about what these words really mean.

I am also intimidated in discussing this subject by my belief in the uniqueness of the individual. Elder Neal A. Maxwell and C. S. Lewis believe that people become more alike as they move away from the Savior's teachings. The reverse might be true as well—that as each individual becomes more Christlike, the uniqueness of his or her personality becomes increasingly evident. Each of us can be helpful to our Father in Heaven in diverse ways in accordance with our varying life-styles and opportunities. The topic is immense. Please allow me to take a very simple approach.

I have just returned from the Holy Land. The red poppy blooms, as does the purple locust tree. The Galilean hills are lush and green. Even the sun's heat at Masada and the Dead Sea is subdued. A friend wrote, "The land takes hold and touches deeply." So it was. So it is. Thus my thoughts are influenced by recent happenings in Jerusalem.

Marlene Wessel Owens was born in New York City and graduated with a bachelor of arts degree from the University of Utah. She has taught elementary school, most recently in an inner-city school of Washington, D.C. She served a mission to France and with her husband presided over the Canada Montreal Mission. Her Church service has included being Relief Society president in three wards. She is married to Wayne Owens, and they are the parents of five children and the grandparents of two.

The last day we were in Jerusalem, a friend and I walked through the Hezekiah Tunnel. As you may recall, fearing that Jerusalem would by attacked by the Assyrians, Hezekiah, according to 2 Kings, "made a pool, and a conduit, and brought water into the city." (2 Kings 20:20.) The source of the water was hidden from the enemy, and a six-hundred-yard tunnel was cut to bring water inside the wall.

It would be wonderful if life were like the experience I had that day. We were led to the rocky opening of the tunnel by warm friends. They expressed concern as we descended into the cold waters with our thin candles lit. They said they would await us at the end of the tunnel.

The water at times was waist high, but for the most part only to our knees. My friend led the way. The tunnel is about two and a half feet wide; the height varies. As we walked along, my friend often turned to tell me of holes to avoid or to warn me of jagged rocks. When my candle would go out, she would stop and relight it. I did the same for her. Midway through the tunnel, my friend's alto voice could be heard singing, "Lead, kindly Light, amid the encircling gloom." After about twenty-five minutes, we could see sunlight. We were soon embraced by those who had led us to the entrance.

Unfortunately, the journey through life is not like my journey through the tunnel, although divine guidance can help to make it so. Our paths are not always well lit. Most of us stumble, and we carry burdens of grief along the way.

Life is difficult. Recently, the Palestinian cook at the Brigham Young University Jerusalem Center was beaten near his home, and his ten-year-old son was shot through the arm. A Jewish entrepreneur tells with moist eyes of leaving home at seventeen when his parents got divorced. An eighteen-year-old discovers a lump on the back of her head — at nineteen she is dead of cancer. An only child is killed in a car accident in the mission field. A stake president leaves home with no notice, deciding he wants another life-style. A child in Washington, D.C., tells his teacher that his mother has left home, saying she was going to kill herself. Another third-grader says that she can't stay after school because she will be stopped and asked to carry a packet of drugs to a certain home. And on and on it goes.

If our dispensation is one of heaviness and darkness, it is also one of restoration, hope, enlightenment, and joy. It seems to me that part of our Father's business is to lift the downtrodden, give hope, direct others toward the tunnel, and light candles along the way. May I share some simple experiences that I believe have something to do with our Father's business. In each case, love, tenderness, kindness, and mercy have been the guiding force. I have first-hand knowledge of most of these accounts.

Elder Richard L. Evans had had only three conversations with a young member of the Church regarding missionary work. He heard a year later that this young woman was having intellectual problems with the Church. He could have easily called her in and reprimanded her, but Elder Evans, in his quiet, understated way, went often to the temple and pleaded with the Lord to intervene and help this member. His prayers were answered.

A Relief Society president reported to her bishop to name her two counselors. The first counselor she requested was divorced and on welfare. The bishop was aghast, suggesting an alternative. But the president insisted. "You don't understand, Bishop. I knew this woman was to be a counselor even before I was called." The bishop was willing to accept her choice, notwithstanding his own adverse inclination.

My mother used to be on the Young Women General Board, responsible for camping programs. After she passed away, I received a letter from a woman who had been a camper at Brighton. This woman told me that all her youthful life she had felt big and awkward and shy and was often excluded from social activities. But she has always remembered my mother. She wrote to say that the way my mother had interacted with her at camp had made her self-esteem soar and changed her entire life. The woman was serving as a superintendent of schools in Southern California.

Sister Ruby Haight visited us when my husband was mission president in Montreal, Canada. She took the arms of one of our sons, who was much taller than she, and said, "You'll be a wonderful missionary." He was a boy who needed to hear that.

One of my husband's young missionaries came to him and said, "President, I can't teach the way this is set up—I just don't feel right challenging people to be baptized. I will teach them, but I feel like I have to wait for them to ask me to be baptized." My husband responded, "Go ahead, Elder, do it your way—you have the right spirit." This young man was something of a loner but very sincere. He did do it his way and was a very successful missionary.

In Montreal, a fourth-grade teacher allowed one of our sons to show a Church film to the class, and she became a favorite of that son. Years later, Stephen was sent back to Montreal as a missionary and looked her up again. When he found her, she gathered a group of her Jewish friends together and let him teach them, just as she had done a decade earlier.

In Chicoutimi, a remote city in northern Quebec, an elder was kind enough to allow a Church member to baptize a new convert. When the convert came out of the water, the members surrounding the swimming pool all spontaneously clapped for joy. (See Mosiah 18:11.)

When my husband was called to go to France on his mission, his seven brothers and sisters, all married, each provided ten dollars a month to his mother, who added a similar amount, sustaining him on his thirty-six-month mission. One of Wayne's treasures is the small memo book in which his mother lovingly recorded the amounts received from each family member.

I called Maureen Beecher last year from Washington, D.C., to ask about a historical script about the beginnings of the Relief Society. The planned celebration, to be held in a historic room of our nation's Capitol building, was less than two weeks away. She promptly called back but had nothing we felt appropriate for such a celebration. I was thrilled to hear her volunteer to write a script for the occasion. Her spirit of love and devotion infused the manuscript, and the appropriateness of her words led to an extraordinary event. New converts from Africa and inner cities in the East, as well as fifth-generation

Mormons, enjoyed an outpouring of the Spirit. Because of Sister Maureen's sacrifice and kindness, a marvelous happening occurred amid the marble halls of Congress.

I know someone who taught the Laurels in the Young Women program. Her calling completed, she went on to other assignments, but she never has forgotten her young women. She has kept track of them with personal talks, letters, and gifts of books. She has given showers for the brides and even ironed their wedding dresses.

A Mormon woman visited a large Catholic family in Massachusetts who were struggling with a seriously ill child. She courageously suggested that they all kneel and take turns offering a prayer in behalf of the child. The young girl eventually recovered. The woman left an indelible, loving impression on that devout Catholic family.

Last fall, a Salt Lake Greek Orthodox Church sponsored a Thanksgiving meal for the homeless. One man asked for two pies, then four, then suggested he might take six. The woman in charge gladly gave him six pies. When he left, she said to me, "You wonder whether he needs them." Then pausing, added, "But it doesn't really matter, does it?" I don't believe she'd ever even heard of, much less read King Benjamin's sermon.

I was sitting in Washington, D.C., having dinner with a group of people who had just returned from the Middle East. Seated next to me was a very prominent American businessman. He said to me, "I have met the most extraordinary person," and I asked why he thought that person so extraordinary. He replied, "He is so kind, even to those he does not know; it doesn't matter who they are."

Last year while living in Washington, D.C., with my husband and our youngest son, I returned to the classroom after twenty-five years' absence to teach a third- and fourth-grade combination in one of the District's poorest areas. They were obviously desperate for teachers. During one of the parent-teacher conferences, a woman came to see me, saying she was the aunt of one of my students. She said the girl's mother was on drugs and had left home. I was distressed by her story, but she responded happily, "How grateful I am that I am alive and can take care of my sisters' three children."

In these daily occurrences, the individual has been of prime concern, and the second great commandment has had priority.

Chaim Potok, in his book *Wanderings,* calls our world "broken and beloved."[1] I believe the Church of Jesus Christ, and we as individuals, are to bring hope to our broken and beloved world. I have felt the all-encompassing love of my Father in Heaven and have received kindness and comfort from the heavens. Thus I believe that for me to be about my Father's business means that I am to nourish, comfort, and speak kindly unto my fellowmen, that their faith might be increased in themselves and in our Father in Heaven.

Note

1. Chaim Potok, *Wanderings* (New York: Fawcett Crest, 1978), p. 525.

Women and Learning

Learning and being instructed refer not only to the traditional definition of getting an education but to the continuing education presented to us in our circumstances as women, whether we are wives, mothers, sisters, daughters, granddaughters, or aunts and to the changing kaleidoscope of opportunities that each of us has to think, to comprehend, to contribute, and to create.

— KATE L. KIRKHAM

"By Knowledge Shall the Chambers Be Filled"

MARILYN ARNOLD

*E*very few years I find myself pulling a slender gray volume in a blue dust jacket off my shelf and reading in it. I am always better for it and always incredulous that I could have neglected it so long. The book is a collection of essays about watching birds and about contemplating life. The title is *Something about Swans*, the author a woman named Madeleine Doran, whose roots happen to be in Salt Lake City but whose life led her to become one of the world's foremost Shakespearean scholars. I had the good fortune to come to know her when I began taking courses in Shakespeare from her at the University of Wisconsin nearly twenty-five years ago. A small, graying woman in horn-rimmed glasses and suede hushpuppies, she quietly, surely, opened the eyes of my understanding and instilled in me a love for Shakespeare that has become one of the rocks upon which I have built a quarter century of reading, writing, and teaching.

But Madeleine Doran knew more than Shakespeare. She knew the sounds and habits of birds; she knew flowers in their thousand species; she knew the pleasure and importance of discovery; she knew what fed the human spirit. She was a staple of wisdom and knowledge from which I drew sustenance through the taxing rigors of graduate school. And I never got past feeling tongue-tied in her presence.

Just a few weeks ago, I lifted the volume on swans again

Marilyn Arnold, professor of English and dean of graduate studies at Brigham Young University, is a widely published scholar and lecturer in modern American fiction, most notably the work of Willa Cather and Eudora Welty. She received her doctor of philosophy degree from the University of Wisconsin. Her service with auxiliary organizations of The Church of Jesus Christ of Latter-day Saints has included extensive writing assignments on lesson manuals for the Young Women and the Relief Society and membership on the Sunday School General Board.

from its familiar place. In the collection's second essay, Miss Doran writes of the pleasure of knowledge pursued and discovered with no thought for its utility:

"Think how much of the world's knowledge is in a strict sense 'useless,' how much of it has been acquired for its own sake, by amateur and scientist alike. It matters to me not at all in any practical way that this heavy, dark rock on my desk—a memento of a morning on a summit in the Rockies—is a piece of granitic gneiss, sparkling with biotite mica, dotted with orange lichen, and recording a history of the building up and the wearing down of a mountain range. Or that this piece of red scoria, idly picked up from an Oregon lava bed—a stone light in the hand and full of holes—has a very different history to tell. But how agreeable to try to read these histories! ... learning in this pure sense is detached from ourselves and therefore gives the pleasure and freedom that go with the absence of self-concern. . . . If knowledge were only gained to be put to uses we could foresee, we should have by now learned very little. Anyhow, for whatever reason, the accumulation of 'useless' knowledge is one of the pleasantest things in life. It commits us to nothing, it costs us nothing (except time, and sometimes money, both of which might be worse spent); it is a pursuit without danger of boredom, and without any necessary period."[1]

Then she alludes to her first sighting of the elusive prothonotary warbler that appeared quite unexpectedly and unearned in a branch above her head while her friends in the Audubon Society searched for it elsewhere. The thrill of the first sighting is good, she says, but so will the second and third sightings be good. "If one of them comes back next spring, we shall have a keener pleasure than just recognition. Its return will give us the pleasure of recurrence at the same time and place and therefore a sense of the stability of things."[2]

She had never seen the bird before, and yet she knew it on the instant because she had studied its picture, had read of its habits and habitat, and knew that one such bird had been seen in the area. She will recognize it if it returns another year, and she rejoices in the sense her knowledge gives her of "the

86

stability of things." We are gathered here to consider many things, but most important among them, the truth spoken by Isaiah that "wisdom and knowledge shall be the stability of thy times" (Isaiah 33:6), meaning our time or any time.

Another woman of my acquaintance whom I deeply revere, now eighty years old, tells of the beginnings of her wisdom, and of her stability, in a wonderful book titled *One Writer's Beginnings*. The epigraph to Eudora Welty's small, personal memoir is a passage from the book itself, but it tells a good deal about an environment that opened doors to wisdom and knowledge for a small child, that led her to her loves and steadied her in her pursuit of them:

"When I was young enough to still spend a long time buttoning my shoes in the morning, I'd listen toward the hall: Daddy upstairs was shaving in the bathroom and Mother downstairs was frying the bacon. They would begin whistling back and forth to each other up and down the stairwell. My father would whistle his phrase, my mother would try to whistle, then hum hers back. It was their duet. I drew my buttonhook in and out and listened to it — I knew it was 'The Merry Widow.' The difference was, their song almost floated with laughter: how different from the record, which growled from the beginning, as if the Victrola were only slowly being wound up. They kept it running between them, up and down the stairs where I was now just about ready to run clattering down and show them my shoes."[3]

There, surely, is a child's anchor in knowledge — parents conversing through the medium of art and the child recognizing not only the music but also the nature of the song and the relationship that produced that rather wonderful, spontaneous duet.

What Eudora Welty remembers about her childhood is mainly how she learned what she would need to know her life through. (And in some sense, hers is the best book ever written on child rearing, even though — or maybe because — it offers not one word of conscious advice.) On her book's first page, Eudora Welty recalls that her "father loved all instruments that would instruct and fascinate." She remembers the drawer in the "library table" where he kept maps and a "telescope with brass extensions, to find the moon and the Big Dipper after supper in our front yard, and to keep appointments with eclipses." That drawer also contained "a magnifying glass, a kaleidoscope, and a gyroscope," along with "an assortment of puzzles composed of metal rings and intersecting links and keys chained together."[4] Christmas to her father always meant "toys that instruct" and teach a child how to build things. And there were also the "elaborate kites" he made himself. "With these gifts," she says, "he was preparing his children." Then she adds, "And so was my mother with her different gifts." Welty continues:

"I learned from the age of two or three that any room in our house, at any time of day, was there to read in, or to be read to. My mother read to me. She'd read to me in the big bedroom in the mornings, when we were in her rocker together, which ticked in rhythm as we rocked, as though we had a cricket accompanying the story. She'd read to me in the diningroom on winter afternoons in front of the coal fire, with our cuckoo clock ending the story with 'Cuckoo,' and at night when I'd got in my own bed. I must have given her no peace. Sometimes she read to me in the kitchen while she sat churning, and the churning sobbed along with *any* story."[5]

Welty says further: "It had been startling and disappointing to me to find out that story books had been written by *people*, that books were not natural wonders, coming up of themselves like grass. Yet regardless of where they came from, I cannot remember a time when I was not in love with them — with the books themselves, cover and binding and the paper they were printed on, with their smell and their weight and with their possession in my arms, captured and carried off to myself. Still illiterate, I was ready for them, committed to all the reading I could give them."[6]

Welty remembers that even during the years when her father was struggling to establish himself in his profession, her parents regularly sent off for books, selecting them carefully. She recalls that in addition to the "bookcase in the livingroom, which was always called 'the library,' there were encyclopedia tables and dictionary stand under the windows in our dining-room. Here to help us grow up arguing around the diningroom table were the *Unabridged Webster*, the *Columbia Encyclopedia, Compton's Pictured Encyclopedia*, the *Lincoln Library of Information*, and later the *Book of Knowledge*."[7] She remembers reading all of the books in her parents' bookcase, each one in turn as it came on the shelf, top row to bottom.

Welty speaks gratefully of her parents' initiating her early into knowledge of the word, especially by way of the alphabet, which in her day, she says, "was the keystone to knowledge. You learned the alphabet as you learned to count to ten, as you learned 'Now I lay me' and the Lord's Prayer and your father's and mother's name and address and telephone number, all in case you were lost."[8] She remembers strict Mrs. Calloway at the library, who had a rule that only two books could be checked out at a time. "So two by two, I read library books as fast as I could go, rushing them home in the basket of my bicycle. From the minute I reached our house, I started to read. Every book I seized on, *Bunny Brown and His Sister Sue at Camp Rest-a-While* to *Twenty Thousand Leagues Under the Sea*, stood for the devouring wish to read being instantly granted. I knew this was bliss, knew it at the time. Taste isn't nearly so important; it comes in its own time." She remembers that her mother's insatiability matched her own: "Now, I think of her as reading so much of the time while doing something else. In my mind's eye *The Origin of Species* is lying on the shelf in the pantry under a light dusting of flour. . . . I remember her picking up *The Man in Lower Ten* while my hair got dry enough to unroll from a load of kid curlers."[9]

Surely, all of this takes you back, as it does me, to childhood and the books we treasured — for their covers, their smell, their illustrations, and the words that spoke magic to our eager eyes and ears. Even the heft of them, the comforting presence of them — like weights on the corners of a map of the universe — held things in place for us. I don't have a great many specific childhood memories, but I do have vivid memories of some early experiences with books. When I was very small, I had a treasured storybook, which I discovered one rainy day to be missing from its place on the bookcase shelf. Alarmed, I searched the house for it, then ran outside to interrogate my brothers. Sure enough, one of them had carried it to a neighbor's and left it outside, in the rain. It was, of course, ruined, and I have never recovered from the loss. I wish I could stroke its dear cover even now.

It was always my job at spring housecleaning time to dust individually every book in the glass-doored bookcases in our living room. This dusting was a ritual of June, as surely as it was a ritual to haul the bedsprings outside, lean them against the garage, and with the hose squirt a year's accumulation of dust from their wire coils. I remember turning the books over in my hands, dawdling over them, feeling their slick or rough paper, running my finger down the grooves in their covers, pondering their titles: *Illustrious Americans*, *Ethelbert Hubbard's Scrapbook*, *Tom Sawyer*, *Heart Throbs*, the complete stories of O'Henry, *Popular Mechanics*, gold-trimmed encyclopedias, *The Comprehensive History of the Church*, my father's high school grammar book, signed in a boyish hand, and my mother's college yearbooks. And each year, new Christmas and birthday books swelling the collection.

I, too, fell in love with words, and as I have grown up cherishing good books and well-turned phrases, I, too, remember a mother who read daily, no matter how late the hour or how weary the day. My mother is one given to proverbial sayings as well as to reading. How many times I heard her say, "It'll never be seen on a galloping horse" (if we children were making too much of something), or, "It's an awful lot on the end of your nose" (if we were paying too little attention to something). One of her favorites was, "Don't go to bed until you have learned something new." How well I remember her predictable quip at each fine new idea or worthwhile piece of information: "Well, I can go to bed now." She also knew many wonderful poems and stories by memory, learned from her mother. Countless times I dried dishes or rubbed her feet to "Little Orphan Annie came to our house to stay," or "Lambikin and Drumikin," or "Three little kittens one stormy night."

Forgive the personal reference, but this is a woman who

loves reading so much that she refused to give it up even when she lost most of her vision several years ago. With a specially crafted eyeglass, she worked and struggled in discouraging but dogged persistence to make what peripheral vision remained in her left eye focus on a text through this glass. It took weeks and months, but now, by holding the page right against the glass she wears, she can make out a few blurry letters at a time, if the text is not too small. She puts these letters together to make words and she reads. Not rapidly, not without frustration, but she reads. And my father, too, is a reader, though he has no taste for fiction or "official" poetry. It was a history book, a biography, or a religious book that I saw always by his reading chair. Surely, it is this hunger for knowledge and this love of wisdom and words that have undergirded my life. "Wisdom and knowledge shall be the stability of thy times."

I am not a poet, except at heart, but occasionally I try to give clarity to an experience or a feeling by jotting a few words in something resembling poetic form. Last August presented one such occasion, my unexpectedly coming upon three pairs of pajamas my mother had made for me in the days when she was able to sew. It was an emotional moment for me, and only words could capture it and hold it.

> It is a perilous thing
> to clean out drawers
> in storage rooms.
> They contain not simply
> the scarves and gloves and socks
> of other seasons,
> but the apparel of other lives.
>
> In the last drawer of the old chest,
> stacked neatly in pastel checks —
> pink, aqua, beige — lie three pairs
> of short pajamas, in collarless,
> cool summer cotton. One worn old,
> one middle-aged, one young. All three unworn
> since that cloudless summer morning
> eight years past when my mother awoke
> to find her vision gone,

dissolved permanently in dusky haze.
Those pajamas she made for me
when she saw, when she was invincible.

And I am middle-aged,
and there will be no more pajamas.
But these I will not wear and make old.
These are what I have that she
made for me when she saw,
when she was invincible.
Here they are safe. They will never fray
at the edges or grow thin with wear.

And now she is old,
and she is not safe after all.
My love is no protecting drawer
of closeted security,
and I crumble with the thought
of her fragility.

Perhaps too seldom do we properly credit the power and importance of the word. Too often we forget that wisdom is never couched in slovenly language. In his moving, powerful discourse on faith, Alma has a good deal to say about words, in particular about the word of God as it is planted like a seed in our hearts, there to swell and sprout and grow. His test for confirming the goodness of God's word can apply, I think, to other kinds of words as well: "It must needs be that . . . the word is good, for it beginneth to enlarge my soul; yea, it beginneth to enlighten my understanding, yea, it beginneth to be delicious to me." (Alma 32:28.) Even the nonscriptural books we read should, I believe, enlarge the soul, enlighten the understanding, and be delicious to us. The books I read from in the beginning are not ponderous books, nor are they heavy with learning, but because of the writers' great gifts and keen insights, they are wise and delicious; they taste good.

This talk very nearly had two titles because I could not part with either of the two I had chosen. Both candidates are from Proverbs, one from chapter 25, verse 11: "A word fitly spoken is like apples of gold in pictures of silver." The passage that yields the other title, the one finally chosen, is in chapter 24, verses 3 and 4: "Through wisdom is an house builded; and by understanding it is established: and by knowledge shall the chambers be filled with all precious and pleasant riches." In this scripture the link between wisdom, knowledge, and stability is explicit, just as it is in Isaiah. Note the language. A house is "builded" through wisdom, and "established" by understanding. The poet is speaking of stability here, of a strong, enduring structure built and maintained through wisdom and understanding. But verse 4 lifts the value beyond utility: "And by knowledge shall the chambers be filled with all precious and pleasant riches." Here the poet speaks not only of the stability that comes through wisdom but also of the stabilizing richness and joy that knowledge brings to our lives. Wisdom and knowledge not only build the house of our intellect and spirit but furnish it in wonderful ways. Words fitly spoken, like "apples of gold in pictures of silver," offer spiritual nourishment, the sustenance of beauty and wonder. They give stability to the soul.

Certainly, there is scarcely more beautiful language anywhere than is found in scripture. It is obvious that the Lord cares very much about language and that many of his prophets were inspired poets. We are fortunate that the King James translators of the Bible were sensitive to aesthetic values. To illustrate the importance of the way something is said, let me compare one passage from the King James Version, 1 Corinthians, chapter 13, with two much later versions, rewritten in an effort to make scripture more accessible to the modern reader. What the revisers forgot is that people learn things from poetry at a secret level that may be more important than explanations or familiar expressions.

The King James Version reads:

> Though I speak with the tongues of men and of angels, and have not charity, I am become as sounding brass, or a tinkling cymbal.

The Revised Standard Version reads:

> If I speak in the tongues of men and of angels, but have
> not love, I am a noisy gong or a clanging cymbal.

I could say a lot about what has been lost in meaning,
power, and beauty in the revision, but your ear has already
registered its disappointment.

Now listen to the verse as it is printed in the Living New
Testament:

> If I had the gift of being able to speak in other languages
> without learning them, and could speak in every language
> there is in all of heaven and earth, but didn't love others, I
> would only be making noise.

The poetry has been lost entirely, and with it the capacity
of the passage to touch and inspire us. Art has its own wisdom,
and we tamper with it only at some peril.

The wise books that bring joy and stability to our lives are
the books that carry knowledge and truths that endure in language worthy of them. It is well to remember that all books
are not created equal, that all books are not rooted in principles
that lead us to understanding and stability. Bookstore shelves
are lined with volumes that contain the so-called popular wisdom of the day, how-to books that guarantee everything from
slender hips to mystic communication with rocks. For the most
part, the theories on which these books are built do not last
even as long as the cheap paper on which they are printed.
Today's cure-all is tomorrow's Edsel. The most offensive, and
yet sometimes inadvertently the funniest, of these hard-sell
wonder books are those claiming that spiritual rewards follow
material pursuits, or vice versa. You will be enraptured to know
that the latest in the "Millionaires of the Bible" series is titled
The Millionaire Joshua: His Prosperity Secrets for You! Inside, the reader is told, "Yes, the Bible is the finest prosperity
textbook that has ever been written! The great people of the
Bible had no psychological hang-ups on the subject of prosperity and success being a part of their spiritual heritage. They
intuitively knew that true prosperity has a spiritual basis."[10]
This stuff is more comical than the comics. Surely, here is proof

of Proverbs 15:2: "The tongue of the wise useth knowledge aright: but the mouth of fools poureth out foolishness."

Capitalizing as it does on our desire for the quick cure, this sort of thing is surely a contributor to the instability of our time. Furthermore, it is the antithesis of the Savior's gospel. You might be interested in some of the titles I encountered in a quick browse through a small bookstore: *How to Invest $5,000 Even If You Don't Have It, Think and Grow Rich, You Can Have It All: The Art of Winning the Money Game and Living a Life of Joy, The Magic of Getting What You Want.*

And now consider: "Lay not up for yourselves treasures upon earth, where moth and rust doth corrupt, . . . but lay up for yourselves treasures in heaven." (Matthew 6:19–20); "where your treasure is, there will your heart be also" (v. 21); "take no thought for your life, what ye shall eat, or what ye shall drink; nor yet for your body, what ye shall put on. Is not the life more than meat, and the body than raiment?" (v. 25).

Consider these titles: *Inspire Yourself: One Hundred Guides to Victorious Days, The Psychology of Winning, Looking Out for #1, Celebrate Yourself, Winning through Intimidation.*

And now consider: "Blessed are the poor in spirit: for theirs is the kingdom of heaven" (Matthew 5:3); "blessed are the meek: for they shall inherit the earth" (v. 5); "he that findeth his life shall lose it: and he that loseth his life for my sake shall find it" (Matthew 10:39); "for what is a man profited, if he shall gain the whole world, and lose his own soul? or what shall a man give in exchange for his soul?" (Matthew 16:26).

Instead of racing to scores of self-help books whose principal inspiration is the dollar sign and whose object is to focus our attention solely on ourselves, why not take the Savior at his word: "Come unto me, all ye that labour and are heavy laden, and I will give you rest. Take my yoke upon you, and learn of me; for I am meek and lowly in heart: and ye shall find rest unto your souls. For my yoke is easy, and my burden is light." (Matthew 11:28–30.)

Add to the books I have just mentioned, the advertisements that bury us daily and the headlines of the grocery store tabloids that insult us even as they entertain us, and you begin to understand why Isaiah made a special plea for the stability of true wisdom and knowledge. Of course, were these sensational scandal sheets to disappear, we might find waiting in checkout lines quite a drag, with only the gum and lifesavers to contemplate. What on earth would we do without this sort of edification: "Hell found in outer space: Scientists listen to screams of the damned on Satan's planet"; "Surgeons from UFO save my life, sailor claims"; "Pilgrims say they see Moses appear above old apple tree."

As an antidote to all of this printed noise, we might remember that the word is so important that it is used in scripture to designate the Savior himself: "In the beginning was the Word, and the Word was with God, and the Word was God." (John 1:1.) In the nonscriptural reading we do, how much better, surely, to read the well-crafted words of intelligent beings who have learned new things in this world and shared their discovery—or, more likely, who have shared their quest for understanding—than to suffer the assault of graceless language and extravagant claims.

With your indulgence, I want to share just a few "apples of gold in pictures of silver" with you, a few of the many things that over the years have stuck in a groove in my gray matter. Emily Dickinson has long been a favorite. Try this teasing taste of her cryptic wisdom:[11]

> It dropped so low—in my Regard—
> I heard it hit the Ground—
> And go to pieces on the Stones
> At bottom of my Mind—
>
> Yet blamed the Fate that flung it—*less*
> Than I denounced Myself,
> For entertaining Plated Wares
> Upon my Silver Shelf—

Just as I had difficulty selecting a title, so did I have difficulty selecting from the long list of things I would like to have shared with you. This will surely come as a great surprise, but I decided to read something from Willa Cather, a brief portrait of Ántonia

Shimerda, an immigrant pioneer to the plains of Nebraska, a woman of integrity who had a hard life, but a good life, a woman whose strength of character showed in every aspect of her being, in every gesture. Jim Burden, seeing her after twenty years, says of her:

"Ántonia had always been one to leave images in the mind that did not fade—that grew stronger with time.... She lent herself to immemorial human attitudes which we recognize by instinct as universal and true.... She was a battered woman now, not a lovely girl; but she still had that something which fires the imagination, could still stop one's breath for a moment by a look or gesture that somehow revealed the meaning in common things. She had only to stand in the orchard, to put her hand on a little crab tree and look up at the apples, to make you feel the goodness of planting and tending and harvesting at last. All the strong things of her heart came out in her body, that had been so tireless in serving generous emotions.... She was a rich mine of life, like the founders of early races."[12]

We began with a Shakespearean scholar; let's end with Shakespeare, with *King Lear*, to me the greatest of his plays. I think nowhere else in English literature is so much said so powerfully about human values and character. You remember the story. The aging king, desiring to be done with kingly responsibilities but wishing to retain all the symbols of power, decides to divide his kingdom among his three daughters. The size of each daughter's portion is to be determined by the eloquence of her overt profession of love for him. The youngest, Cordelia, the only one who truly loves him, pridefully refuses to submit to his foolish test and is disinherited. The two older daughters, lavish in their expressions of love, inherit the kingdom but soon show their true colors. They refuse their father his retinue of knights and abuse him to the point that he is cast out on the heath in a terrible storm. Suffering and deprivation cost the once selfish old man his wits, but they also ennoble him. We sense the change when he steps back and invites his fool to enter the protective hovel ahead of him. Moreover, he realizes for the first time what it is to be an

outcast, living in unsheltered poverty. His thoughts extend to
the ragged and homeless in his kingdom:

> Poor naked wretches, whereso'er you are,
> That bide the pelting of this pitiless storm,
> How shall your houseless heads and unfed sides,
> Your loop'd and window'd raggedness, defend you
> From seasons such as these? O, I have ta'en
> Too little care of this! Take physic, pomp:
> Expose thyself to feel what wretches feel,
> That thou mayst shake the superflux to them
> And show the heavens more just. (III:iv)

Here is a changed man. And the change becomes even
more apparent near the end of the play when in the midst of
battle he and his daughter Cordelia — whose husband's forces
have waged war against those of her wicked sisters — are re-
united. Here is this ragged, honorless, half-mad, deposed old
man, and this is how his loving daughter addresses him. She
refuses to diminish him; she accords him the respect due a
mighty king:

> How does my royal lord? How fares your Majesty?

Then that chastened man, who earlier would not have
bowed to anyone or anything, falls on his knees before his
daughter. She begs him not to kneel, and he replies:

> Pray, do not mock me.
> I am a very foolish fond old man,
> Fourscore and upward, not an hour more nor less;
> And to deal plainly,
> I fear I am not in my perfect mind.
> Methinks I should know you, and know this man;
> Yet I am doubtful; for I am mainly ignorant
> What place this is; and all the skill I have
> Remembers not these garments: nor I know not
> Where I did lodge last night. Do not laugh at me;
> For (as I am a man) I think this lady to be my child Cordelia.

Greatly moved, she cries, "And so I am! I am!" He continues,

> Be your tears wet? Yes, faith, I pray weep not.
> If you have poison for me, I will drink it.
> I know you do not love me; for your sisters
> Have, as I do remember, done me wrong.
> You have some cause, they have not.

And she replies, "No cause, no cause." (IV:vii.)

Cordelia forgives him; in fact, she had never blamed him. His joy in that realization is so full that he forgets all about the battle and the wrong done him by his other daughters. Even when the tides of war turn and he and Cordelia are taken prisoners, his only thought is to be with her:

> Come, let's away to prison.
> We two alone will sing like birds i' th' cage.
> When thou dost ask me blessing, I'll kneel down
> And ask of thee forgiveness. So we'll live,
> And pray, and sing, and tell old tales, and laugh
> At gilded butterflies. (V:iii)

Here, my dear sisters, are riches enough to fill a thousand chambers.

Notes

1. Madeleine Doran, *Something about Swans* (Madison: University of Wisconsin Press, 1973), pp. 26–27.
2. Ibid., p. 27.
3. Eudora Welty, *One Writer's Beginnings* (Cambridge: Harvard University Press, 1984) p. [xi].
4. Ibid., p. 3.
5. Ibid., p. 5.
6. Ibid., pp. 5–6.
7. Ibid., p. 6.
8. Ibid., p. 9.
9. Ibid., p. 30.
10. Catherine Ponder, *The Millionaire Joshua: His Prosperity Secrets for You* (Marina del Ray, California: DeVorss, 1978), p. 3.
11. Emily Dickinson, "It dropped so low—in my Regard," in Thomas H. Johnson, *The Complete Poems of Emily Dickinson* (Boston: Little, Brown, and Co., 1960), p. 366.
12. Willa Cather, *My Ántonia* (Boston: Houghton Mifflin, 1918), pp. 352–53.

Learning Is Nurture

EMMA LOU THAYNE

Something every one of us will eventually deal with is the fear of aging. Even as one who is well into the delicate ruin, I would like to announce that I like *now*. Every day is a new awakening and a new chance at something I've never experienced. I'm convinced that life is indeed a stage and is made up of stages. Out of those stages comes learning.

Remember the wonderful Lily who says in a Maurice Chevalier movie of long ago, "You don't learn; you just get older, and you know." So true. In getting older you come to know a lot, most of it enriching, some of it not so. In the *Deseret News* recently there was a telling Small Society cartoon on the editorial page. Bill Yates's two little globby figures say, one to the other, "The only happiness I can seem to find anymore is finding my glasses soon enough to remember why I wanted them."[1] I had 20/20 eyesight till I was forty-five. Now I'm into trifocals — and seeing just fine.

Things happen along the way. Things just happen. And we're all having them happen to us, no matter what stage we're in. The secret is to learn from them. What is learning? education? What is it that attracts us to any learning? To me, it's *nurture*. I love the word *nurture*. Nurture is feeding; nurture

A native of Salt Lake City, Utah, Emma Lou Thayne earned her bachelor and master of arts degrees from the University of Utah and taught part-time in the English department of that university for more than three decades. Her extensive publications include ten books as well as poetry and articles in many periodicals, both Church-related and general. Her novel Never Past the Gate *was a New York Book Club selection, and she has received major awards from Lambda Delta Sigma, the Association for Mormon Letters, Brigham Young University, and the University of Utah. Her other interests include skiing, hiking, and tennis. She and her husband, Melvin E. Thayne, are the parents of five daughters and the grandparents of fifteen.*

is faith; nurture is learning, education. It can be what frees me from fear—at any stage.

Education turns my leaves green, brings my blossoms out, and allows me the full measure of my creation. I have to know a lot of things before I am free to do many things. My formal education freed me to receive nurturing from books. Now, at age sixty-four, I need my glasses to be free to receive that nurturing.

Still, beyond any aging and for all the credence I would give to formal education, it takes dealing with life to really teach us—the handling of the things that just happen to happen. In this nurturing, this discovering, this becoming familiar with, this never losing touch with what nurtures us, the constant growth ingredient has to be, "I want to know more." I need to *expect* in order to be educated, to be taught, to be filled. I have to have a prepared mind that says, "I wonder." What a gift, the ability to wonder. Not doubt, but wonder. Think what that persuades me to pursue—an education indeed.

About formal education. Yes, I did go back for a master's degree in creative writing, when our youngest daughter started school. I had been teaching part-time, one class a quarter, three hours a week, for most of thirty years. I had loved it! When we had five little girls under ten, teaching had given me a touch with the adult world, and I came back to my children better able to talk their language, having talked a grown-up tongue for even a little while.

During those hectic years we had unwed mothers from Relief Society Social Services live in our home. We were selected together as a match, our family and each of those young women, and they took creative care of things while I was gone. Since theirs had been a temptation I had not had to confront, I had been a moral snob, thinking, why didn't they just say no? But I found they were wonderful people, friends. And oh, did I learn from them—humility, understanding, graciousness, pain. They taught our children much about nurturing that I might never have known enough to teach.

Over the years, as I had had the fun of teaching those students—and oh, it was fun—I decided that when our youngest, Megan, started first grade, I would go back to school. I did—at age forty-five and scared to death. Talk about fear. I'd been colleagues with the people in the department, and all of a sudden I was going to be one of their students, writing in bluebooks and meeting all the terrifying demands that I'd been inflicting on other students all those years.

But I made a quite lovely discovery in going back. My fears were not grounded. I had learned in those twenty-five years out of school. I had learned a lot. As the poet Rilke says, all the things that I lavish myself on, grow rich and lavish me. I had lavished myself on my home, on my Church work, on the General Board, on whatever was happening in our neighborhood. On a tennis court, on friends, sometimes on people very unlike me, on my children, my family, my husband, I had lavished me and loved it. And it all came back to lavish me.

As I sat in my first class—Shakespeare—I listened to Dr. Harold Folland talk about such things as Aristotelian unities and I thought, Did I ever know this? Petrified, I found that the bright young minds around me knew a lot more of some things than I did. But, oh, I knew some very important things, too, one of which was that I wanted to learn. As an undergraduate I had received a lot out of college that had much more to do with sociability than studying, and I'd bluffed my way through lots of tests. Now, as a graduate student, I was one of the "old alumni in tennis shoes" that we had moaned about when we were undergraduates—they were so intense!

Here I was, sitting in class, drinking it up, loving it. I remember my first trip to the library. I had all that space in a day—nobody coming home for lunch, nobody needing me. I had from nine to three—that's *six* hours to play. In that library I thought, hey, lady, you've got it all. I could go anywhere and pull any book off the shelf and read it and stay with it and talk about it and think about it. I was a rich woman.

I learned a lot in that formal education—my thesis, a collection of poems, was my first published book—at age forty-six. But along the way, in my anything but formal education, I had learned a lot from people, especially from the people I worked with in various capacities. Oh my, I had been fed! And it all came home when I took it to school.

I had learned a lot and I have learned more since about silence and solitude for nurturing. There were years when I felt totally accompanied with five little people. From room to room and wall to wall, even in the bathroom. What mother doesn't know the story? Silence and solitude were never mine. Unless I stayed up all night one night a week, which I did. Or I worked on my writing and projects between 11 P.M. and 3 A.M. when the rest of the house was quiet.

Stillness not only can give me acquaintance with where I am but lets me know what I have learned. I like to think what Neruda said when he accepted the Nobel Prize for his poetry: "I have always found somewhere the necessary affirmation, the formula which lay waiting for me, not to be petrified in my words, but to explain me to myself."[2]

Only in stillness did I find that affirmation and explaining, because then I could write. Write in a journal, at best. My friends, get it down, think about it, filter it out, all that keeps happening and happening. Let it appear on the page like invisible ink and tell you where you are and who you are and how you feel. Then feel cleansed and clarified for having found the stillness in yourself.

By that writing for school, I learned and was nurtured in my home, in my work. And most of all, I have learned and been nurtured by prayer and meditation to find the ultimate nourishment that has always come in the night. My mother's adage, "Pray at night; plan in the morning" has been as natural as breathing.

To be truly nourished, I must allow everything that happens to me to be assimilated — not only ingested but assimilated — if it is to be of value to me. If it is going to turn knowledge into wisdom, it has to work itself inside me and find a place. Theodore Roethke says it:

> I wake to sleep, and take my waking slow.
> I learn by going where I have to go.[3]

If I pay attention, I do learn by going where I have to go.

I had an accident two and a half years ago. Early on a Saturday morning, I was driving home on the freeway with a son-in-law. We had been camping with his family and my husband, and the two of us had to get back early, he to the hospital where he was a resident surgeon and I to help a friend who was having a party for her daughter.

We were driving up past Provo, almost to Murray. I was looking down, reading to him from the manual about how the car worked. We were driving my husband's new car that had multiple buttons on the dashboard, and we were laughing and trying them all out.

It was lucky that I was looking down. Without warning there was a crash, like a shot. I didn't see or know anything except that suddenly my hand was at my eye and was full of blood. I said, "Jim, I've been hit." I looked at the windshield, and there was a gaping hole. Glass was all over my lap. I said, "What hit me?"

Jim looked around and saw lodged in the back window a huge piece of metal, like an L-shaped crowbar. He said, "Grey, you'll never believe what hit you." It turned out to be the six-pound metal shaft that holds a mud flap on a big rig. It had fallen off and somehow gotten airborne and come through the windshield. We were going sixty-five miles per hour. It hit my face, missing my eye by a centimeter, then hit my temple and flew into the back window.

If you want to have an accident like that, you want to be riding with your plastic surgeon son-in-law. He got us to the hospital, to emergency, by going ninety miles per hour with his flashers on. Everybody—policemen, reporters, doctors—said, "Impossible. Nobody could have survived."

I never lost consciousness. I never was afraid. I never cried. Weeks later I began trying to understand what had happened to me in that time. It was a learning that I needed, and it was probably the most precious learning I've ever had. I had eight fractures in my face. Surgeons had to move my eyeball to operate, to screw my broken cheek and forehead to metal plates, most of the surgery done up through my mouth so the scars wouldn't show.

But scarring was the least of my worries. I wanted to be alive and able to read, to put my face down to do my work, to jiggle and run and hug. Reading had been my access my whole entire life. But for seven months I couldn't read; I couldn't bounce; I couldn't move fast. I couldn't lean my head down, so I couldn't write. I couldn't do any of the things I was used to doing.

But, oh, did I learn. I learned that the greatest learning of all comes from inside and is proffered always from a divine hand—if we pay attention. I remember Jack Adamson, one of my mentors at the university, saying as he confronted getting older, "You know, I'm reading less and thinking more." And I thought, I get to do that now, Jack. It wasn't that my recovery was not without peril or that I didn't have times of real concern. It's been only in the last little while that I've been able to understand that accident and to write about it. But now I know that I had a death experience. I went somewhere and knew a feeling way beyond joy, but by choice, I came back without fear. It was a remarkable privilege, both the going and the coming. Since then I have sensed a light that occupies me. And I see more of it in other people, even more than I knew was there before. I had to slow down, be slowed down, to find the stillness that allows it to be.

And that light is accessible if we simply let ourselves be lavished by it. I go to sleep to find out what I'm thinking, and without ever an exception, I find out in the morning what I'm thinking and where I am. The answers are there and very real.

Yes, I think formal education is important, that it's valuable. But I don't think it is all there is. The thing we do learn as we grow older and are nurtured is that we can abide in that place of no fear. Graciously it is given, that peace, to move us through this stage and these phases with at least some equanimity—if we simply stay in touch with the light that I know is so availably there.

Years ago in 1965, when I was a young mother with all those little girls, I wrote a frail poem to end my first collection, which I quiveringly entered in the Utah State Fine Arts contest so long ago. Such faltering beginnings, long before any formal education in the writing of a poem. But I dug that collection up last year and made copies for each of my daughters for Mother's Day because they're all now at the stage that I was in then—each a young wife and mother. And each expectant and wondering and sometimes afraid.

So Come, Tomorrow

Security is not in knowing
what will come
nor if it will be
bad or good.

It is a faith drawn taut
with having learned
and seen and done
that says, Tomorrow, come.

The absence of fear, the presence of faith. It has to be a little like the prayer our seven-year-old granddaughter ended with, "Thanks so much. We've had a good ol' time."

Yes, thanks so much to learning, to being nurtured by all that comes along at any stage, in any time.

Notes

1. *Deseret News*, 5–6 Apr. 1989, p. A–7.
2. Pablo Neruda, *Toward the Splendid City: Nobel Lecture* (New York: Farrar, Strauss, and Giroux, 1972), p. 17.
3. Theodore Roethke, "The Waking," in *Collected Poems* (Garden City, N. J.: Doubleday, 1966), p. 108.

On Being Teachable

KATE L. KIRKHAM

*J*n the Book of Mormon we read: "And the church did
meet together oft, to fast and to pray, and to speak one
with another concerning the welfare of their souls." (Moroni
6:5.) The BYU Women's Conference is also a time to meet
together to fast and to pray and to speak one with another
concerning the welfare of our souls. But some of us may experience too many meetings—are we not meeting and talking
together all the time? There is in this scripture, and in others,
a particular spirit of meeting one with another. That spirit is
a mutual caretaking, a spiritual reciprocity—even as the Apostle
Paul entreated: a kindness, a desire to be tenderhearted one
to another. (Ephesians 4:32.)

But what readies us to learn of the welfare of other souls?
What readies us to be taught? And why, when we as a people
are engaged in teaching the gospel of Jesus Christ, should we
also be concerned with being teachable?

Several years ago, a theme of the Relief Society was "Learn,
then teach." Sometimes, however, we think about learning only
when we are in a classroom. We associate being teachable with
being in attendance. In a campus setting we can further link
learning to a required curriculum, specified prerequisites, se-
quenced electives, and defined areas of study. We develop
beliefs about who can and should be teaching us. So, as stu-

*Kate Kirkham is an associate professor of organizational behavior
at Brigham Young University. She received her doctor of philosophy
from the Union Graduate School, Union of Experimenting Colleges
and Universities, in 1977. Formerly associate director of the MBA
program at BYU, her research has focused on race and gender diversity in organizations. She has written numerous training and
educational materials for programs on institutional racism and
discrimination and is a consultant to government, educational, volunteer, and business organizations. She has also served on general
Church committees and as stake Relief Society president.*

dents, it is fairly easy to adopt the attitude, "Well, I'm here. The rest is up to you."

As a teacher, I share with you who have faced a classroom the challenges of looking at faces, watching body postures, listening to questions, and trying to determine each person's "readiness to learn." There is a responsibility and a requirement to be ready to teach, but today I want to focus on that powerful part of the interaction we influence as learners.

What are we like as learners? Over the years I've watched and had students describe to me (usually after grades were in) their roles as learners. Some take the posture, "Go ahead; get my attention, if you can," or "I already know about this subject." Some say, "I don't want to know about this subject — it's required," or "I need to know exactly what I'm supposed to learn here," or "You've got my attention, but I don't understand you." There are also those who come inquiring, ready to risk asking the "dumb question," ready to contribute to the learning of others.

My point is: Are we willing and able to look at what we are like as learners? Are we paying attention to how we ready ourselves to learn — our style, assumptions, expectations, attitudes, and so forth? Are we aware how much we really influence, if not control, how teachable each of us really is?

Now, if the place of learning is not the traditional classroom but a congregation or an interdenominational community, and the curriculum is not math or English but the gospel of Jesus Christ — the character of our being one with another heretofore, here, and hereafter — then what would describe us as learners? Who may instruct us? What does it mean to be teachable?

This concept is difficult for me to explain. I have experienced it in myself and in others with more certainty than I can articulate in a description. Because of our individuality, the expression varies. And though I list these common characteristics separately, they form a whole. They seem to be a sense of one's incompleteness — a gnawing awareness of a desired, divine, and future state; a contrite spirit; a humble heart; a knowledge of one's worth; a reverence for the worth of others;

the trusting readiness often most apparent in little children; a belief in one's abilities and one's capacity to grow and to contribute; and an acknowledgment of our interdependency as sons and daughters of our heavenly parents. Perhaps, fundamentally, being teachable means that we daily open ourselves to the consistency of God's love for us. We accept that we are loved and make real in our complex, earthly lives the cornerstone commandments to love our God and our neighbors as ourselves. We can acknowledge that no matter who we are or where we are, encoded into each of us are two things: this common language of learning that is love, and a most common bond of purpose—we came to learn and to "speak one with another concerning the welfare of our souls"—in fact, to progress eternally.

Our capacity to be taught is infinite—whatever our current circumstances, whatever the conditions of our physical abilities, and whatever status we may hold in the eyes of others. It is easy to move away from such a compelling awareness of our potential. We can allow and assist others to get in the way of our being teachable. We can find for a variety of reasons—fear, doubt, convenience, comfort—ways to deny our capacity for learning, to lose faith in ourselves, to lose faith in the love of those around us, or to lose faith in God's love for us. By not believing in our capacity to learn (even from our mistakes), by not believing in our capacity to influence others for good, we deny the power of God in us.

I hope I have conveyed to you my belief in our capacity and responsibility to remain ever the learning children of our heavenly parents and my belief as well that this condition of being teachable is fundamentally linked to God's love for us and ours for Him and for one another. I hope that it is also evident that learning and being instructed refer not only to the traditional definition of getting an education but to the continuing education presented to us in our circumstances as women, whether we are wives, mothers, sisters, daughters, granddaughters, or aunts and to the changing kaleidoscope of opportunities that each of us has to think, to comprehend, to contribute and to create.

Now I would like to suggest five things that can affect the quality of being teachable and comment on three areas where we can edify each other as we speak one with another.

To Improve Our Teachableness

Let us demonstrate what we already know, so that our preparation to learn even more is evident to our earthly parents, to our Heavenly Father, and to others around us in the congregation.

Why are we constantly reminded of things? Why are basic principles repeated so frequently? Perhaps we have not demonstrated in our daily behavior our ability to do those things. Long ago, King Benjamin advised his congregation, "If you believe all these things see that ye do them." (Mosiah 4:10.)

If we are demonstrating what we have learned, even a reminder will be heard without offense. When I was sixteen I backed out of our steep driveway directly into the only car parked on the other side of the street. I think that over the decades I've now proven I can navigate my parents' driveway, and because of that, their reminders are not heard the same way they were the first few times after the accident when I had not yet "proved myself."

Sometimes we treat requests to visit teach, home teach, prepare for meetings, or even to be compassionate as things we could do if we really had time or if we really wanted to do them. I have experienced the deception that can come when we confuse thinking about possible actions with the actual effort required to do them. I don't learn as much from thinking about opportunities to be charitable as I do from exercising charity in my conduct with others and learning from those very real experiences. What if, as a ward or stake congregation, when we next met together, we had all paid our tithes, made clear our love for our neighbors in how we had treated them, had proven obedient to the commandments, and in diverse ways of expression given evidence of the fullness of our faith? What would the speakers say to us? By our efforts, wouldn't we have demonstrated a readiness to learn that would call forth even greater instructions? And what if in our daily interactions with each other as women we helped each other learn more fully that we are daughters of deity, that we have an infinite value to the Lord, as do men, because each of us is required in building up the kingdom of God.

If we can experience with one another being a daughter of God and affirm who we are and why we are here, we will be less likely to compete for proof of that through our daily interactions whether at home, in employment, or in callings. A woman who serves in a calling with men who believe they have nothing they can learn from her, a woman who works full time in the home but meets with women who think she is not developing her potential, a woman who seeks a non-traditional major and career only to have the members of her ward think that she is not interested in men or marriage—all of these women expend energy defending their experience and proving their worth in ways that lessen their ability to contribute to the congregation and feel of value. If we could in fact demonstrate that we know men can learn from women, that we know women with the opportunity to be in the home full time are developing their own potential, that women with the opportunity to pursue a nontraditional career are also still interested in men and marriage, we could create conditions where we could really affirm the value of others and call forth even greater contributions. In these circumstances we could learn a lot more from one another.

In discussing the glory of the city of Enoch, Elder Neal A. Maxwell presented a narrative progressively illustrating the readiness of a people and included these observations: "Our unity is not the unity born of compulsion or of mindless rapport, but of the realization that such unity is a necessity. . . . It helps greatly to do first things first, not only because these are most important, but because the order of things does matter. . . . In our meetings we recount our own blessings, and as we hear the blessings of others, we both feel and see the accumulations of affection from God to his people."[1]

As Alma said, "By small and simple things are great things brought to pass." (Alma 37:6.) Let us demonstrate our ability to do "small and simple things" in ways that value the differences in the lives of people around us, and enable us to learn much from their experience.

Second, we learn about being teachable when we seek to balance being directed and being anxiously engaged. There are absolutes in life — things we are not supposed to do. But there is also ambiguity — several possible ways to do good, to influence others, and multiple ways to excel. In the face of ambiguity, some of us will be directed and will know for certain what to do; for others of us, it will be up to us to figure out what to do! Sometimes what I personally should be learning is painfully obvious to myself and to others. Sometimes I have struggled for years to understand, to discern the meaning of an experience, or to embrace a principle.

Being receptive and being active are both ways to enhance our teachableness. Some of us want the recipe: we want the ingredients explicitly identified and their relationship clarified. On the other hand, some of us just want the basic principles and will make do with whatever materials or conditions are around us. Our differences in how we approach learning should invite interest from each other and not judgment. I hope we spend as much time trying to transcend our experience and understand the experience of someone else as we do defending our own experience.

If we err in the extreme — either in thinking "if we are not told, we don't have to try" or "I resent being told; I can figure it out for myself" we diminish our ability to be taught. We can find a balance between these extremes in the circumstances of our lives which enable our own righteousness to grow. Last fall I began my third year as Relief Society president in one of the BYU stakes. If there is ever a time to be anxiously engaged, it is at the beginning of a new semester on campus. I felt overwhelmed and uncertain about what I was going to contribute that could be any different from the prior two years. I felt that I should know with more certainty what I was doing if I was going to serve another year as the Relief Society president. As I sat in the back row during a Relief Society lesson in one of the wards on campus, a strong feeling came over me. It was as if a voice said, "If you are uncertain, you can get up, go get a blessing, and find out." I thought, "I can't get up and walk out in the middle of this meeting, and, besides, the stake president will probably be very busy." The feeling came back, "You can get a blessing." Finally, I got up and left the meeting. I went back to the office where I had been not ten minutes before. I said to the stake president, "I just felt like I should come back for a blessing." I told him I was a little anxious about the start of the semester and needed more clarity about what I should be doing.

What came out of the blessing was a very clear message that I was to pray about what I should pray for. Understanding that I could pray to know what to pray for helped me achieve a balance between being directed and facing the ambiguities of my calling. I received a calm assurance that I could employ prayer to achieve this balance.

Third, we can seek to increase our capacity to discern. Our lives are complex; our circumstances varied. Failure to develop our spiritual capacity to discern could leave us overwhelmed, overdependent on others for meaning, overcommitted, or overreacting to the next thing that pops up. We are here to make choices. That purpose was made evident to me quite powerfully in another priesthood blessing in which I was told, in essence, "You will know what is good to do if you do not reason it away." I have often remembered that instruction and thought about the criteria it suggests for discerning what is good to do in my life.

I believe we develop discernment by exercising it. We can combine our efforts with the guidance of the Spirit. We can compare our experiences with those of others without feeling we are competing. We can rejoice in their excellence and still know there are ways we can also excel. If we were dressed alike, had none of the possessions of the world—jewelry, purses, wallets—and no information about marriage, children, education or employment, what would we possess? What would you possess? If the things we sometimes rely on to "see" are things of the world, then we are not able to discern the spirituality of the people around us. If we were in a room without those other trappings, we would have to rely more on the

Spirit to teach us about others and about how to be of service to them. We would be able to discern by the same spiritual resources that we have now, only their availability to us would be more evident.

We can monitor our own progress and discern the gains we make and the patterns in which we are vulnerable to temptation. I am indebted to a wise old friend (both in years and in association) of another faith who taught me to take an active interest in learning about the patterns in my life and how temptations occurred. He struggled a long time with some of his temptations and finally decided to take a proactive interest. He tried to anticipate where in his life he might encounter that "old trickster devil" again. He became a good scout. He watched the terrain of his life and could tell where it looked like his own form of quicksand might be. He rerouted and gave up trying to see how close he could get to that quicksand without getting caught.

Fourth, we are teachable when we can trust in the Lord. Sometimes we won't know in advance; sometimes in our lives we will "wait upon the Lord" for a long time. But we still need to ready ourselves. We need to be learning, even though the specific opportunities to express what we are learning may not be as apparent or as exciting as we wish.

I gained an appreciation of this point a few weeks ago when I accompanied my sister to Saint George. Her three children sing in the Utah Valley Children's Choir, and she wanted to hear their concert. I wanted to sleep or read; she convinced me I could do both in the car while she drove.

The kids had worked hard, paying attention to Beverly Thomas's direction, learning lyrics, rehearsing harmony, and trying to show up at performances in the appropriate outfits. They did a good job. After their last concert the kids had a chance to stop in Zion National Park on the way home. Diane and I pulled up alongside the bus as it unloaded sixty noisy kids who raced up the path to Weeping Rock. We decided it would be safer to wait in the parking lot.

All of a sudden it was strangely quiet in the canyon. We couldn't see the kids. And then truly angelic sounds filled the canyon. People in the parking lot who were not in our group stopped. We all heard the words echoing in the canyon: "We will sing for the Lord is listening. He hears the praise of our hearts. We will sing for the Lord is listening. We lift our voices and start to sing for the Lord."[2]

It was a beautiful moment of clarity and harmony. When the song ended, there was a joyous shout followed by the more familiar chaotic noises of kids racing back to the bus. When they got back their excitement and joy was tangible. "Did you hear us?" They relayed the story of an older couple who were nearby as they started. When they offered to sing for them, the couple smiled and started to back away, only to stand transfixed as the kids began singing. Now when my niece and nephews joined the choir, nobody promised them a perfect moment in Zion Park on April 29, but there it was. If they had not been ready—individually prepared and collectively willing to participate—they could not have had that experience. It is one thing to arrive at a place like Zion's Weeping Rock and realize, "Yes, this could be a great place for a group of kids to spontaneously experience the product of their learning and the Lord's love through music," and quite another to feel, "Oh, here is the place you have prepared, and having been taught, I am ready." And so sometimes we don't know where our experiences will be put to service, and we prepare for moments we are not sure of, but they come.

In the same way I am instructed by the women who preceded us. The women who stood by the well, who went to the inn, who sought out the tomb, who remained a loyal daughter-in-law, who stood before the king, who taught their sons well. These are women who trusted that their lives would be available to the Lord no matter what their circumstances. Their lives in a wide variety of circumstances had purpose. I also am instructed and learn much from women today who also trust in the Lord no matter their circumstances.

Earlier, in describing the qualities that contribute to being teachable, I listed self-worth. How we understand self-worth greatly affects the degree to which we are teachable. So, my fifth point is that self-worth is different from self-importance.

God loves us, and we are of value to him. If I am teachable, I can learn from those who acknowledge their worth without becoming vain, I can assess their strength and talents without becoming boastful, and, when surrounded by the blessings of a loving God, I can remember Alma's caution to his son: "Do not say: O God, I thank thee that we are better than our brethren; but rather say: O Lord, forgive my unworthiness, and remember my brethren in mercy." (Alma 38:14.)

If we do not care much for ourselves, then to love our neighbor as ourself doesn't mean much. Loving ourselves can magnify our charity toward others. If we overvalue or undervalue ourselves, we are less able and ready to learn from others. We either think we can't learn much from them, or we don't trust their motive for interacting with us.

Helping someone to love himself or herself is harder than just telling that person that you love him or her. We each have a gift. We can learn how to remind each other of the value of our part and the contribution we can make to the whole.

A few weeks ago my counselors and I were asked as a Relief Society presidency to present a fireside to one of the wards. The four of us were asked to talk about the range of our experiences because our lives are so diverse. One of us is married with teenagers, one of us is a single parent, one of us is newly engaged, and one of us has never married. We also run the gamut on education and experience. One of the questions that came to us was intriguing, "How can the four of you be so self-confident?" When we first heard the question we asked ourselves, "How could they see us as confident?" Then we realized that it wasn't just the expression of confidence; we did have something in common that they were picking up on. In each of our lives, for very different reasons and under very different circumstances, we had faced a time when we had to believe in our own self-worth. We had to recognize that we individually were of value to the Lord — something that we often have to face alone, even though we are sustained by others and the Spirit.

Strengthening Our Interactions

Now, having discussed our need to seek to be more teachable, I want to suggest three aspects of our interactions where being teachable seems to be a very needed goal.

First, we might better know the experience of being a woman or a man in our congregation. What is it like for someone who is different from us? If we are women, what can we know of the experience of men as fathers, husbands, siblings, and brothers in the gospel? If we are men, what can we know of the experience of women? The four of us in my Relief Society presidency began asking some of the men we worked with what they thought Relief Society was, what it did, what it accomplished, what it's purpose was. We wanted to know how they saw us, what their experience with Relief Society was, what they thought went on in the meetings. And in the BYU stake we were in we periodically invited the wards to exchange instructors—to have an elders quorum meeting taught by a Relief Society teacher and to have Relief Society meeting taught by an elders quorum teacher. The ward leaders, on two occasions, decided that they needed to exchange information about visiting teaching and home teaching. And so the sisters were invited to the elders quorum and said to the men, "This is what we value about home teachers." And the men were invited to Relief Society to talk about what they hear about visiting teaching. It is extremely important that we know more about the experience of men and women in our congregations.

If we too quickly assume we know what the experience of someone else is or should be, then we are less prepared to learn from "speaking together concerning the welfare of our souls." One of the most disheartening experiences I have had recently was when a neighbor child showed up one day in my yard while I was weeding and said, "My dad says you are inactive." I had just completed five years of service on a general Church committee and was serving as a BYU stake Relief Society president. I explained to this young twelve-year-old that because I didn't attend his ward didn't mean I was inactive. But it reminded me how little we know about the

117

circumstances and lives of others and how we judge with so little information.

Elder Maxwell's description of the quality of conversation in the city of Enoch is instructive to us as both men and women: "You should observe . . . how . . . they listen to each other instead of seeking to display their own learning. They are more willing to be impressed than they are eager to impress."[3] This description is important whether we are eager to impress others of our conservative or our liberal values. We have much to learn from one another in living the gospel, and we can best do that by staying in relationship to each other. I know in my own life that it is easier to talk about somebody than to talk with that person—but my learning is different when we are speaking together. I have learned to listen without fearing that others will think my listening means agreement. And I have learned that being too anxious to tell others where our differences exist hasn't helped me understand them.

In my class on diversity and discrimination, I asked the men and the women to talk about their perceptions of each other, what they had learned from each other, and what they expected from each other. The men said they felt more comfortable in relationships with women that were defined by dating or marriage. When asked about friendship within a congregation, they said they didn't know much about being friends with women. Men and women need to learn more about how to work together on committees and in church assignments, how to be appropriately interested in each other's well-being and caring about each other's work. So we spent time in our class talking about how friendships can be formed that sustain commandments and covenants but allow people to experience one another as brothers and sisters in the gospel.

A second area where being teachable can strengthen our interaction has to do with the quality of our service to one another in our congregation and communities. I have sometimes allowed my own need to serve to determine what I did rather than paying close attention to the needs of others. Seeking to meet the needs of others is more of a challenge than doing what is convenient for me to be helpful. Paying attention to others is a powerful factor in how well we serve. Tim Gallwey wrote about the necessity of paying attention to service. Interestingly enough, he was talking about tennis. He suggested that to improve our serve, we had to learn to love the tennis ball.[4] "What!" I remember saying. "Love a tennis ball?" But he meant pay attention to it, see how it bounces, see where the seams are when it comes at you — concentrate. When we love, we concentrate our attention. By truly paying attention to others around me and concentrating on them, I can place myself in their service and am taught what is needed. I saw a very pragmatic example of this a few semesters ago when a study group member who obviously had better computer skills than the others didn't take the attitude "I learned it, so can they," and didn't say, "I'll do it since you'll never learn this anyway." Instead, he watched, he made himself available, he answered questions, he encouraged. He didn't exaggerate. In his daily interactions with his study group, he was taught how he could best teach them, and he did.

Now, last of all, the best expression of our willingness to be teachable is to be ever ready to say at any moment in our lives, "Nevertheless, not my will, but thine be done." Elder Maxwell states, "The Lord loves both the teachable and the unteachable, but it is through the obedience of the teachable that God can help these helpers, that all might be benefited thereby."[5]

For each of us and for myself, I pray that we will realize that our obedience; our agency; our acknowledgement of God's love for us and our love for Him, for our neighbor, and for ourselves; our testimony of the truthfulness of His gospel; and our willingness to trust His further instruction are never more evident than when we can echo in a small way in our lives the words of our Elder Brother: "Here am I, send me."

Notes

1. Neal A. Maxwell, *Of One Heart: The Glory of the City of Enoch* (Salt Lake City, Utah: Deseret Book Co., 1975), pp. 44–45.

2. Steven Kapp Perry, "Sing for the Lord Is Listening," in *A Child's Prayer:*

Children's Songs, Janice Kapp Perry, Steven Kapp Perry, Lynne Perry Christofferson (Provo, Utah: Prime Recordings, 1986), pp. 15–18.

3. Maxwell, p. 15.
4. Tim Gallwey, *The Inner Game of Tennis* (New York: Random House, 1974).
5. Maxwell, p. 48.

Women and Men

It is my opinion that we are observing, in the changing position of women, a significant and far-reaching revolution in the history of the world. I ask myself and my brethren, what should be the role of men in relation to this revolution? I believe it is to facilitate and support these changes.

—ALLEN E. BERGIN

Power and Intimacy

ALLEN E. BERGIN

*S*o that you can know something about me, I will tell you that my wife's name is Marian and that she and I are the parents of nine children—including triplet boys—and the grandparents of nine grandchildren. Marian invested herself first in the wife-and-mother role, but she was driven by the dynamics of the family to become a psychotherapist! She now practices at Utah Valley Hospital, and we have many interesting experiences together.

It is my opinion that we are observing, in the changing position of women, a significant and far-reaching revolution in the history of the world. I ask myself and my brethren, what should be the role of men in relation to this revolution? I believe it is to facilitate and support these changes. In that connection, I will discuss the Melchizedek Priesthood manuals of the Church and the role that they play in the instruction of men in relation to women.

Let me summarize a couple of themes that I believe are contained in the priesthood manuals of the past ten years, though they are not well known to women—nor to many men either. One theme has to do with power and the other with intimacy. My perception is that we men are being taught that we need to reduce the tendency toward domination and control and increase nurturance and self-sacrifice. Women need to change less than men do because most women do not aspire to control and they already know how to nurture. But each

Allen E. Bergin is professor and director of the clinical psychology program at Brigham Young University. He taught at Columbia University for eleven years and has been a visiting professor at the University of Minnesota and the University of Utah. He received the 1989 Distinguished Professional Contribution to Knowledge award from the American Psychological Association. He is a counselor in the presidency of the BYU Eleventh Stake.

woman does, as a woman, need to increase her willingness to be a complete person, a person with an independent identity and the right to equal respect and opportunity.

Power, which is the capacity to make a difference, needs to be shared and managed with mutual consent and participation. Intimacy, likewise, needs to be shared and managed with mutual consent and participation. Sexual intimacy needs to occur in a context of emotional, intellectual, and spiritual intimacy. This context requires tenderness, commitment that endures, self-control, and self-sacrifice.

Those are themes that I derived from the priesthood lessons. Maybe they surprise you, and if they do, you ought to get a current priesthood manual and read through it. If you are married, invite your husband to discuss the lessons with you. Let me quote from the 1989 manual, Lesson 11, entitled "Encouraging Your Wife's Growth and Development." (There are seven lessons in the manual concerned with these issues.) In the opening section President Spencer W. Kimball is quoted as saying, "Our sisters do not wish to be indulged or to be treated condescendingly; they desire to be respected and revered as our sisters and our equals. I mention all these things, my brethren, not because the doctrines or the teachings of the Church regarding women are in any doubt, but because in some situations our behavior is of doubtful quality."[1]

Power

Let me give examples concerning the kind of power that is being endorsed in our instruction. I knew a member of the Quorum of the Twelve who supervised our work in the New York City area. He was a powerful individual, and when he was called to be a member of the Twelve, he asserted himself vigorously in the high councils of the Church. But one of the senior Brethren said to him, "Don't you know that when you have the power you can't use it?" What did he mean by that? Certainly he did not mean for the new apostle to give up his priesthood power. He simply meant that there was a way of using it that is divinely sanctioned, a way that all righteous men

124

must learn, a way that is explained in Doctrine and Covenants 121:34–46.

With respect to decision making, which is one of the most important uses of power, my friend Carlfred Broderick, former president of the Cerritos, California Stake, asserts that husband and wife should share equally, a view with which I agree.[2] Decisions should be mutually agreed to. There is no place for one-sidedness. In all family matters, husband and wife should be one and function as a unit in which they come to unified decisions together.

This principle was enunciated in the last century through the Prophet Joseph Smith and is recorded in Doctrine and Covenants 107. The priesthood decision-making principle laid out there can be applied as well to the home situation, in which husband, wife, and perhaps children may be making important decisions. Section 107 refers to decisions of the high quorums or councils of the Church: "Every decision made by . . . these quorums must be by the unanimous voice of the same; that is, every member in each quorum must be agreed to its decisions, in order to make their decisions of the same power or validity. . . . Unless this is the case, their decisions are not entitled to the same blessings which the decisions of a quorum of three presidents were anciently, who were ordained after the order of Melchizedek, and were righteous and holy men." (Vv. 27, 29.) These decisions must be made in holiness, lowliness of heart, and meekness. The promise, then, is that if a decision is unanimous, it receives the greater sanction or blessing of the Lord.

In this mode of making decisions, all participants have a veto power that is to be respected, both by each individual and by the group as a whole. I submit to you that if we make unanimous decisions in the home in keeping with this principle, those decisions will also receive the greater sanction and blessing.

Let me refer again to President Kimball, who said, "When we speak of marriage as a partnership, let us speak of it as a *full* partnership. We do not want our LDS women to be *silent* partners nor limited partners in that eternal assignment! Please be a *contributing* and a *full* partner."[3] Another great man, Theodore M. Burton of the First Quorum of the Seventy, had this to say about unity of husband and wife: "When I personally think of Elohim, or Father, I think of mother also. To my mind they are one because they are one in perfect knowledge, power, purity, all-wise, all-knowing, and all-loving. At least that is how I personally think of my heavenly parents. They are united in all wisdom and in doing what they do together."[4] These remarks are his personal opinion, but I believe they fit President Kimball's model of equal partners. Consequently, we might think of husband and wife as sharing authority, as being together in decision making. The wife is not in a secondary position, as is a counselor in a stake presidency or bishopric.

In our home, my wife and I have attempted to make decisions jointly. A few years ago when we decided to move from the New York-New Jersey area to Provo, we fasted together; we prayed together. It was an important and consequential decision that affected everyone's life. Never would I have considered deciding on my own without my wife's counsel and consent. If there were disagreement, we would do the same thing we have observed in the councils of the Church: we would postpone the decision, gather information, and evaluate the problem until we could reach a consensus. If that is the way the councils of the Church operate, shouldn't we apply the same principle in our homes?

Intimacy

Let me refer to the concept of intimacy in a little different way from the ordinary. It seems to me that masculinity ought to be expressed in the intimacy of the home as sacrifice, that is, men's giving up some of their personal interests for the sake of serving their wives and families in the same way the Lord serves us, even though he presides over us. I might refer here to Ephesians 5, in which husbands are enjoined to love their wives even as Christ loved the Church and gave himself for it. "So ought men to love their wives as their own bodies. . . . For no man ever yet hated his own flesh; but nourisheth and cherisheth it, even as the Lord [loved and cherished] the church." (Ephesians 5:28–29.)

President Kimball asked what it means for men to love their wives even as Christ loved the Church and gave himself for it: "Christ loved the Church and its people so much that he voluntarily endured persecution for them, suffered humiliating indignities for them, stoically withstood pain and physical abuse for them, and finally gave his precious life for them. When a man is ready to treat his household in that manner, not only the wife but all the family will respond to his leadership."[5] We need to consider that the Savior, who is the author of the priesthood, came not to be ministered unto, He said, but to be a minister and "to give his life a ransom for many." (Matthew 20:28.)

Let me return now to the 1989 Melchizedek Priesthood manual: "You can give your wife emotional support by—

"1. Keeping your promises and commitments.

"2. Expressing love and appreciation daily.

"3. Giving her sincere compliments.

"4. Spending time alone with her.

"5. Sharing thoughts and feelings and listening to her." And then at the end of the lesson we're given a worksheet to fill out, which says: "What are your wife's social needs? What can you do to help her meet those needs? What are your wife's intellectual needs? What can you do to help her meet those needs?"[6]

It is wonderful that we are being taught in the priesthood quorums how to be men consistent with the divine concept of masculinity outlined in scripture and in the teachings of the prophets.

Let me conclude by saying that I believe that contemporary women are transitional figures between the old ways and the new ways yet to come. Therefore, they struggle with change rather than stability, ambiguity rather than certainty. Those I know best are being valiant in this process, both married and single women. Single women have a great role to play in this process, whether they have never been married or have been married and widowed or divorced.

Valiant Latter-day Saint women are carving out of the social matrix a new destiny for women in the generations to come. This is the day of women. The daughters of Zion are rising to the fulness of their eternal natures as intelligent beings who understand the principle of agency and act from it. For myself, I say God bless all who are participating in what seems to me a heroic effort, however public and dramatic or private and quiet their contributions may be. May the processes of change that they elect have the sanction of the Lord Jesus Christ, that thereby peace may be in their hearts and in the hearts of all those who are affected by this revolution. May it not be a revolution of this world but rather a revolution against the standards of the world and thus a latter-day witness of what eternal womanhood means. May we as men embrace the divine concept of masculinity and thereby nurture the processes of self-actualization in which so many women are now engaged.

Notes

1. Spencer W. Kimball, in *Seek to Obtain My Word: Melchizedek Priesthood Personal Study Guide, 1989* (Salt Lake City: The Church of Jesus Christ of Latter-day Saints, 1988), p. 71.
2. Carlfred Broderick, *One Flesh, One Heart: Putting Celestial Love into Your Marriage* (Salt Lake City: Deseret Book, 1986), pp. 31–32.
3. Spencer W. Kimball, "Sharing Priesthood Blessings with Our Wives," in *Seek to Obtain My Word*, p. 226.
4. Theodore M. Burton, *God's Greatest Gift* (Salt Lake City: Deseret Book, 1976), p. 17.
5. Quoted in *Prepare the Way of the Lord: Melchizedek Priesthood Personal Study Guide 1978–79* (Salt Lake City: The Church of Jesus Christ of Latter-day Saints, 1978), p. 10.
6. "Encouraging Your Wife's Growth and Development," in *Seek to Obtain My Word*, pp. 73–74.

Snapshots and Observations

STEPHEN G. WOOD

*A*s I was thinking about what I might say on the theme of Women and Men in the 1980s: A Male Perspective, I decided the relationship I knew the most about was the relationship that I have with my wife, Mary Anne. We are the parents of five children: our oldest is eighteen; our youngest is five.

What I would like to do, then, is to provide you with five snapshots of our relationship and to draw from those snapshots some observations that I think are true for Mary Anne and me and, more generally, are true for other married couples.

Five Snapshots

First snapshot: 1968. In the summer of 1968, I attended a fireside where I met my future wife. I was impressed. She was impressed. Being the dynamic and decisive person that I am, I waited six months before I asked her out on our first date. That first date did not go very well. We double-dated with good friends whom we both knew, and together we decided that we would see a movie. We went to the movie theater and discovered that the movie was sold out. The four of us then spent the next two and a half hours driving around the Salt Lake Valley trying to decide what we would do. We never did decide, and we finally delivered my wife to work at midnight

Stephen G. Wood, professor of law at the J. Reuben Clark Law School, Brigham Young University, received his juris doctor degree from the University of Utah and his doctor of science of laws degree from Columbia University. He has written two books and numerous articles in his field and teaches courses in administrative law, collective bargaining, comparative law, fair employment practices and standards, international business transactions, and labor law. He has served as a bishop and high councilor. He is married to Mary Anne Q. Wood, and they are the parents of five children.

because she was a police dispatcher for the Bountiful Police Department.

That was our first date. Things did progress from there, and, by the time we had come to the end of the school year— I was a third-year student at the University of Utah College of Law; Mary Anne was a first-year student—we had decided that we would marry. We went to inform Dean Samuel Thurman that Mary Anne was going to discontinue her legal studies. He did not receive this news enthusiastically. The reason for his response was that Mary Anne had done exceptionally well in her first year at the law school—she was third in her class— and Dean Thurman wasn't anxious to lose a woman who had done well at a time when there were relatively few women attending law school.

Nevertheless, when we decided in 1968 to get married, that decision meant that Mary Anne would discontinue her schooling and accompany me first to New York City and then to Munich while I continued my studies. We hoped that we would have children. Our plans, if we were blessed with children, were to raise them, and after they were raised Mary Anne would return to law school.

Second snapshot: 1973. Mary Anne and I were living in the Virginia suburbs of Washington, D.C., in 1973. I was practicing law in the Washington office of a New York City law firm. We were the parents of two children: our first child had been born in Germany; our second child had been born earlier that year. My wife was restless. She did not find life satisfying, circumscribed as it was by activities in and around a housing subdivision in northern Virginia. She wanted more. We talked about our situation and decided that the appropriate thing to do was for her to return to law school.

Mary Anne applied to be admitted to the law school at George Washington University. The initial reaction of the admissions office was that although Mary Anne had been good enough to attend the University of Utah, she might not be good enough to attend George Washington University. They eventually relented, and she returned to the legal studies she had interrupted when we married.

Third snapshot: 1976. In May 1976 Mary Anne graduated first in her class from the law school at George Washington University. In the months before her graduation, we had been talking to Brigham Young University's law school about coming here as members of the faculty. The more we thought about that option, the more attractive it became. We had two children. Mary Anne had had several miscarriages, but we hoped to have more children. Both of us felt a responsibility to be good parents. Teaching and researching at a law school seemed to offer us more flexibility than we would have if I were to continue and Mary Anne were to begin practicing law.

Interviews with a General Authority are part of the hiring process at Brigham Young University. Mary Anne was the first woman to be considered for a full-time appointment at the law school. No one was quite certain what would happen in our interviews.

President Romney was the General Authority who interviewed us. We had a delightful conversation with him, in which we told him about our children and explained why we had chosen to join the law faculty. He wanted to see pictures of our children. President Romney counseled us to be excellent teachers at the law school and to be equally excellent parents to our two daughters. The interview ended successfully, and we began teaching at the law school later that year.

Fourth snapshot: 1981. In 1981 my wife was selected as a White House Fellow, and we moved our family from Provo, Utah, to Washington, D.C. Mary Anne worked as a special assistant to Secretary of Defense Casper Weinberger. Her assignment with Secretary Weinberger was very demanding. I was a consultant to the Department of Labor and the Administrative Conference of the United States.

We had four children by this time, and one of those children was brand new. We and our children had a wonderful time reacquainting ourselves with a part of the country that we dearly love.

Fifth snapshot: 1989. Today, I am a husband, a father of five children (one of whom was born to us after our return to Provo), a teacher and a scholar at the law school, a bishop, a parent who is attempting to establish a school for my children, and an officer in several bar associations, state and federal. I have a very full plate.

Mary Anne is a wife, a mother of five children, a partner in the Salt Lake City office of a Denver law firm, a member of the Utah Constitutional Revision Commission, and chair of the Institutional Council at Utah Valley Community College. She has an equally full plate. We have an exceptionally busy, full life, a life that has evolved over the last twenty years.

Observations

Thinking about Mary Anne and me and what has happened to us and what happens to other couples leads me to the following observations.

My first observation is that there is no "right" choice of roles for any couple. Women and men have a variety of roles. I have mentioned some of the roles that my wife and I currently have. You can think about the roles that you and your spouse, if you are married, have. I want to suggest to you that the right choice of roles for one couple is not necessarily the right choice of roles for another couple. I am not here to say to you that somehow Mary Anne and Steve Wood have discovered the celestial order of things and that all of you must fall in line behind us and do exactly what we do. I am saying that we feel comfortable and happy with the choices we have made.

I want you to know that I think my wife is a better wife and mother to our five children doing what she is doing than if we had made some other choice. I want you to know that we counseled with each other and with our Father in Heaven before making the decision we made and that the decision was made only after the Spirit had whispered to us that the choice we were contemplating was the right choice for us. I am not saying that our choice would be the right choice for you, but I am saying that our choice was the right choice for us. I also want you to know that we continue to counsel with our Father in Heaven about the decisions we are making.

My second observation is that a choice of roles once made may have to be altered because of subsequent events. Flexibility is required. Not all of us marry, even though we may wish to. Not all of us are able to have children, even though we may wish to have them. Not all spouses live happily ever after, even though they may wish to. Those are the realities. Our initial plan was that Mary Anne would interrupt her legal studies, that we would have children and would raise them, and that when our children were raised and perhaps when Mary Anne was forty-five or fifty years of age she would return to law school. That is not what happened. Events change the course of our lives, and we have to be flexible enough to adjust to those changes.

My third observation is that all choices involve benefits and costs. We have to be realistic about both the benefits and the costs when we talk about choices that we ourselves make and as we give counsel to our children. There are benefits and costs in every choice. For example, the choices Mary Anne and I have made involve costs. One of those costs is that my wife spends less time with her children than other mothers spend with their children. Our judgment is that that particular cost is offset by the benefit that I probably spend significantly more time with our children than many fathers spend with their children. There also are other costs. Our lives are so busy at the moment that we essentially have time for each other, our children, our work, and our church responsibilities. Everything else in life simply doesn't receive much attention.

My final observation is that I hope some day we reach the point where each of us has sufficient confidence in the choices we have made that there will be no need to apologize for our choices or to criticize others for the choices they have made. I view with sorrow something that I observe frequently in our community: people criticizing others for the choices they have made and suggesting that the choices others have made are somehow at odds with the "right" choices.

If we are honest with ourselves, we have to admit that conflicting signals are frequently sent about what women should do with their lives. On the one hand, we have all been taught in the Church that the place for women to be is in the home as wife and mother. On the other hand, when my wife was named the associate dean at the law school of Brigham Young University, there was a full-page article in the *Church News* touting her appointment. Sorting out and making sense of these conflicting signals is a challenge.

My own view is that our testimonies of what the gospel requires of us ought not to be based on one talk. I do not think that President Ezra Taft Benson intended to say all that there is to say to the women of the Church in his recent talk in which he stressed the importance of being a wife and mother. That talk was motivated, I think, by wonderful desires on his part. One concern expressed in that talk is that many women — I would add men as well — in the Church are forgoing the opportunity to have children in order to pursue other interests. President Benson, in that particular talk, is reminding all parents that one of our highest priorities in this life ought to be to have children if we are fortunate enough to have them. Another concern being expressed in the talk is that parenting involves more than mere procreation. President Benson is reminding us that when we have children, we have a responsibility to nurture them. Many of you are blessed to be mothers, and, as mothers, your nurturing responsibilities are obvious. I am here today to say that fathers also have a responsibility to nurture their children.

When our choices have been made after consulting our Father in Heaven and after receiving a spiritual confirmation that what we are about to do is right for us, we have no need to apologize to anyone for that decision, and others have no right to criticize us for the decision we have made. If we insist on criticizing others for their choices, realizing that they have consulted their Father in Heaven and that they have received a spiritual confirmation about the appropriateness of the decision they have made, our actions are un-Christlike and the judgments we are making are the kind of unjust judgments our Savior warned us to avoid.

My wife's mother, Alice Quinn, is a "traditional" mother. She raised eight children and is one of the most interesting people I know. She is now eighty-three years old and lives with us. One of the things I admire about her is that she is continually interested in exploring new ideas. She represents the traditional model. I love her and respect her for the choice she made. She has no need to apologize for her choice. My wife made another choice. She represents another model. I love her and respect her for the choice she made. She has no need to apologize for her choice, either. Alice Quinn and Mary Anne Wood are two different people. Horace Quinn and Stephen Wood are two different people. The Quinns made the right choice for them. I fervently believe we made the right choice for us.

A New Era for Mormon Women and Men

EUGENE ENGLAND

*M*y main credential for being here is that I've now been married for thirty-five years to Charlotte Ann Hawkins. She is a remarkable combination of forthright honesty and generous love, and she has educated me a great deal during the eighties, as have my five daughters and my daughter-in-law. I have three granddaughters and two grandsons, and I think they, too, will educate me in the coming new era that I want to describe later. One of the main things that I have learned in the eighties about men and women is that it is presumptuous and usually not helpful to generalize about women — or men either. So I will mainly offer some personal testimony that may be useful to some of you.

Last Monday Charlotte and I saw the Ballet West production of act 2 of Swan Lake. I could not resist seeing the ballet as a parable of men and women in Western culture. Remember, Prince Siegfried has come of age and, in keeping with the central human tradition, must choose a bride. He is out hunting swans with his court companions but is in a meditative mood about his upcoming responsibilities. He sees a swan come out of the lake and turn into a beautiful woman. She tells him that

Eugene England is professor of English literature at Brigham Young University, where he has taught courses in Shakespeare and American and Latter-day Saint literature. He received a doctor of philosophy degree from Stanford University. He has written three books, Brother Brigham, Dialogues with Myself, *and* Why the Church Is as True as the Gospel, *and is preparing two others,* Shakespeare's Avengers and Healers *and* The Quality of Mercy, *a collection of personal essays. He is the editor of* The Best of Lowell L. Bennion, Harvest: Contemporary Mormon Poems, *and* Converted to Christ through the Book of Mormon. *He has served as bishop, branch president, and high councilor, and is currently a counselor in a Provo bishopric. He is married to Charlotte Hawkins England, and they are the parents of six children.*

she and her companions are under a spell and only at night can take on human form.

When the sorcerer, Von Rothbart, appears in the form of an owl, the prince wants to shoot him but is prevented by the woman, Odette. She and the maidens dance in the glade as the prince searches for her among them, and then in a marvelous *pas de deux* they fall in love. But with the dawn Odette succumbs again to the spell and turns back into a swan.

This ancient story (I've given only part of it, of course) has become perhaps the most popular modern ballet partly because it tells us much about Western perceptions and anxieties concerning men and women in marriage. Extended commentary about its relevance to us in the eighties is tempting, but let me mention only two things.

First, there is a strange confusion in the prince's companions, who aren't certain whether to shoot the owl or the swans—that is, whether to attack what it is in our culture that enslaves women and turns them into passive, less-than-human swans or to attack the women. Perhaps they recognize their kinship to the owl, the male sorcerer, and cannot attack what is in themselves. Second, viewed from our seats back in the mezzanine, the dancing of Daniela Buson was elegantly shaped, flawless, wonderfully expressive of Ivanov's classical choreography for Odette's transitions from swan to woman to lover. But as I looked through my binoculars at Buson's face, I saw a constant mask of pain, tragic yearning, and fear combined in this woman escaping enchantment in response to her womanly nature. I remember that most of the great ballerinas, beginning at least with Pavlova, have naturally taken on that face.

Is it fear of being drawn back into enchantment or of being taken out into something even more terrible and demanding — love and marriage? I found it hard to watch that face, perhaps because I have seen such a face of combined fear and yearning on Mormon women, young and old, who have come to my office for counsel in the eighties, perhaps even more because I have begun to recognize such fear and yearning combined in myself as a married Mormon man. In the past ten years I

have become increasingly unsure about the value and satis-
faction of my traditional male role as aggressive achiever, doer,
decider, spokesman, which for all my achievements has left
me lonely and defensive and in some ways emotionally im-
mature. I become uneasy about what our culture has traditionally designated the masculine virtues of courage, pride,
self-confidence, rational assertion, generalization, and deci-
siveness, which for all their apparent value, seem to leave
individuals and whole societies in constant unsatisfied desire
and constantly engaged in envy, rivalry, and imitative violence.

I have found inadequate for my own needs as a poet and
essayist the traditional male style of straightforward narration
and logical conclusiveness, which for all it says leaves what is
most important to me unsaid. Instead, I find myself, though
I'm still not very good at it, wanting to listen, to cooperate, to
nurture with presence, to learn rather than to teach. I yearn
to *be* more than to *do*, to give mercy more and to seek justice
less, to heal rather than to help. I yearn to be meek. I want to
listen to my inner voices record their circling presence, trust
my unconscious mind as it moves upon silence, as it responds
to the unpredictable, uncapturable breeze of the Holy Ghost.
I do not want to be the sorcerer, to hold power that changes
women into something else.

Charlotte is also changing in some directions that are quite
different from mine, as she moves out of some of the destructive
enchantments of her youth and culture. She is doing, achieving,
asserting, and deciding. She is cultivating courage, speaking
out, writing, and learning by refusing to put up with nonsense,
manipulation, and exploitation. I find myself growing in admiration and love for her, yearning and delighting to know
her as well as be with her. I am also fearful sometimes. But
mainly I am excited about this adventure we are having together
and hopeful for ourselves and the many others who are having
a similar adventure. We are changing and growing partly because of the challenging time in which we live, challenging
for the Church and for women and men.

Forgive me, but I am still reprobate male enough that I
want to generalize about this challenging era a bit. I draw on

two important books that Mormon women and their friends have produced in the eighties, *Sisters in Spirit: Mormon Women in Historical and Cultural Perspective* (University of Illinois, 1987), edited by Maureen Ursenbach Beecher and Lavina Fielding Anderson, and *As Women of Faith* (Deseret Book, 1989), talks selected from the BYU Women's Conferences and edited by Mary E. Stovall and Carol Cornwall Madsen. In these two blue-covered books, which I recommend that you read, we are reminded of two rather sharply different periods the Church has gone through, and some new possibilities are suggested.

During most of the nineteenth century, the Church was in what has been called a mode of radical restoration. Mormon women were fully involved in—and their involvement was crucial to—the success of a literal building of the kingdom of God that required heroic efforts, and not only in the traditional women's roles of establishing homes and caring for the sick and needy, as the Saints were uprooted time after time. That restoration also required women, because polygamy and continuing proselyting often kept men absent, to become heads of households and thus to develop occupational and professional skills. They did this, as non-Mormon scholar, Jan Shipps, has pointed out, "in far greater numbers than [women did] elsewhere in the Western world."[1]

Mormon women, individually and collectively, developed unusual independence, participated in public life (including publishing and politics), voted, involved themselves in the national suffrage movement, and so on. And they enjoyed remarkable equality within the Church itself. The Relief Society, one of the first women's organizations in the world, was seen by Joseph Smith as an extension of the priesthood, and the temple was revealed as a place where men and women were equally yoked in a kingdom of kings and queens, priests and priestesses. As Carol Cornwall Madsen has documented, Mormon women enjoyed great opportunities in connection with the temple ordinances, opportunities for healing and for giving blessings to pregnant women and others.[2]

The success of the Mormon kingdom generated opposition

from Victorian society and the United States government that by 1890 had nearly destroyed the Church, and the Lord led us into a period of conservative accommodation and preservation, including the end of polygamy and of theocratic politics and economics. Mormon women took their places essentially as wives and supporters of male Church, business, and political leaders, and women's lives centered more exclusively in home and family. Their prominence in politics and publishing and the independence of their auxiliary declined. The evidence suggests that even their roles in relation to the priesthood in the temple were diminished.

This stage of retrenchment may have been necessary to build a strong family and economic base for taking the gospel to all the world in preparation for Christ's coming. But now in the eighties I believe we are entering a third stage, one more like the first, where radical restoration is needed again more than conservative preservation. New nations are opening up to the Church almost monthly in a way unthinkable just ten years ago, including Kenya, Zimbabwe, India, Ghana, Poland, Hungary, East Germany, China — and we have hopes for Russia. The Book of Mormon is being placed everywhere with almost exponential increases, sweeping the earth, as President Ezra Taft Benson has prophesied, like a flood. The need for leaders and teachers, for talent, energy, and ideas, is growing just as fast, very much like in the early Church, when women had to contribute beyond the customs of the time for the kingdom even to survive. Once again, I believe, we are seeing and will see women emerge in new roles in the Church, not because of someone's theory about equality but simply because their abilities and energies are desperately needed.

Julia Mavimbela of South Africa is a marvelous example, emerging as a Mormon woman leader in the efforts to heal that torn nation, efforts that will be tied, I believe, directly to the gospel and her participation in it. [See her own account on pages 61–72.] My youngest daughter Jane became the district leader over the sister missionaries in her mission, even a kind of an assistant to the president (which would have seemed an impossible idea not long ago), simply because a pragmatic leader saw the need and saw her value. Women—more than half the membership of the Church—simply must not be relegated to anything less than full participation in building the kingdom.

As we move into this new stage, I feel a need to leave behind some cultural baggage inherited from our sexist Western traditions, some popular doctrinal ideas that are unworthy of our worldwide mission and are directly damaging to it. A central liberating truth restored by God to Joseph Smith was that the Fall was not a bad thing, a *thwarting* of God's plan, but instead was a *part* of the plan, a courageous act by our great first parents, Adam and Eve, that began the process of mortal probation and atonement. Christ completed the Atonement, leaving us all, men and women, free forever to choose and progress through repentance towards godhood.

But during the conservative, preservation stage of this century, when I believe we were unduly influenced by American values, including traditional Judeo-Christian sexism, there was gradually insinuated into popular Mormon theology a destructive ancient notion. It is the notion that Eve succumbed to Satan's temptation and in turn tempted Adam and brought about our downfall, and thus she and all women had to be punished and controlled. This notion has been used to justify the horrible suppression of women in Western culture, including the terrible persecution of so-called witches, in which as many as hundreds of thousands of women in Europe were executed in the name of Eve because they thought for themselves or were a little different.

Unfortunately, this notion of Eve's responsibility for the Fall has been buttressed for Mormons by a too-literal reading of the Genesis story. But I believe the idea is false. Modern scripture clearly denies it, and the temple ceremony warns us we must see the Genesis story dramatized there as only *figurative* so far as the man and the woman are concerned.

The book of Moses makes absolutely clear that what Eve correctly refers to as *"our* transgression" was part of God's plan, a correct decision and something to be thankful for, not a reason for punishment or suppression. (Moses 5:11.) Further,

God tells Adam and Eve after they are baptized that they are both forgiven of their transgression in the Garden. (Moses 6:53–54.) The Doctrine and Covenants explicitly denies the idea of Eve's prior transgression by saying Adam was responsible for the Fall: "The devil tempted *Adam,* and he partook of the forbidden fruit and transgressed the commandment. . . . Wherefore, I . . . caused that he should be cast out from the Garden." (D&C 29:40–41; italics added.) But of course God is using the term *Adam,* a plural proper noun, to mean Adam and Eve, Mr. and Mrs. Adam, if you will, together. They made that crucial decision as you would expect that our great, divinely chosen first parents, the first couple married on earth and the model for us all, would do — through consultation and agreement, in exactly the way that we have heard recommended for *all* couples in our priesthood and Relief Society manuals. Much of the pain I have seen on the faces of Mormon women could be removed, I believe, if we aggressively taught this true doctrine, which honors women and men equally and gives them equal responsibility.

The Book of Mormon tells us that all are alike unto God, both black and white, both male and female. (2 Nephi 26:33.) Elder Bruce R. McConkie, shortly after the revelation giving blacks the priesthood, quoted that scripture about all being alike unto God and said, "Many of us never imagined or supposed that these passages had the extensive and broad meaning that they do have."[3] If we didn't understand for a long time what it means that "black and white" are alike unto God, perhaps we still don't understand fully what it means that "male and female" are alike unto God. I look forward in this third era of church history, opening up in the late eighties and the nineties, to discovering more fully what that equality means — and also to discovering more fully what it means when Christ tells us, also in the Book of Mormon, "what manner of men [and women] ought ye to be? . . . even as I am." (3 Nephi 27:27.) If we can do so, I believe we can come out of our enchantments to full human lives as daughters and sons of Heavenly Parents.

Let me close by reading something from Sister Mavimbela. It is a kind of prophetic description of the role all of us, who are alike unto God, black and white, male and female, can take in the new era opening up to the Church and to Mormon men and women throughout the world:

"I give thanks to God that He has made me a woman. I give thanks to my Creator that He has made me black, that he has fashioned me as I am, with hands, heart, head to serve my people. . . . It can, it should, be a glorious thing to be a woman. It is important for women to be aware of their common lot. It is important for women to stand together and rise together to meet our common enemies — illiteracy, poverty, crime, disease, and stupid, unjust laws that have made women feel so helpless as to be hopeless."[4]

Sister Mavimbela talked about an interesting phenomenon she has seen in her country: that the men there, when faced with a problem, tend to turn quickly toward confrontation and violence. She said that the women, on the other hand, are not like that. This contrast is not just true of her culture. I suggest as a practical agenda for us all that we need to learn from the "feminine values," and perhaps from women themselves, how to be less violent in our culture, how to get over our natural tendency toward envy and rivalry and escalating violence. A good example, I feel, was the peacemaking talk Sister Joy Evans, counselor in the Relief Society General Presidency, gave near the close of the April 1989 general conference, a very healing message that many of us particularly needed right then.[5]

Notes

1. Foreword to *Sisters in Spirit: Mormon Women in Historical and Cultural Perspective*, ed. Maureen Ursenbach Beecher and Lavina Fielding Anderson (Urbana: University of Illinois Press, 1987), p. viii.

2. Carol Cornwall Madsen, "Mormon Women and the Temple: Toward a New Understanding," in *Sisters in Spirit*, pp. 80–110.

3. Bruce R. McConkie, "All Are Alike unto God," address given 18 Aug. 1978, in *Charge to Religious Educators* 2d ed. (Salt Lake City, Utah: The Church of Jesus Christ of Latter-day Saints, 1982), p. 52.

4. Julia Mavimbela, Presidential Address to Transvaal Region of National Council of African Women, 28th Regional Conference, Aug. 1975.

5. Joy F. Evans, "Lord, When Saw We Thee an Hungred?" *Ensign* May 1989, pp. 73–75.

Confessions of a
Sometimes-Reactionary Mormon Male

TIM B. HEATON

*L*et me explain the title of my remarks. For me, a central tenet of the gospel is that we are all children of Heavenly Parents. We have all inherited the same divine potential and have been offered the same eternal blessings. Any denial of this equality is morally wrong. Any attempt to define a category of persons as inferior, subordinate, or second class on the basis of ascribed characteristics, such as race or gender, is evil. Such an attempt is evil because it may limit the ability of those who are so defined to make the most of their God-given experience on this earth, and it is evil because it is false. The women's movement has made us painfully aware of many ways in which gender is a basis of discrimination, a basis of evil, as I have defined evil. My religious belief demands that I be intolerant of gender discrimination, that I do what I can to eliminate it. From this perspective, the women's movement has been an important source of religious enlightenment.

So why am I sometimes reactionary? Why do I sometimes balk at changes in gender roles? Why do I feel uneasy with some feminists' messages? Why do I want to preserve a large chunk of our values and traditions? These have not been easy questions for me to answer, and my answers are not complete, but I appreciate the opportunity to give you a progress report.

I'm afraid it is my lot in life to feel ambivalent about many things. Let me give you a few examples. I am delighted to see an important leader express love and concern for children, offer them counsel, and tell them how important they are. At

Tim B. Heaton is an associate professor of sociology at Brigham Young University. His research has focused on the demography of Latter-day Saints, the relationship between religion and family, and the interrelatedness of such family changes as marriage, childbearing, and divorce.

the same time, I worry about the subtle and unintended message the children hear when this leader tells them that the best thing in the world to be is a Mormon boy. Women and girls who already question how much they are valued may be hurt. Male feelings of superiority may also be reinforced. I really do not believe the Church leader intended to tell men that they are superior or women that they are inferior. I do believe, however, that we belong to a culture that has given us the message that the best thing to be is a Mormon boy. I personally like the Mormon boy song. It gives boys a sense of pride in belonging to a good organization. I feel ambivalent, however, because we do not sing about being a Mormon girl.

Another source of ambivalence comes from the Church and my teenaged children. I don't like it that there is inequality in the use of Church resources to support my teenaged son. A large portion of our ward budget goes to the Scouts, but very little goes to the Young Women's program. I don't like it when boys' achievements are given more attention than girls' achievements. On the other hand, I am delighted with leaders who care about my children, who create wholesome activities for them, and who set good examples for them. This care and concern is at least as evident for my daughter as for my son. I am grateful to belong to a ward that gives my teenagers so much at a very important time in their development.

I have been accused of being a purveyor of demography. The demographic statistics I have studied are also a source of ambivalence. The first statistic is the recent estimate that two-thirds of new marriages will eventually end in divorce. Several reasons have been offered for the dramatic increase in divorce. One of the most important is that women are more independent now. The ideology of liberation combined with increased opportunities to earn a living allow women more freedom to escape from undesirable marriages. Since I place a high value on long-term commitment in marriage, that is a very distressing statistic. Nevertheless, because I believe that no man or woman should be compelled to remain in a bad relationship out of economic necessity or ideological repression, I also see a good side to that statistic.

145

The second statistic is that gender-based socioeconomic inequality is greater in religious groups that hold to traditional values. In a study of Canadian religious groups, we found substantial variation in the ratio of male to female education, labor force participation, and income. The socioeconomic gap between males and females was greater in The Church of Jesus Christ of Latter-day Saints than in most other religious groups. Moreover, religions with lower divorce rates and larger family sizes generally have greater gender inequality. I like commitment to children and marriage, but I don't like systematic gender inequality.

The third statistic was presented by Marie Cornwall in this conference. On the average, Mormons score lower than average on depression. Contrary to popular speculation, Mormon women do not score higher on depression than do other women. Overall, however, Mormon women are more depressed than Mormon men. Mormon men are the least depressed in all the major religious groups. This statistic reaffirms my belief that the social support and purpose in life offered by our religion are beneficial; however, the gap between male and female depression is greater for Mormons than for most other groups. Perhaps there is something about our gender-role structure that is more beneficial to men than to women. Perhaps the best possible thing to be is a Mormon boy. But if the positive mental condition of Mormon men comes at the expense of Mormon women, then something is wrong.

The last set of statistics concerns women in third-world countries. In the United States, the women's movement has focused on issues of gender equality. The goals are to eliminate gender differences in power, prestige, and economic position. Third-world women are more concerned with escaping poverty and with achieving some degree of dignity. It will be many years before equality will be an achievable goal. The conditions of third-world women vary dramatically. We have just completed a study of women's work patterns in Bogotá, Bangkok, and Cairo. Only about a fourth of women in Cairo will ever have gainful employment. The restrictions of Islamic culture severely limit women's roles. In Colombia the percentage of women who will work for pay is closer to fifty percent. Catholic religion and culture are not so restrictive. In Bangkok more than 80 percent of women will work for pay. It seems that cultures based on Buddhist beliefs are even less restrictive about the economic role of women.

My ambivalence comes because we have a very important message to share with the world — the gospel. I hope the message we deliver is not overburdened with our Wasatch Front notion of appropriate gender roles. More importantly, I hope the message will promote rather than prevent an improved quality of life for third-world women in a wide variety of cultural and economic circumstances.

In sum, my ambivalence arises because I find many things I value in Mormonism. At the same time, I find other elements that stand in the way of our achieving greater equality of the sexes. I want change, but not change that will destroy the things I value, such as strong and stable commitment to marriage and children.

At this point we could spend some time agonizing over an interesting question, namely, will gender equality destroy our ability to have stable marriages and good child care? The problem is that I don't think we have a definitive answer. I do believe that increasing gender equality in the last few decades has led to a higher divorce rate and a decrease in the amount of time children spend with parents. This fact does not necessarily mean, however, that there has been a decrease in the quality of marriage or of parenting. Nor does it mean that there are no alternative ways of creating greater gender equality without detracting from family life.

It is more beneficial to ask a different question, namely, are there ways we can promote greater gender equality that will not detract from, and indeed may even improve, family life? My answer is a resounding yes:

We must find ways to enhance the status of women. "Mother of the Year" awards are great but will not fit all women. For some, a job may be the best solution. Jobs can provide a sense of accomplishment and self-worth. Many important contributions to society are also made through jobs. To assume that women work only for the money is unfair. I still remember a friend's distress at the suggestion that she was materialistic because she was employed; she felt her work made a valuable contribution to society. Our own home has benefited from my wife's return to school. She has gained self-esteem and knowledge; her studies have enhanced our conversations; and she, being a diligent student, is a great role model for our children. I would also recommend that husbands send their wives away for a week from time to time so that the men can take responsibility for homemaking. My wife insists that our food budget cannot afford her absence very often, but I have gained some appreciation for her contribution by trying to manage the family on my own.

I also wish we could find ways to give more status to fathers who are fathering. The most respected men seem to be those who accomplish much in their work or church callings. Neighbors have sometimes complimented me after seeing my name in the paper, but I get no recognition for taking the neighborhood kids to the swimming pool or to movies. Of course, we don't do either for recognition, but recognition does help us feel appreciated.

Children need to be encouraged to learn the importance of both breadwinning and parenting-homemaking. (My wife is due the credit for implementing this instruction in our home.) Our society is beginning to realize that women may be the sole supporters of a family and that there are many other good reasons for women to develop employable skills. Schooling and good grades in all subjects — including math and science — are equally important for girls and boys. Our society is slower, however, in learning that boys also need to learn about homemaking and childcare in order to be good fathers. Boys should learn to cook and clean toilets just as girls learn to do physics and chemistry. And of course, daddy needs to be willing to do whatever jobs are assigned to the kids.

I could mention many other things, but I hope you see the point. There are many things we can do to enhance women's status in society and help families at the same time. After we achieve these goals, we may be ready to start answering broader questions about gender equality. I look forward to the day when it will be just as meaningful and pleasurable to sing about being a Mormon girl as to sing about being a Mormon boy. I doubt we can achieve such balance without strong families, but I also doubt we can do it until gender bias has been eliminated.

Women as Parents

In the parable of the prodigal son, the Savior taught clearly what our response to the wayward should be. We give our best to our children for as long as they will let us, and when they insist on leaving, we let them go. Then we wait and pray. We are constant in our love, even though we have to endure the pain of their sinning. When they return, we rejoice.

— RICHARD C. FERRE

As Parents, What Do We Do with the Pain?

MARIAN S. BERGIN

*I*t hurts to have wayward children. It hurts deeply. When a precious child becomes a stranger to us, we may feel betrayed. We may lose faith in ourselves, in the family unit, in everything we've counted on for a sense of happiness and hope for the future. We may become a stranger to ourselves, driven to accuse, attack, blame, reject, belittle, judge, deny, until— overwhelmed—we may turn it all off and sink into depression. Maybe you are there right now.

Our pain can either teach us or defeat us. We can use our emotional pain to drive us to positive action, or we can let ourselves be swallowed up in self-pity and feelings of victimization. In trying to understand the experiences life gives us, especially ones as emotionally painful as a child's rejecting his or her parents and family values, it helps to hear from those who have been there. With that in mind, I drew upon bonds of friendship to obtain several remarkable statements on this subject and permission to share them with you.

As you listen to these accounts, it might be helpful to keep in mind Elizabeth Kubler-Ross's five stages of grieving: denial, anger, bargaining, depression, and finally acceptance.[1] Whenever we face significant, ongoing pain, we go through these emotional stages, or a variation of them. The process and the result can ultimately be positive, leading to personal growth.

Marian S. Bergin, homemaker and clinical social worker, serves as the program director of Adult Psychiatry and the Depression Center at Utah Valley Regional Medical Center in Provo, Utah, and also has a private psychotherapy practice. She received a bachelor of science degree in psychology and a master of social work degree from Brigham Young University. She has served in many auxiliary positions and on the Church Evaluation Correlation Committee. She and her husband, Allen, are the parents of nine children and have nine grandchildren.

Or we can become stuck in one of the stages and never reach the resolution of our pain.

First, listen to this mother, who describes her experience with several children who rejected the values she and her husband had taught them:

"[Having children reject your values and standards] makes you deal with the subject of the fairness of life. You examine yourself and discover where and to what you are anchored. You suffer, you sacrifice, and you wonder if this is where you really want to be, if this [suffering] is what you want to continue doing. As you resolve these issues, you become more tolerant, less judgmental, more pliable.

"Great truths are revealed about yourself. I know I have a more healthy detachment from my children, so that they can soar or dive as they need to, to also discover life and experience their own choices. . . .

"The Church did not help me. In fact, I felt betrayed by some of the promises. *But the Lord did*, and I bear testimony of this with my whole heart and soul."

Second, a mother describes her experience with a son who was involved in drug abuse and, though now drug-free, has rejected his Mormon upbringing:

"I went through a period of real mourning. The information about our son's behavior came to us over the period of a month or two. We kept the specifics of the behavior within the family and shared some general information with our closest friends. I pretty much worked out my own grief. My husband and I differed about what we thought were some of the reasons for the behavior.

"I didn't ignore the pain or try to cover it with busyness or whatever. I expressed the pain as well as the anger to Jimmy. I tried not to spill my pain all over the family since everyone had their own pain. . . . The grieving process came to its own end. The pain was replaced by hope, which I still feel. I have acted on the hope in every positive way I could think of to provide a healthy, healing relationship with Jimmy."

Third, a father relates his experience with a son who heavily abused alcohol and drugs:

"Looking back on the situation, I find that I was much too willing to accept denials and even implausible explanations. None of us wants to have a troubling or troubled child, and denial is often the point of first defense. Once the behavior had escalated to the point where denial was no longer possible, I went through a whole kaleidoscope of emotions. I was alternately fearful for his safety and even his life. I felt guilty that I had somehow failed him as a father. I was hurt that he would do these things to us, and I was angry over his behavior and sometimes belligerence. I can remember desperate hours searching the streets and hangouts looking for him when he had suddenly taken off. All sorts of dire consequences passed through my mind. I can also recall situations where I wanted to literally beat the hell out of him.

"As I look back on the situation, I think part of the guilt is attributable to our desire to have answers. It seems logical that every behavioral pattern must have some causative reason. Finally, we came to the conclusion that although we had parental shortcomings, the problems were ultimately his. Our ability to step back and to deal with his behavior in a more positive and unemotional fashion took years to achieve; however, it was at that point that we really were able to offer him the kind of assistance and support that he needed."

Fourth, listen to a father who typed three single-spaced pages, pouring out his private tale of pain over a wayward child:

"I expected more direct relief through prayer and sincere appeals for insight and cures of the problems. I cried for help, but what I got were bits and pieces of understanding and hope here and there over a long period of time. I found that God does not work the way I do. I want to relieve distress quickly and directly. He stretches it out to the limit, until we are revealed for what we are.

"One of the most wonderful resources was having two male friends whom I trusted and who were my confidants. Their support and more objective perspective and nonjudgmental attitudes were an enormous help. They provided relief for my pent-up emotion, and they engendered hope.

"Accepting fault in myself instead of trying to deny or distort it has given me hope, because I realize that if I am part of the problem, I can change, and change in me can make a difference in my children. I found that pain helped me to see myself. I was surprised by the personal learning this brought about. Seeing myself in personal conflict revealed my traits to me in a way that might not otherwise have been possible.

"I found some bishops to be essentially useless and others to be wonderfully helpful. The Church, though, is still far from being the kind of mutual therapeutic community of believers that it ought to be and that I think the Lord intends it to be. As I counsel with members of our stake, I find numerous ways in which we could do better in helping one another through crises and actually solving or curing the crisis.

"I think my pain was increased by the idea that lots of other families were succeeding very well and that ours wasn't. I wanted to hide our private realities. Since then, I have learned that virtually every family faces one or more major moral crises, and I have learned that many of those who are put before us as outstanding examples or who promote themselves before us are about as inadequate as the rest of us."

Fifth, a mother describes her pain over a child's drug problems and abusive behavior:

"There came a point for me when I knew I was going to die. One day I told my husband, 'I can no longer survive in this situation. Either he must leave, or I will die.' Everything inside me was shutting down — my will to produce and nurture and love and live was slowly but very surely disintegrating.

"We, through much heart wrenching, prepared for him to leave and try life in another area with another family. I shall never forget the feeling I had the morning he left. It was complete sadness. I remembered only once before in my life when I'd had this feeling. It was the day after my dad died, when I was fifteen.

"The only way I knew to deal with my feelings was to eliminate the evidence of him in recent years, to try to erase those memories. So almost immediately I cleaned out his room, mostly with a big garbage can from the garage that I set right in the middle of his room. It did help because I found the longer I could go without thinking deeply about him, the more productive I became. I was slowly healing. Time and distance were allowing me to see the world again as it really was. I could feel my strength return.

"It may sound like 'out of sight, out of mind' was my solution, but that's not the way I view it. He stayed away for awhile, and I healed, and he grew older — not necessarily better but also not worse. He came home again, and that was okay. I had regained enough strength to cope with him and at least some of his problems, although it never was easy.

"The last time my son was home, I felt cheated that he had to leave again so soon. He had finally pulled himself out of his hell both physically and spiritually, and I longed for some 'little boy' days again with him. They, too, are gone, and I can only hope that his newfound strength will last him through a lifetime.

"For myself, the lesson has been one of agency. As the Father does not in any way try to force us, we cannot force others, our children included, into believing or living or accepting our will. Nevertheless, we can always be there for them in a supportive, caring, loving way."

I was surprised that in these accounts there was only one mention of talking with close friends or seeking out trusted loved ones to share the pain. Perhaps that is a commentary on our culture. Do we hesitate to share our pain? Do we build walls to keep each other out and protect our images rather than build bridges to reach out to one another? I wish we were more open and trusted each other more — loved each other more.

I work in therapy with people in deep pain. I have heard incredible expressions of emotional anguish, some that have never been voiced before. I stand in awe of what some of us are called upon to endure and also what some of us put ourselves through.

M. Scott Peck, whom you may know as the author of *The Road Less Traveled* (New York: Simon and Schuster, 1978), recently spoke in a seminar that I attended. He had a lot to say about pain. He said that pain is a quintessential part of living. He believes pain is the pure essence of living, the most perfect part. He likened our pain to going into the desert to discover ourselves, as the Savior did. Paradoxically, the more we face our pain—the more we experience awareness of our pain—the more joy we are capable of. Even as we suffer in the desert, experiencing its hunger, thirst, and searing isolation, we become acutely aware of the "little green places"—the oases we never noticed before or never valued. Therein lies true joy.

I hope the experiences I've communicated have helped us begin to sort out the meanings of our pain, to understand it better and to move toward acceptance of whatever challenges we face. Acceptance does not mean that we give up. It means we accept where we are, and only then start making changes and finding solutions—no longer paralyzed by guilt or denial or depression or anger. Some of us might need professional help as we seek this acceptance. I encourage us to get the help we need, choosing it carefully.

The process of accepting our challenges might be likened to an upwardly spiraling staircase. We may have the sense of coming back on ourselves, but in reality we are on a higher level. I cannot teach you *how* to face your pain, but I will say I believe that none of us can do it without becoming more and more honest with ourselves. Therein lies the secret—and the growth.

Note

1. Elizabeth Kubler-Ross, *On Death and Dying* (London: Collier-Macmillan Ltd., 1969).

My Way, Slip Away, Find a Way, Leave a Way

> "No, no!" said the Queen. "Sentence first—verdict afterwards."
>
> "Stuff and nonsense!" said Alice loudly. "The idea of having the sentence first!"
>
> "Hold your tongue!" said the Queen, turning purple.
>
> "I won't!" said Alice.
>
> "Off with her head!" the Queen shouted at the top of her voice.[1]

*I*s that your family? Wouldn't it be wonderful if that's all we had to do to deal with wayward children? Off with their heads! All ways in Wonderland are the queen's ways. "Off with your head" would be an easy solution. The premise in such a world is that everything must be done in the same way.

That is the queen's way of thinking, but it is a one-dimensional way of thinking. If we fail to open our minds to the many alternative ways to solve problems with our children, we are more likely to have trouble coping. We fail when we are more concerned about "the way" than about "the wayward."

Any study of families in the scriptures will reveal that almost none of the scriptural families was without its own wayward children—Adam and Eve weeping for Cain, David weeping over Absalom, Lehi and Sarah weeping over Laman and Lemuel. An alternative premise, therefore, is that we live in a wayward

Richard C. Ferre is a native of Salt Lake City. He studied at Stanford as an undergraduate and received his doctor of medicine degree from the University of Utah. He has served as the chair of the Child Psychiatry Department at Primary Children's Medical Center and as associate clinical professor in the Department of Psychiatry at the University of Utah. He and his wife, Janis M. Baker Ferre, are the parents of three children.

world. Everyone has agency. Things are not under our control. Things go wrong.

The wayward world is the ubiquitous state of things. Let us consider, then, learning *how* to respond to and accept children, *how* to learn from children, *how* not to worry so much about controlling children, but to work at accepting and teaching them. Then the wayward teach us. To love is to let go of trying to control.

I would like to point out something from my experience that I think is important. Genes — those funny things that create our personalities, our bodies, and how everything functions together — are wayward. Somehow it's okay if our ear lobes aren't quite right, or if one hand is slightly different from the other — genes cause those differences — but sometimes we don't appreciate that genes can cause similar differences in our brains. These differences may create such difficult problems as learning disabilities, mental retardation, mental illness, and other disorders of many different kinds. Sometimes the problems are subtle: predispositions to pathology in temperament, personality, and intelligence.

With the wayward, I have found that those with the most significant problems may have biologically based deficits that are often not their fault. They are struggling with unseen handicaps that no one really knows are there. If we are going to understand these children and work with them, we need to understand the biological traits that limit them. These biological problems are predispositions to deviancy, which the child will need help to understand and cope with. Sometimes these problems can be eased with medication, for example, attention problems, predispositions toward anxiety and worry, predisposition to depression, or insensitivity to social reinforcement.

All of these problems can be very real burdens. Children with such traits may have difficulty adjusting to their environment and develop other, major problems. Educational or psychological testing can identify children who may need help in these areas. These tests may tell us, for example, what specific learning style a child has.

Sometimes the wayward are stuck. They are less flexible,

more intense, easily overwhelmed, or frighteningly rigid. Or they may be very independent, more outgoing, not willing to sit and simply conform. Recognizing these differences in children, we are better able to support them as we better understand them.

Let me tell you about a young man who was angry and defensive and who had run away. He had been doing very well in elementary school and was a superior student. When he entered junior high school, however, he began to fail his classes. Eventual evaluation after many failures revealed he had a previously unrecognized learning disability.

Another child, eleven years old, who was irritable and withdrawn, had been going to school and doing reasonably well. He then began having more temper tantrums and became almost totally uncooperative. After thorough evaluation, it was discovered he had a depressive trait. Although it was not a major depression, his predisposition to depression clearly accounted for the problems we observed.

We need to understand that we did not all get an equal start. Wayward genes get in the way. Sometimes their effects are obvious, and sometimes they are subtle. We need to be less judgmental of others and be ready to listen and to understand. We need to respect what a child brings to us. We need to respect the child's agency.

What do we do to help when we feel a child is wayward? I would like to share two things *not* to do and two things *to* do.

The first thing *not* to do is control, to insist on what I call "my way." The queen in *Alice* was always yelling, "My way." We give the message to children that they are not valued or adequate unless they do it "my way." No matter how righteous our intentions, when we have decided that it has to be "my way," we often fail. We all have thought, "If my children are wonderful then I am wonderful. If my children are bad, then I am bad." If we see our children as an extension of ourselves, then we will expect them to be what we think they should be and we do not allow them to become their own person. If we are overly responsible, our need to control can lead to dependency, contention, power struggles, and eventually open conflict with our children.

Sometimes we disguise our control by calling it love: "I am doing this for your own good." The need to control is motivated by fear. It has to do with needing our child's life to follow our specific expectations in order for us to feel comfortable. The child intuitively knows that the control comes from our need and is not necessarily for his or her benefit. Listen to this conversation:

Child: "But I don't want to go to the dance."

Parent: "Well, you won't be happy just staying home."

Child: "It's OK."

Parent: "Well, what about that nice Smith girl?"

Child: "I don't like her."

Parent: "She's very accomplished. I'm sure you'll enjoy her company."

Child: "I don't relate to her."

Parent: "How come you never make friends with any of the respectable kids at school?"

Child: "Leave it alone!"

Parent: "I only want you to be happy. The friends you pick — they don't make you happy. Why are you always in trouble with your friends?"

Child: "Forget it."

The child leaves at this point, annoyed. The parent is not listening — the parent is trying to make things right for the child.

The second thing *not* to do is what I call "slip away." The parent in this situation says, "I just don't know how my child slipped away. Sure, I was very busy, concerned about a lot of things — my church work, my business. I was going to be there later. Later never came." The parent who has slipped away will say, "I'm defeated. I give up. You win! You really are a turkey, and let's let it be that. I am helpless. I am frustrated. I cannot listen, and you are to blame. That feels better to me. You are the problem." In this situation, discipline goes out the window and so does the relationship with the child. The motivations behind this anger are defeat and helplessness. In the guise of giving children agency, we abandon them.

Child: "Mom, I'm going out Friday night and I'm taking the car."

Parent: "What?"

Child: "I'll be gone Friday night."

Parent: "We are going out that evening."

Child: "Dad said I could go."

Parent: "Did you check with your father?"

Child: "I won't be back until late."

Parent: "Well, be sure to be in early."

Child: "Thanks. See you."

This parent is not listening because this parent is not involved.

These two tactics I have just highlighted compound the difficulty with a wayward child. We need to move from control or abandonment to understanding, accepting, and consistent support. To help the wayward child, we need supportive ways to respond to their struggles.

The first thing *to* do is to "find a way." We need to find a way to stay connected with the wayward child, to actively pursue a rewarding relationship with the child. Picture, for a moment, what it was like when the child was little. Remember the fun times when you laughed together or when you read stories together. That child you delighted to know still exists.

First, respond to the child as someone who lives by principle. A good model is always the best advice. Remember the child has grown and lost his innocence, feels pain and alienation, but the child still wants good things, just as do the children he sees who are more obviously successful. We don't need to condone bad behavior while remaining connected to the child. The child must know the principles that we value and that bring us happiness. Then we must stop worrying about how the child is making *us* feel, and start listening to how the *child* feels. Let us look at the dance situation again.

Child: "I'm not going to the dance!"

Parent: "I don't understand. What's the problem?"

Child: "I don't want to go."

Parent: "Okay. I thought you said you wanted to be with your friends."

Child: "They're not going."

Parent: "It's hard to go to the dance when your friends aren't there."

Child: "Yeah, it's no fun at all."

Now we are listening to the child.

As we try to "find a way" to stay connected with our children in a positive relationship, we also need to find a fair structure of rules and discipline that will help us live with them. Make your rules clear and be consistent.

Child: "Mom, I'm going out Friday night. I'm taking the car."

Parent: "You've earned the privilege, so I guess that's fine. Of course it is your brother's night for the car."

Child: "Well, I've got to have it."

Parent: "I guess you'll have to work that out with your brother. It's his night for the car. You can go ahead and negotiate with him."

Child: "But I'll be out real late."

Parent: "You'll need to remember that you have agreed on the time to be home, which is midnight."

Child: "Well, I'm going to be later than that."

Parent: "We expect you at twelve."

Child: "Can we talk about this? I have got something special going on that night, and twelve won't work."

Parent: "Okay, I'll talk about it, but you should know I think we should follow the rules we have established."

This discussion sounds too good, perhaps, but communication and consistent rules can lead to better interactions with our children. We respond to the child within the structure we have set and not out of anger or an attempt simply to control.

Another point to remember about "find a way" is that the passage from childhood to adulthood is difficult. In our society we do not have a clear rite of passage. This lack makes becoming an adult and discovering a meaningful personal identity difficult. Children perceive extensive license in adult behavior,

164

and they assume that adults simply act on their desires. But children have a much poorer concept of what becoming adult means for them in terms of accepting responsibility. They often get lost in their extended adolescence and feel they do not have a meaningful role. We may at times impede our children in finding a meaningful adult role by continuing to treat them as irresponsible children. Children need to experience increasing responsibility, especially with work. Often, if other things are going wrong in their life, they can feel successful by having meaningful work.

The second thing *to* do to help the wayward is "leave a way back." Do not close the door. Do not disown the child. Have patience. Great things can be accomplished with long-suffering, endurance, and patience.

Search for the soul of the child you loved so long before things went wrong. Look past the child's ways, and remember the child's heart. We see numerous examples of wayward children in the scriptures, but we also find messages of the importance of prayer and endurance. The Savior taught clearly what our response to the wayward should be in the parable of the prodigal son. We give our best to our children for as long as they will let us, and when they insist on leaving, we let them go. Then we wait and pray. We are constant in our love, even though we have to endure the pain of their sinning. When they return, we rejoice. They may no longer have an inheritance, but they have our love. And so we set ourselves again to the task of helping them learn the ways of correct principles as far as they will allow us.

We have many opportunities to be guides on our children's journeys. Finally, however, our stewardship requires us to let them go. As we separated from our Father in Heaven, as He let us go, so we let our children go—trusting in Him. Our Godlike task is to shepherd them in order that they may leave us. He suffers for us in our agency. We suffer for them in their agency. Leave a way, leave the heart open, for them to return.

Note

1. Lewis Carroll, *Alice's Adventures in Wonderland* (New York: Random House, 1946), pp. 146–47.

Women and Religion

There is neither male nor female: for ye are all one in Christ Jesus.

— GALATIANS 3:28

He inviteth them all to come unto him and partake of his goodness; and he denieth none that come unto him, black and white, bond and free, male and female; . . . and all are alike unto God, both Jew and Gentile.

— 2 NEPHI 26:33

Women and the Book of Mormon: Tradition and Revelation

FRANCINE R. BENNION

*H*ow do we decide what is good? In the Book of Mormon, some clues are suggested by relationships among women and men, tradition, and revelation. Before we examine the relationships, it may be well to remember some of the women.

First is Sariah, who leaves friends, precious things, and comforts of civilization forever to go into the wilderness. Lehi knows the Lord will provide a land of promise and deliver their sons out of the hands of Laban, but Sariah does not have that assurance for herself. Only after she mourns, believing her sons have perished, and then finds comfort in their return does she say, "Now I know of a surety that the Lord hath commanded my husband to flee into the wilderness." (1 Nephi 5:8.)

In the wilderness, Ishmael's daughter, wife, and son persuade Laman and Lemuel not to kill Nephi when Nephi himself is unable to do so. (1 Nephi 7:19–21.) In the wilderness, women bear children, eat raw meat, give suck to their children, and become strong "like unto the men." (1 Nephi 17:2.)

In the land of promise, daughters of Laman and Lemuel are blessed by Lehi. (2 Nephi 4:3–9.) In Jacob's time there are women whose hearts are broken by their husbands' whoredoms, and there are women with whom those husbands commit whoredoms. (Jacob 2:22–35.) In Ammonihah, women who "believed or had been taught to believe in the word of God"

Francine R. Bennion has served on the Young Women General Board and the Relief Society General Board. She was for many years a parttime instructor at Ohio State University and Brigham Young University. She and her husband, Robert, have one daughter and two sons.

are cast into the fire and burned alive while Alma and Amulek watch their pains. (Alma 14:8–11.)

A Lamanite queen saves her husband, Lamoni, from being placed in a sepulchre, announcing, "To me he doth not stink." (Alma 19:1–5.) Later, Ammon tells this queen, "Blessed art thou because of thy exceeding faith; I say unto thee, woman, there has not been such great faith among *all* the people of the Nephites." (Alma 19:10; italics added.)

The queen's servant is remarkable partly because we are given her name, Abish. When she sees the servants of Lamoni fallen to the earth and also sees the queen, king, and Ammon prostrate upon the earth, she knows it to have been done by the power of God. Supposing that people will believe in the power of God if they view this scene, Abish runs from house to house to tell them about it, a female missionary in early times. (Alma 19:16–17.)

When a multitude assembles and contends sharply about the apparent state of affairs, Abish takes the queen by the hand and the queen arises. The queen then raises the king, and later Ammon arises: "And thus the work of the Lord did commence among the Lamanites." (Alma 19:28–36.)

In another part of the country, the queen's determined mother-in-law commands that Aaron be slain when she thinks he has killed her husband, the king "over all the land save it were the land of Ishmael." (Alma 22:1, 19–24.) A later Lamanite queen is the duped pawn in Amalickiah's treacherous rise to power. (Alma 47.) The harlot Isabel steals away the hearts of many, including Corianton, son of Alma. (Alma 39:1–11.) Mothers teach two thousand stripling youths such faith and courage that without loss to themselves, the striplings overcome an army of mature men. (Alma 56.)

Late in their history, Nephite women are forced by Lamanites to eat the flesh of their own husbands. The women go without water and wander where they can for food. Old women faint by the way and die. Lamanite women fare no better: they are raped by Nephites, who then torture them to death and devour them like wild beasts as a token of bravery. (Moroni 9:8–10, 16.)

Three women in the Book of Ether are memorable to me. Two are the wives of good King Coriantum, who had no children till he was "exceedingly old. And it came to pass that his wife died, being an hundred and two years old. And it came to pass that Coriantum took to wife, in his old age, a young maid, and begat sons and daughters; wherefore he lived until he was an hundred and forty and two years old." (Ether 9:23–24.) The original couple stay married to each other for most of a century, though they have no children and need them for succession to the throne. Then a young maid marries the royal widower, who is probably at least five times older than herself, and bears his children. One can only speculate on the quality of the marriages.

The other memorable woman in the book of Ether is the fair daughter of a later Jared. "Exceedingly expert," she sees that her father wants to regain his father's throne, and she devises a plan to get it for him. She reintroduces the old secret combinations and dances so seductively for Akish that he agrees to kill the old king, her grandfather, to obtain her as his wife. When Akish, by killing Jared, obtains the throne for himself, we hear no more of the woman responsible for his getting it. (Ether 8.)

The power of men over women in Book of Mormon societies produced abuses, as does any hierarchy not based on virtue alone. Even when good men did not abuse their power but protected women and were tender with them, men did have the power. Men made the decisions. Men did the ruling, the judging, and the prophesying. Men did the preaching, and addressed it to "my brethren." Men defined the history and recorded it.

Women were primarily accessories to men, dependent upon them not only for survival but also for identity, which is presented as a matter of relationship to a man, usefulness to a man, or use by men. Whatever their strengths or virtues, women were subsidiary to men, shown making decisions only when their men were absent or helpless.

Nevertheless, Book of Mormon prophets give us powerful sermons that seem to contradict such inequities, sermons that

171

differ remarkably from assumptions elsewhere about the place of women in God's eyes. The sermons are remarkable both for what they say and also for what they do not say.

There is no suggestion that women are to be forever subservient to men because of Eve's choice in Eden. On the contrary, Lehi says, "And the Messiah cometh in the fulness of time, that he may redeem the children of men from the fall. And because that they are redeemed from the fall they have become free forever, knowing good from evil; to act for themselves and not to be acted upon." (2 Nephi 2:26.)

There is no statement that women are responsible for the sexual misconduct of men. Jacob and Alma hold men responsible for their own sexual transgressions. (Jacob 2:34–35; Alma 39:4.)

There is no suggestion that women are inherently inferior to men or less important to God than men are. On the contrary, Nephi writes, "He inviteth them all to come unto him and partake of his goodness; and he denieth none that come unto him, black and white, bond and free, male and female; . . . and all are alike unto God, both Jew and Gentile." (2 Nephi 26:33.) Jacob says, "And the one being is as precious in his sight as the other." (Jacob 2:21.)

There is no proclamation that gender determines communication from God, access to God, or inheritance in God's kingdom. Alma preaches, "He imparteth his word by angels unto men, yea, not only men but women also." (Alma 32:23.) Benjamin proclaims, "And now, because of the covenant which ye have made ye shall be called the children of Christ, his sons, and his daughters; . . . ye say that your hearts are changed through faith on his name; therefore, ye are born of him and have become his sons and his daughters." (Mosiah 5:7.) Christ says, "And whoso believeth in me, and is baptized, the same shall be saved; and they are they who shall inherit the kingdom of God." (3 Nephi 11:33.)

Why did good men with such doctrine keep women in subsidiary roles? Why did they seldom name the women, or portray them as individuals, or apparently expect them to read

172

or lead? Why was gender so prime a determinant to Book of Mormon men and women if it apparently is not to God?

"All are alike unto God" seems powerful and clear to me and probably did to them. We may each think it an eternal, universal truth but define it differently and act differently upon it. If we are to understand what the verses I have quoted may have meant to the writers or their people, we must understand something of their culture. I will suggest only a few considerations, a few broad strokes in the history without attention to temporary or fragmentary changes. I do not include the Jaredites in this discussion.

The importance of tradition is clear in the Book of Mormon. What matters is not only *what* the traditions were but also *that* they were the traditions. What matters is not only that the people inherited Old Testament, Middle Eastern, patriarchal traditions but that adherence to traditions of the fathers was equated with rightness and honor for Nephites and Lamanites alike.[1] They fought wars for hundreds of years because of "the traditions of their fathers." (See, for example, Enos 1:14 and Mosiah 1:5.)

To people who called themselves Nephites, Father Lehi was good, and therefore his ways were good and were the measure of goodness. To examine the roles of women would be to question core traditions of Lehi, and if such questioning were to occur (which, apparently, it did not), that questioning would by definition be neither right nor righteous. The place women had apparently was assumed to be the place God wanted them to have, as unchanged and unquestioned as ordinary air.

Any new revelation would be interpreted within the context of traditional beliefs and assumptions and would take its meaning from those beliefs and assumptions. Thus, persons for whom tradition was in itself a significant value might well assume that all are equally precious to God in their separate, traditional roles. All in those roles are alike in access to love and redemption. All who hear, believe, and are baptized can continue filling their traditional hierarchically determined roles eternally, loved and appreciated, in God's kingdom. Interpretations other than these would require beliefs and customs different from those that Nephites had.[2]

For Old Testament Israelites, all moral traditions but their own were heathen and polluting. For Book of Mormon peoples, there are no traditions but their own. They meet none but those they carry or create. Nephites, Lamanites, and the people of Zarahemla are a closed community, lacking exchange or intercourse with the world beyond their own. They do not encounter foreign visitors. They know only their own pots, fabrics, tools, and weapons. They are not a nation of readers with widely available books, scripture or otherwise, for every book must be copied individually with rare skill and valuable materials. They do not have easy access even to persons on the other side of their country. Ideas, rebellious or conventional, exist within a local framework, and the place of women is unexamined and constant in that framework. Even had they known the whole world in their time, it is unlikely they would have encountered better circumstances for women, and they probably would have encountered worse; however, interchange is more likely than isolation to prompt useful examination of the assumption that one's own traditions are the only good ones.

The Book of Mormon is primarily a history of groups, and the groups' major activities are war and religion, usually intertwined. In these activities the roles of men, like the roles of women, are affected by tradition as well as practical considerations. It is primarily sons of leaders who become the leaders. The people are usually united under one man: though there may be teachers, judges, or other prophets, more often than not a military leader leads both Nephite religion and government. Leaders are men of large stature, wielding weapons and tools apparently unchanged in a thousand years — bows and arrows, slings, stones, swords, spears, pruning hooks and plowshares. (See, for example, 1 Nephi 2:16 and Mormon 2:1.)

Even where inspiration or intelligence contributes to success, tools or weapons must also be exercised. Thus, Nephi the seer makes a bow and arrow, slays wild beasts on the mountaintop, and carries them back to his hungry people. (1

Nephi 16.) Benjamin the preacher protects his people by driving Lamanites out of Zarahemla. (Words of Mormon 1:12–18.) Ammon the missionary slings stones and cuts off arms. (Alma 17:36–39.) Physical, intellectual, and spiritual stature are traditionally one in a leader in his prime. We read of no cripples, blind men, or healthy women becoming public leaders.

But, says a critical twentieth-century reader, whatever the assumptions of the people, couldn't God tell the men to record women's names and make opportunities equitable, even if the men didn't know enough to ask about it? The Book of Mormon tells much about revelation that I find profoundly relevant to such a question.

The visions of Nephi, Enos, and Moroni suggest a model: revelation is given to a seeker who takes his own questions and puzzlements to God. He expects God to answer, even if the answer is long in coming. He is an active participant in the revelation. Consider these excerpts from Nephi's account: "I *had desired* to know the things that my father had seen, and *believing* that the Lord was able to make them known unto me, as I sat *pondering* in mine heart I was caught away in the Spirit of the Lord. . . . the Spirit said unto me: *Look!* And *I looked and beheld*. . . . And he said unto me, *What desirest thou*? And I said unto him, *To know* the interpretation. . . . And he said unto me: Knowest thou the condescension of God? And I said unto him: *I know* that he loveth his children; nevertheless, *I do not know* the meaning of all things." (1 Nephi 11:1, 8, 10–11, 16–17; italics added.)

Nephi thinks, looks, answers, asks, acknowledges his limitations. What is shown is directly relevant to what he has asked and is represented with symbols familiar to him—an iron rod and a stream, not a nylon cable and a freeway.

God does not erase the prophet's understanding with His own. God gives respect for agency, experience with His love, and awareness of Christ's mission as integral parts of the revelation, whatever the seeker's question, because these are relevant to all questions. But God speaks to us according to our own language and understanding, which at the same time both aids and limits us. (See, for example, 2 Nephi 31:3 and 3 Nephi

5:18.) Moroni specifically cautions against regarding faults of men to be the faults of God, including possible faults Moroni doesn't know about. (Mormon 8:17.) Moroni himself addresses specifically to "my *brethren*, the Lamanites" his exhortation, "And when ye shall receive these things, I would exhort you that ye would ask God, the Eternal Father, in the name of Christ, if these things are not true." (Moroni 10:1, 4; italics added.) Moroni does not address these words to women.

Christ showed Moroni our fine apparel, our love for money and substance more than for the poor or afflicted. Moroni saw our pollution and pride more clearly than our own society apparently does. Moroni, however, does not report seeing nations of women who will read his words. He does not report seeing men and women alike searching and asking questions, or a nation in which nearly half the adult women have no husband. He does not report seeing our latter-day church in which leaders preach that his exhortation is for all women and men alike. If we teach women today to read the Book of Mormon and know it for themselves, then we are teaching them to transcend the apparent expectations of Moroni.

Directly and indirectly, Nephi and Moroni suggest that God does not imprint revelation upon a blank mind. God answers, shows, tells. The receiver asks, sees, hears, takes part in creating understanding, and then acts upon that understanding. In turn, translators, hearers, and readers of the words do the same. As Nephites, Lamanites, or Latter-day Saints, we bring our own sight and assumptions to scripture. God does not destroy this ability but has preserved it. (See Moses 4:3 and D&C 93:29–31.)

Our people are both like and different from the people of Nephi and Moroni. Like them, we know righteousness, wickedness, and war. We have concern for our people, and our earth, and we seek for what is good. We have a more diverse heritage, valuing many traditions and discarding others—we value the letters of Paul, but we invite women to speak and teach in Church. Some of our breaks with tradition have changed the history of the world. Latter-day Saints in the United States celebrate national independence from England, a break not only with traditional rulers but also with traditional systems of rule. Latter-day Saints value divine revelation, but also prize technological equipment that receives and records signals from objects at the far side of the known universe. We are part of a world community in which people can travel and use cars, pots, fabrics, books, and food from many nations. Without physical strength or stature, one person can blow up our planet.

The wonder is not that there is so little about women in the Book of Mormon but that there is so much, given the times and traditions. Given the times and traditions, the wonder is not that the practices seem to contradict the doctrine but that the doctrine so powerfully proclaims the worth of women and men alike. Contradictions appear between doctrine and practice not only because of the writers' assumptions about hierarchy and gender but also because of our own.

Many of us fail to notice what mention there is of women in the book, either because it is what we expect or because it is not. Like Nephi and his people, we bring our own meanings to the phrases "all are alike unto God" and "the one being is as precious in his sight as another." We may come closer to understanding God's intent by means of the strenuous, familiar process: ponder, ask God, humbly listen, and ponder again.

An additional element in the process is suggested by relationships in the Book of Mormon between gender, tradition, and revelation: it is important to examine our assumptions and traditions and consider whether they are enhancing or limiting our ongoing quest to do what is good. It is important to try humbly to learn God's ways rather than to assume we fully comprehend them.

We need assumptions; we cannot live without them. But we must be able to examine them if we are to be able to transcend them. If we want to understand our sisters and brothers in the Book of Mormon and also to understand ourselves, we do well to inquire as well as we can of our God, who knows us all and loves us beyond our present meager contexts for understanding.

Notes

1. Lamanites believed that Laman should have inherited from Lehi the traditional right to rule the family by virtue of his being the oldest son. Nephites believed Laman, and in turn Lemuel, lost that right by purposefully disregarding traditional obedience to their father and his ways. Thus Lamanites felt robbed of their birthright, including the brass plates, and Nephites believed Lamanites had strayed from the fold. Tradition was a major consideration for both.

   Changes did occur, of course; however, when either group changed residence, government, worship, and so on, they made some specific changes within a traditional general framework. During the thousand-year Nephite-Lamanite history, no large-group changes permanently destroyed the traditional fabric of society until the final disintegration.

2. After Christ's visit to the Americas, there were temporarily no rich or poor, bond or free, Lamanites or Nephites, "nor any manner of -ites, but they were in one, the children of Christ, and heirs to the kingdom of God." (4 Nephi 3, 17.) The disciples of Christ served the people, but there is no evidence that they ruled the people. (4 Nephi 5.) Nevertheless, 4 Nephi 1:11 states ambiguously, "And they were married, and given in marriage, and were blessed." It is impossible for us to know whether indeed all forms of human hierarchy were temporarily erased, or whether it was assumed to be quite consistent with rightness, love, and freedom that, as in traditional Old Testament times, men *married* and women *were given* in marriage.

Mothers in Israel: Sarah's Legacy

CAROL CORNWALL MADSEN

*A*s a girl of fourteen, I felt the hands of my grandfather, a patriarch, rest heavy on my head while he pronounced a blessing that would open up to me possibilities of spiritual riches throughout my life. Among the promises he made to me that day was that as a descendant of Ephraim and a mother in Israel, I would share in all the blessings of Abraham, Isaac, and Jacob. At the time I little noted those words, but since then I have grown in knowledge and have come to a measure of understanding of the significance of that promise. My study of past usage of the term *mother in Israel* has increased my understanding of its meaning and enhanced my appreciation for its contribution to my identity as a Latter-day Saint woman.

With some exceptions, the term has little currency today, considered by many to be a quaint peculiarity of earlier times. But while its usage may have diminished and its connotation become anachronistic for many, its significance for women in Mormon theology and practice has not. While all Mormon women were entitled to the appellation, and still are, only a few in the past century were acknowledged publicly as mothers

Carol Cornwall Madsen is an associate professor of history and senior research historian with the Joseph Fielding Smith Institute for Church History at Brigham Young University. She has served as associate director of the Women's Research Institute. Dr. Madsen received her doctor of philosophy degree from the University of Utah. She coauthored Sisters and Little Saints: One Hundred Years of Primary, *and coedited* A Heritage of Faith *and* As Women of Faith, *collections of speeches given at BYU women's conferences. She has written several articles on the history of early Mormon women and is working on a biography of Emmeline B. Wells, suffragist, editor, and fifth general president of the Relief Society. She has served as Relief Society president in her ward. She is married to Gordon A. Madsen, and they are the parents of six children.*

in Israel and even fewer were addressed by name as mother, such as Mother Whitney (Elizabeth Ann), Mother Chase (Phebe), and Mother Sessions (Patty). The breadth of meaning this title held for an earlier generation is best illustrated by the women who bore it.

In 1916 the *Relief Society Magazine* ran a series of articles entitled "Mothers in Israel." Included was a piece on Eliza R. Snow, the childless wife of both the Prophet Joseph Smith and Brigham Young. "By nature and grace," the article stated, she was "the mother of all mothers in Israel. Everyone thought of some Hebrew prophetess when she was near. She was and is a pattern for all Latter-day Saint women to emulate."[1] The author of the article made a heavy demand on Mormon women, for Eliza R. Snow was not of a common mold. As wife to two prophets and possessor of extraordinary faith, commitment, and capability, she was, according to the article, "the high priestess of the religion of Jesus Christ, ministering as such among her people." No other Mormon woman has been so characterized nor so venerated.

In the vernacular of her day, she was identified at once as a poetess, presidentess, prophetess, and priestess.[2] In each role she created a pattern by which Mormon women measured the expectations of each vocation. As the preeminent Mormon woman poet of her time, she wrote verses to comfort, build faith, and explicate gospel principles. As presidentess of all the women of the Church, she generated and supervised a broad range of female enterprises even as she motivated women to tap their own well springs of initiative. As a prophetess, no veil of mystery shrouded the future in uncertainty for her, for the narrow and straight path she followed and urged others to seek led unerringly to clearly defined and predictable ends. Of all the titles she bore, she may well have preferred that of priestess, by which she ministered among her sisters in ways she found intrinsic to gospel living—blessing, healing and comforting them, washing and anointing them, and administering the temple ordinances to them. A mystique attached to her name and presence that lingered long after her death.

This, then, was the woman who was mother to all the

mothers in Israel, a childless woman who became the paradigm for Latter-day Saint women, and whose self-appointed mission was to awaken her Mormon sisters to a consciousness of their own position and potential as women in the forefront of a new religious dispensation.

Usage of this revered title thus combined biological and theological concepts of womanhood, and, like many other aspects of the Restoration, the title reached across the centuries to its strong Hebraic roots from which both its literal and symbolic meanings took shape. Eliza R. Snow, the modern-day "Hebrew prophetess," became exemplar of that connection, a relationship continually invoked during early Mormonism.

The biblical models of mothers in Israel initiated a tradition of pro-active religious women that penetrated an otherwise uniformly patriarchal religious community. In the tightly constrained society of ancient Israel, motherhood was the chief identifying feature and major source of authority for the Israelite woman. Barrenness was her reproach and denied her validity in the eyes of her husband, her society, and her religion. Barrenness was the dramatic element upon which turned the story of the four great matriarchs of the Old Testament, for it was through them that God's covenant with Abraham was to be fulfilled.

On the surface, these four women are significant in Bible literature because they gave birth to significant sons, certainly a major characteristic of a mother in Israel, both in ancient times and in early Mormonism.[3] But a close reading of their stories discloses that they were more than passive participants in the establishment of God's covenant people. They were active agents whose choices dramatically affected the historical course of events. Sarah willingly gave Abraham her handmaid Hagar so that Sarah might "obtain children by her," thereby providing Abraham with posterity but also removing her reproach and securing her own status through the son that would be accounted hers through her maidservant. The contempt Hagar unexpectedly demonstrated toward Sarah after conceiving, however, set in motion the unfortunate events that resulted in Hagar's eventual exile and the fulfillment of the covenant through Sarah and her son Isaac. Sarah was to be the mother of promise, her son, Isaac, heir to the birthright. Hagar was outside the chosen lineage and Sarah's gift of her servant would not satisfy the terms of the covenant. To protect the birthright and prevent Hagar's son, Ishmael, from making any claims to the inheritance, Sarah counseled Abraham to banish Hagar and her son, which he reluctantly did. With Isaac's eventual birth, Sarah fulfilled her destiny as mother of the royal birthright and with Abraham became the fountainhead of Israel.[4] She was the first of the mothers in Israel, for the yet unnamed kingdom began with Isaac's birth.

In Hebrew legend, Sarah emerges as a strong, beloved woman, unique among her sex in piety and preeminent among the twenty-two legendary Hebrew women of valor. For two years after their marriage, Abraham and Sarah devoted themselves to "turning the hearts of men to God and His teachings," Sarah specifically addressing herself to and instructing women. According to legend, "she was a helpmeet worthy of Abraham." Her prophetic gifts were renowned. Indeed, in prophetic powers she ranked higher than her husband. She foresaw Israel's history and implored God to assist Israel in its tribulations. She was sometimes called Iscah, "the seer," on that account. Her compassion was heralded throughout the land, the gates of her tent always "opened for the needy, wide and spacious." At her death, the peace that had reigned gave way to tumult and confusion as the people mourned. She was honored among her people as the only woman to whom God spoke directly.[5]

The characteristics of the latter-day mother in Israel found roots in the legendary life of the first mother in Israel, attributes that also displayed themselves in varying degrees in Sarah's successors, Rebekah, Leah, and Rachel.

Like Sarah, Rebekah struggled with the humiliation of barrenness. But through Isaac's pleading, the Lord made her fruitful and she bore twin sons. Esau, the first, removed himself from the covenant blessing by marrying out of the chosen lineage and then compounded that disqualification by selling his birthright to Jacob. Rebekah, however, stepped into the drama when the Lord disclosed to her that "the elder shall serve the younger." She it was who ensured fulfillment of that prophecy, even though it required deceiving Isaac. It was also Rebekah who later devised a plan to protect Jacob against Esau's wrath when Esau discovered he had lost the covenant blessing. Rebekah risked much to preserve the covenant through the chosen lineage. She also was known in legend as a woman of valor and a prophetess and hailed as the counterpart of Sarah. Like Sarah, she symbolized the joining of the maternal and the theological in their mothering.

While Leah, Jacob's first wife, provided numerous sons to Jacob, Rachel was destined to repeat the pattern of barrenness. Both sisters gave their handmaids to Jacob to increase the number of his posterity, and only after this gesture did Rebekah become fruitful. Like Sarah and Rebekah before them, Leah and Rachel were instrumental in the fulfillment of the Abrahamic covenant. Through these biblical matriarchs, Israel was established, the chosen line preserved, and the covenant honored.[6]

Although the title of mother in Israel did not appear in the Old Testament until the story of Deborah, a judge and prophetess, who coined it for herself after leading the Israelites successfully in battle, modern-day Mormon prophets and patriarchs used Sarah more than Deborah as the prototype of latter-day mothers in Israel.[7] Yet Deborah added another dimension to the title that gave it transcendence over the wholly familial. In her victory song, Deborah identified herself as a mother in Israel for unifying and empowering her people to overthrow their oppressors:

> In the days of Shamgar the son of Anath,
> In the days of Jael, the highways were unoccupied,
> And the travellers walked through byways.
> The inhabitants of the villages ceased, they ceased.
> In Israel, until that I Deborah arose, that I arose a
> mother in Israel. (Judges 5:6–7)[8]

Although Eliza R. Snow and other early women of the

Restoration were certainly equal to the task of judging, prophesying, and even leading their people against oppression, and
did so in varying ways, it was Sarah of the covenant who became
the spiritual mother of Mormon women.

The biblical expression *mother in Israel* passed out of usage
in the early Christian period primarily because Christ's egalitarian message expanded the spiritual boundaries of Israel and
universalized God's elect. His teachings were a socially and
spiritually liberating force as he preached the spiritual equiv-
alency of all people.[9] As disciples of Christ, women experienced
the equality of esteem that Christ offered to all of his followers.
The scriptural image of womanhood represented by the quartet
of Hebrew mothers, Deborah, and other singular Old Testament women, now included the mother figure of Mary. Christ's
tender relationship with His mother added a holy dimension
to the maternal experience. Mary's song of joy, "Behold, from
henceforth all generations shall call me blessed," prefigured
the promise of patriarchs to Mormon mothers centuries later.
Yet the transcendant role of Mary in medieval Christianity and,
later, Catholicism, derived not only from her honored role as
mortal mother of the Savior but from her escape from original
sin in the miraculous circumstances of her own conception
and that of her son. It was her virginal state, not her motherhood, that represented the highest plane of holiness in the
religious tradition that so honored her, and the celibate woman,
not the chaste mother, more nearly attained the state of holiness
that Mary represented in that tradition.[10]

Only when the Protestant reformation rescued women,
marriage, and procreation from their spiritual bondage was
mortal motherhood once again an honored status for women.
The image of womanhood in Protestantism was vital and life
affirming. Maternity rather than celibacy crowned a woman
with glory, and the home, not the convent, became the center
of woman's highest religious vocation. Childbearing was cel-
ebrated in Protestantism as the pinnacle of womanhood and
the means to her redemption. It turned Eve's curse into a
blessing; the pangs of birth brought the joy of life. As in Old

Testament times, barrenness, not fertility, was the reproach of women.[11]

Eve, the mother of all living, provided a feminine symbol that gave fruitful women social as well as spiritual status. "God placed his creation of all men in woman," Luther wrote. "Thus," he said, "among the worst vices and evils this unspeakable good shines forth." Even after the Fall, he continued, woman "saw that the glory of motherhood was left to her." The pain and sorrow of childbirth, he explained, "should be rightly seen as a cheerful and joyful punishment."[12]

In Puritan America, the famed minister, Cotton Mather, also addressed the importance of Eve as a symbol of womanhood, capable of effecting her own redemption and her husband's as well:

"And that brave Woman, being Styled, The Mother of all the Living, it has induced Learned Men to conceive, That Eve was, by being the First of them all, in a peculiar manner, the Mother of all that Live unto God; and that she was on this account, (Oh! most Happy Woman!) a Mother to her own Husband, and the Instrument of bringing him to Believe in the Great Redeemer."[13]

There is no evidence of widespread use of the term *mother in Israel* during the Reformation, despite the renewed regard for motherhood. American Puritans, however, identifying themselves with ancient Israel as God's chosen people, occasionally called up the term and honored individual women as mothers in Israel, a level of esteem that seemed to lie somewhat beyond the more frequently used adulatory title of *Goodwife.* Anne Eliot, who died in 1687, merited the title by a minister who eulogized her accomplishments in verse at her death, entitled: "Upon the Triumphant Translation of a Mother in Our Israel, Mrs Anne Eliot, From This Life to a Better."[14] He heralded her as a sagacious and adventurous soul, created to control weak nature's foes:

Long didst thou stand,
An Atlas, in Heav'n's Hand To th' World to be....

> Heav'n's Richest spices, Choicest Graces were
> [Queen Esther like,]
> Allotted to Thy Share, For to Prepare Thee for
> thy King.

Her motherhood exceeded her domestic tasks as she demonstrated strength, endurance, and the gifts entitling her to a heavenly reward.

As a woman who looked well to the needs of her household, lived in harmony with her husband, and demonstrated piety and meekness, Elizabeth Hutchinson also earned the title of mother in Israel. At her death in 1712 John Danforth wrote a eulogy entitled "Honour and Vertue Elegized in a Poem Upon An Honourable, Aged, and Gracious Mother in our Israel." It concludes:

> She the Bright Vertues of Good Wives,
> Practis'd Her Self, and Cherished in other lives.
> The Greatest Ladies well might Emmulate
> Her Gracious Life and now Her Glorious fate.
> She's Run Her Race. The Glorious Prize is won.
> (Painful to Do; and Pleasing to be Done.)[15]

In Puritan New England, "Good Wives," like Anne and Elizabeth lived lives that entitled them to be gracious mothers in Israel.

The ancient expression emerged a century later in the religious vernacular of some of the early evangelical sects in eighteenth- and nineteenth-century England, acquiring additional layers of meaning in its usage.[16] To a large extent alienated by the dramatic social and economic changes brought about by industrialization, which left their cottage skills and pastoral life well behind in the march of progress, the villagers of rural England sought ways to hold on to their familiar values and way of life. To survive their feelings of personal and spiritual dislocation, they imbued the most commonplace experiences and ordinary tasks with extraordinary signifiance. They attached a spiritual value to the most prosaic act or event.

Central to the belief of some of these offshoots of Methodism was the domestic ideology of the home. It was not only their place of worship in the absence of, or more often, in preference to, a chapel or formal religious edifice but it was also the focal point of their religion, which centered on the flow of life lived within the home, a pattern that ineluctably followed the seasonal cycle of both human life and the natural world. Theirs was a religion of the hearth, as one historian has designated it.[17] It expressed the variegated richness of village life and the simple but fundamental experiences lived each day. Villagers gathered in homes to hear the itinerant preachers who passed through the towns, and between visits these homes were used for cottage and prayer meetings. Under the guidance of an appointed group leader, members related personal religious experiences, discussed personal, familial, and even community problems and generally evoked a sense of group identity and cohesiveness through this mutual sharing. These meetings also promoted an egalitarian view toward religious expression, for women as well as men participated in the discussion and served as group leaders.

The domestic ideology that characterized their religion served as a natural vehicle for the full participation of women who transferred their domestic commitments into pastoral service. In the pattern of New Testament women, they offered their homes for religious gatherings, this service entitling them to be called mothers in Israel. Some included preaching in their pastoral service. These also were accorded the title mother in Israel. Records show that more than two hundred women, both single and married, engaged in rural preaching during this period.[18] They bore personal witness of the intervention of Christ in their lives, their sermons often couched in rural imagery that touched responsive minds and spirits. Their own experiences composed their message, often reflecting lives lived on the extreme margins of existence but rescued by religious awakening. Elizabeth Gaunt was one such woman. After her conversion and later marriage, she became a maternal pastor, holding motherly and pious conversations with her neighbors, assisting in their material welfare, and praying with and for them for temporal provisions as well as spiritual blessings. Her biographer wrote, "Indeed, as a Mother in

Israel, she searched for manna that would aid in maintaining her people."[19] She was a modern-day Deborah.

Another mother in Israel was Betsey Evans, a young woman who spoke to the needs of her neighbors. As a sometime preacher, she followed the preacher's circuit, staying with friends and members in neighboring villages. She conducted cottage meetings in village homes and acted as both a counselor and a midwife to village women, persuading others to her commitment of communal service. "I believe the whole village had a powerful call to serve," she wrote. Her primary mission, she said, was to persuade "those who were in good circumstances . . . to take more heed of the necessities of the poor than they had hitherto been accustomed to take."[20]

Generally bestowed on women like Betsey Evans, who displayed exemplary devotion to the religious cause, the term *mother in Israel* conveyed more distinction than the common term *sister,* applied to all women in the faith, a difference made in Mormonism as well. Women merited the special title for a variety of services that beautifully conveyed the affinity of the maternal and pastoral functions. It linked the spiritual and domestic spheres, identifying both as natural and desirable areas for female ministry.

Whether in preaching, in providing homes for worship, in visiting and succoring the poor, in counseling and encouraging the fainthearted, or in relieving the distressed, these mothers in Israel enlarged the symbolic image they bore while broadening its range of both maternal and religious expression.

Wilford Woodruff encountered one branch of this cottage religion when he arrived in England in 1840. An early convert to Mormonism, William Benbow, introduced Elder Woodruff to his brother, John Benbow, of Castle Frome, a tiny village in Herefordshire. John and his wife Jane were members of the United Brethren, headed by Thomas Kington and numbering about six hundred members. Both Jane Benbow and Kington's wife, Hannah, entered the tradition of mothers in Israel when they offered their homes as licensed houses of worship, first for members of the United Brethren and afterwards for Mormon meetings. Moreover, after conversion to Mormonism, both women contributed their dowries for the first British publication of the Book of Mormon and the LDS hymnal, a major service toward building the kingdom in Great Britain. Nearly all of the members of the United Brethren joined the Church; seventeen of the fifty-five preachers among the converts were women, some of whom were evangelical mothers in Israel.

The term *mother in Israel* did not transfer to Mormonism via the British missionaries, however, but was introduced by Joseph Smith in Kirtland, Ohio in 1833. With a focus on the restoration of Biblical truths and practices, it seems natural that Mormonism would revive this ancient encomium for women, who throughout early Church history would frequently be reminded of their Hebrew heritage. Appropriately, Lucy Mack Smith, mother of the Prophet Joseph, was the first Mormon woman honored as a mother in Israel. After ordaining his father to the office of Patriarch of the Church and conferring all the keys of the patriarchal priesthood, he then blessed his mother, pronouncing her a mother in Israel, "for her soul," he said, "is ever filled with benevolence and philanthropy," and promising her that she would share with her husband "in all his patriarchal blessings."[21] Wilford Woodruff also blessed her as a mother in Israel after the death of Joseph and Hyrum in 1844. "The Old Mother and Prophetess felt most heart broken at the loss of her Children and the wicked and Cruel treatment she had recieved [sic] from the hands of the gentile world," his diary reveals. "She begged a blessing at my hands." He addressed her as "Beloved Mother in Israel," and later called her the "greatest Mother in Israel," for the sons she bore, he said, "are the most noble spirits that ever graced humanity or tabernacled in flesh."[22] Like the matriarchs of ancient Israel, Lucy Smith was honored for her prophetic powers and for bearing and sustaining her sons who had renewed the Abrahamic covenant in the latter days. At the last Church conference in Nauvoo before the exodus, she received a unanimous response when she asked the congregation if they considered her a mother in Israel. Their reverberating "Yes!"

189

secured her place in the female religious tradition of mothers in Israel.[23]

Emma Smith, the Prophet's wife, became an "elect lady" before she was accorded the title of mother in Israel, but she did not learn the meaning of those titles until 1842. In the organizational meeting of the Nauvoo Relief Society, after Emma was elected president, Joseph Smith announced that Emma had been ordained an elect lady twelve years earlier according to revelation (D&C 25) and that elect lady meant one who was "to preside." As an elect lady whom the Lord had personally called, Emma was admonished to "expound scriptures and exhort the church." In confirming her prior ordination, apostle John Taylor broadened Emma's stewardship by declaring her a "mother in Israel" who was to "look to the wants of the needy, and be a pattern of virtue." He blessed her with "all the qualifications necessary for her to stand and preside and dignify her Office."[24] The term *elect lady* was largely reserved for Emma and her successors in the Relief Society presidency, but as a mother in Israel, many would join ranks with her and establish a pattern for a female ministry.

This Old Testament appellative became embedded in early Mormon culture primarily through its private use in patriarchal blessings, which became a major vehicle by which Old Testament language, imagery, and concepts passed into general usage in Mormonism. Patriarchs invoked images of a covenant people, the blood of Israel, a royal lineage, and the establishment of a new Jerusalem in the blessings they pronounced upon the heads of Latter-day Saints. Early Mormons called themselves the "children of Israel" and rejoiced in the literal renewal of God's covenant with ancient Israel. "Camps of Israel" dotted the western trail in the exodus from Nauvoo, itself a replication of Israel's flight from Egypt. An early chronicler of Mormon women, Edward Tullidge, wrote an entire book euphorically describing Mormon women as latter-day Israelites. "The Mormon woman is Sarah in the covenant," he wrote. "She claims her mother Sarah's rights. She invokes her mother Sarah's destiny: 'She shall be a mother of nations; kings of people shall be of her.' "[25] His account of Eliza R. Snow standing on the Mount of Olives with a party of Mormon pilgrims would be but overzealous rhetoric if his words had no foundation in truth: "Woman on the Mount of Olives, in her character of prophetess and high priestess of the temple! A daughter of David officiating for her Father's house!"[26] This characterization was not exclusive to Eliza R. Snow.

Not only did patriarchal blessings assert the link between Mormonism and ancient Israel but they were a primary source for the kind of female spiritual empowerment and ecclesiastical identity that Tullidge so euphorically described. Though deeply personal and individualized, these early blessings also shared several common themes. One, of primary importance then, as now, was the declaration of lineage. Unlike more recent blessings, this announcement was often accompanied by a recital of the extraordinary privilege it was to be a lineal and spiritual descendant of Abraham and come within the bonds of the covenant. Only the royal seed of Abraham could inherit the priesthood, from which flowed all the blessings of salvation and exaltation, explained Patriarch William Smith to Esther Russell, "and the patriarchal blessing," he told Anna Landers, "extends the promises of God throughout the generations of the Royal seed."[27] Lovinia Dame learned of her privileged lot as a descendant of Abraham. "The blessings of holy men and Patriarchs even from days of old are upon thine head," she was told, "and none can stay the fountain of knowledge that shall be opened unto thee for thou art a Josephite in very deed by legal descent of the blood of Abraham through the loins of Ephraim."[28] Louise Y. Robison was told that as a lineal descendant of Joseph through the loins of Ephraim she had become "a legal heiress to the blessings of the celestial world."[29] As a member of this royal lineage Angelina Packer was promised that "if at any time, thou shalt step aside through temptation, from the faith of the Gospel, by means of unbelief, thou shalt be redeemed because of thy blood, thy stock, and the royal family unto whom the promise made by Abraham pertaineth."[30] Similarly, Zina D. H. Young learned that "not one person having one drop of your blood shall be lost, but shall, in time, be brought forth in the Celestial Kingdom of our God."[31] These promises constitute a

191

powerful confirmation that Christ does indeed know His sheep and will not suffer even one to be lost. Those who came within the reach of this ennobling heritage, by birth or adoption, were not only "inheritors of the promises of the covenant" and lawful heirs to the powers and privileges of the priesthood but also "the elect of the new covenant of God," which was destined to unfold to "every nation, kindred, tongue and people."[32]

Like Sarah of old, Mormon women were promised large posterities in this life and the next. But they were also blessed with wisdom and knowledge to instruct and guide those who came within their keeping, a crucial area of their ministry as mothers in Israel. In this calling they perpetuated a tradition that began with time, as women, experienced in the mysteries and rituals of life, transmitted their wisdom from generation to generation. Elizabeth Thompson learned from her patriarch that she would be granted a gift of "wisdom, knowledge, light and also faith, hope, and charity." "Many," he said "shall come to thee for counsel and advice and they shall go away happy and contented and thou shalt have great influence with thy sex for good, also shall the young and rising generation come to thee for advice and instructions and thou shalt bless them and they shall bless thee and thou shalt go forth and do much good."[33] A second blessing announced that her counsel would be sought far and near among her sex because of her great wisdom.[34]

In 1876 Patriarch Zebedee Coltrin told Martha Riggs that she would be numbered among the mothers in Israel, for, he said, "thou will become mighty in the midst of thy sisters . . . and thou shall have a knowledge by which thou shall teach the Daughters of Zion how to live, for it shall be required unto thee from the heavens." She was given the spirit of prophecy and revelation and the promise that none would surpass her in wisdom and many would seek knowledge at her hands.[35] Patriarch John L. Smith acknowledged this gift already residing in Lucy Meserve Smith, wife of George A. Smith. "Many have sought unto thee for advice, counsel and comfort and thou hast had a word for all," he said to her in 1880, adding that "thousands will claim thee in a day to come because of thy blessings unto them, a wise counselor, among thy sex."[36] Patriarch Silas Smith praised Lucy Emily Smith for her faithfulness and ministrations and promised her "abundant wisdom to instruct the youth among the saints and to bless your sex, to encourage and strengthen them in the faith," and told her these labors would increase as she advanced in years and understanding "for the instruction of others will be your life's labour," he informed her.[37] And Brigham Young promised Phebe Woodruff in 1848, shortly before she left on a mission to England with her husband Wilford, that she would be "looked up to as A mother in Israel for council and for Instruction." He promised her "power and wisdom to teach the truth to thy friends and thy sex" and that she would not be at a loss for ideas and words in her teaching.[38]

Even as latter-day mothers in Israel were admonished to protect their own and those who came within their circle from the pitfalls of ignorance and disbelief, they were charged with the responsibility to protect their physical well-being. Patriarchal blessings confirmed the healing art as a woman's talent and task for which she drew from her reservoir of maternal and spiritual gifts to heal the bodies, and often the souls, of those to whom she ministered.[39] Beyond applying what medical techniques they understood, mothers in Israel were told to heal the sick of their families by the laying on of hands and were promised that they would receive the spiritual power necessary in the service they would be called upon to render.[40] Louise Y. Robison was one who was promised that she would enjoy power to "heal the sick, and to cast out evil spirits . . . and to keep the destroyer from her household" as well as to "overcome all the powers of darkness."[41] Patriarch John Smith counseled Charlotte Carter Cornwall that through prayer and faith she would have power to heal the sick of her family and hold the adversary at bay and that as a mother in Israel her fame would be known far and near.[42] Other women were blessed with the power to rebuke the adversary, to discern evil, to speak in tongues, and to interpret. Their steadfast faith entitled them to receive this power from on high.[43]

Patriarchal blessings delineated a unique and visible space

for women within a highly ordered patriarchal structure. The focus of their ministry was in preserving the physical and spiritual integrity and wholeness of the individuals within that structure rather than of the organization itself. The division of labor in building the kingdom left the administrative tasks to men. Not all women, however, distinguished themselves as mothers in Israel or reached the high destiny outlined by their blessings. But the recorded lives of those who earned this title testify of the frequent fulfillment of patriarchal promises. Many exercised the spiritual gifts with which they were blessed. Elizabeth Ann Whitney touched hearts and lives with the songs she sang in "the pure Adamic tongue." She was praised as a "true daughter of Sarah who established the new and everlasting covenant of marriage upon the earth in this dispensation" which secured for her a "more exceeding and eternal weight of glory."[44] Louisa Greene Richards felt the spiritual power of three sisters in the gospel as they washed and anointed her before the birth of her third but first living child. Lucy Smith had occasion to draw from her well of faith to protect her home and family from evil spirits. Eliza R. Snow helped anchor many a young testimony to strong spiritual moorings as she bore witness of Joseph Smith's prophetic calling and gave her own testimony and blessing in tongues.

Women shared this spiritual vitality in other ways as well. Various public channels augmented private ones as conduits of the wisdom they had learned from well-studied lessons of life. Through the written forum of the *Woman's Exponent*, a bi-monthly woman's newspaper, and the networkings of the Relief Society meetings, the Retrenchment Association, and their other organizations, women of all ages and experience came together where they taught, instructed, inspired, and blessed one another. Strong bonds of sisterhood grew out of this sharing. In her eighty-fifth year, General Relief Society President Emmeline B. Wells reflected on the associations developed through her life. Remembering by name the women with whom she had worked for nearly half a century, particularly in the Relief Society, she recalled them as women whom she had loved "as much as if bound by kindred ties, closer perhaps, because our faith and work were so in tune with our everyday life."[45]

Like their Puritan forebears, Mormon women were publicly eulogized as mothers in Israel as they neared or reached the end of long and fruitful lives. Mercy Fielding Thompson, a widow of fifty-seven years and the mother of one daughter, was remembered as a "veteran Mother in Israel, a woman of particularly strong and heroic character, revered as a ministering angel among the daughters of Zion."[46] A sister temple worker wrote of Bathsheba W. Smith: "One has but to look into the kind, gentle features of Aunt Bathsheba to realize that she is face to face with a Mother in Israel. We have but to spend a few hours in her company to realize that the Spirit of God dwells in her being."[47] Marinda Hyde was praised in a poem by Eliza R. Snow:

> With true greatness of soul you have sought out and blest
> The sad and afflicted, and cheered the distressed,
> Until "Mother in Israel," the title your due,
> The pure daughters of Zion accord unto you.[48]

At the funeral of Mary Ann Freeze, a longtime temple worker and president of the young women in the Salt Lake Stake, President Joseph F. Smith praised her life of service and example. "She has been laboring to bring others of the daughters of Zion to the same standard of knowledge, faith and understanding of the principles of the gospel of Christ that she herself possessed, a ministering angel and a mother in Israel, seeking the salvation of other daughters and other mothers in Israel. What can you conceive of grander than a calling like that?[49] Eliza R. Snow's special designation as a mother in Israel was noted at her funeral in 1887:

"Inasmuch as Sister Eliza was deprived of bearing children, she is entitled to be called Mother among this people, just as much as the childless George Washington is to be called Father of the people of the United States. She has been a mother to this people. I pray that whenever we think of Eliza R. Snow Smith, we will not think of her as 'Aunt Eliza' in the future,

but that we may in truth and righteousness call her Mother —
a Mother in Israel."[50]

The image of Mormon women that this title evoked in the
past was as complex as the women who bore it. It is evident
that in Latter-day Saint women it transcended its biological
roots, its familial connotations, and even its biblical associations. "Its meaning has a depth and significance far more important than marrying and bearing children," explained President Joseph Fielding Smith in 1970.[51] It represented a woman
who was both other-oriented and other-worldly oriented, a
woman for whom the hundred little incidents that made up
the "daily sweep of her life," also made her ripe for the "rich
blessings of believing blood," for she was, first of all, a true
believer.[52]

If the concept of *mother in Israel,* as applied to Latter-day
Saint women, seems foreign and unrelated to modern times,
it is, perhaps, that we are too far spiritually distanced from
those who knew themselves to be chosen from out of the
world to lay the foundation of a new dispensation and to restore
and receive the blessings of God's covenant with Abraham. If
the patriarchal promises seem excessive to modern ears, it is,
perhaps, that we are no longer so clearly attuned to the scriptural cadences that informed the religious learning of an earlier
generation steeped in biblical imagery, versed in the biblical
narrative, and grounded in religious symbolism.

The linking of Latter-day Saints with their Israelite heritage
has more than symbolic value, however. It provides a spiritual
as well as lineal continuity that connects Mormonism solidly
with its biblical roots. The latter-day mother in Israel is not an
anachronism but a modern manifestation of a biblical reality.
If any Mormon woman alone lent credence and definition to
the title, it was Eliza R. Snow, the "Hebrew prophetess." Her
high visibility, the reverence in which she was held throughout
the Church, the many positions she held and the influence she
wielded, along with her single-minded adherence to the religious tenets and life pattern of Mormonism, made her distinct
among distinctive women. She used her influence to raise all
Mormon women to an enabling awareness of their favored

position among women, of the nobility of their heritage, and of their singular opportunity "to act in a wider sphere and with higher and more responsible duties devolving upon them, than [upon] all others."[53] To women dwelling in the farthest reaches of Mormondom as well as to her associates among the "leading sisters" of the Church, the message was the same: "Latter-day Saint women occupy a more important position than is occupied by any other women on the earth. Associated, as they are, with apostles and prophets inspired by the living God— with them sharing in the gifts and powers of the holy Priesthood...participating in those sacred ordinances, without which, we could never be prepared to dwell in the presence of the Holy Ones."[54] It was not mere hyberbole by the Relief Society sisters of Kanab in their greeting to Eliza R. Snow and Zina D. H. Young when they visited that small community in 1881: "We welcome Sisters Eliza and Zina as our Elect Lady and her counselor and as presidents of all the feminine portion of the human race, although comparatively few recognize their right to this authority. Yet, we know that they have been set apart as leading priestesses of this dispensation. As such we honor them."[55]

This power-laden image of women, manifest in various ways through the centuries, has rescued women from the shadows of religious history. It has illuminated an historically hidden reservoir of spirituality exemplified across a broad continuum of religious service. All womanhood is honored by those who were called by this richly significant title, mother in Israel, through whose ministrations, as one patriarch declared, "the graces of the gospel have been richly manifested" and who would find those blessings perpetuated for her own posterity through her sons "who would be called to the priesthood and her daughters to the ministry."[56]

Notes

1. *Relief Society Magazine*, Apr. 1916, 183–90. Some few others were also designated mothers of mothers in Israel, such as Emmeline B. Wells, fifth general president of the Relief Society, honored as "a mother of

mothers" by "virtue of her office." (See "A Mother in Israel," *Juvenile Instructor,* May 1913, 297–98. None, however, received the esteem that was accorded Eliza R. Snow, nor have their names carried such historical prominence as hers.

2. Maureen Ursenbach Beecher has detailed how Eliza R. Snow functioned in each of these roles in "The Eliza Enigma: The Life and Legend of Eliza R. Snow," in *Essays on the American West, 1974–1975* (Provo: Charles Redd Monographs on Western History, 1976).

3. Information on women in Old Testament times was obtained from more detailed studies by J. Cheryl Exum, "'Mother in Israel': A Familiar Figure Reconsidered," in *Feminist Interpretation of the Bible* ed. Letty M. Russell, (Philadelphia: Westminster Press, 1985), pp. 73–85, especially pp. 74–80; Rachel Adler, "A Mother in Israel: Aspects of the Mother Role in Jewish Myth," in *Beyond Androcentrism, New Essays on Women and Religion* ed. Rita M. Gross, (Missoula, Mont.: Scholars Press, 1977), pp. 237–55, esp. 245–52; Claudia V. Camp, "The Wise Women of 2 Samuel: A Role Model for Women in Early Israel?" *Catholic Biblical Quarterly* 43 (January 1981): 14–29; Phyllis Trible, "Hagar, The Desolation of Rejection," in Trible, *Texts of Terror* (Philadelphia: Fortress Press, 1984), pp. 9–35.

4. According to legend, Sarah supposedly lived only thirty-seven years from the birth of Isaac to her death, because the years of her barrenness were not regarded as life. See Louis Ginsberg, *Legend of the Jews,* 7 vols. (Philadelphia: The Jewish Publication Society of America, 1909–1966), 5:255, fn. 258.

5. These legendary characteristics of Sarah can be found in various volumes of Ginsberg's *Legends of the Jews,* specifically, 3:206; 5:258; 5:215, fn. 44; 1:203.

6. Exum, pp. 75–80.

7. Though Sarah's unselfish willingness to give her handmaid to Abraham was held as a model for Mormon wives upon the introduction of plural marriage, her subsequent action in removing Hagar from the household suggests that Leah and Rachel are better models.

8. Adler, pp. 247–9; Camp, pp. 27–8.

9. Elisabeth Schussler Fiorenza, "Word, Spirit and Power: Women in Early Christian Communities," in Rosemary Ruether and Eleanor McLaughlin, eds., *Women of Spirit: Female Leadership in the Jewish and Christian Traditions* (New York: Simon and Schuster, 1979), pp. 29–70.

10. For more details about woman's relationship to the medieval Christian church, see Eleanor Commo McLaughlin, "Equality of Souls, Inequality of Sexes: Woman in Medieval Theology," in Rosemary Radford Ruether, *Images of Women in the Jewish and Christian Traditions* (New York: Simon and Schuster, 1974), pp. 213–266.

11. Original sin was still a tenet of Protestantism but carried different theological ramifications for women in that religious tradition. A discussion

of women in the Reformation is Jane Dempsey Douglass, "Women and the Continental Reformation," in Rosemary Reuther, ed., *Religion and Sexism: Images of Woman in the Jewish and Christian Traditions* (New York: Simon and Schuster, 1974), pp. 292–318.

12. In Douglass, pp. 297–8.
13. Cotton Mather, *Tabitha Rediviva, An Essay to Describe and Commend the Good Works of a Virtuous Woman* (Boston, 1713), p. 23; reprinted in Laurel Thatcher Ulrich, *Good Wives, Image and Reality in the Lives of Women in Northern New England, 1650–1750* (New York: Oxford University Press, 1983), p. 153.
14. Broadside, Boston, 1687.
15. John Danforth, "Honour and Vertue Elegized in a Poem Upon an Honourable, Aged and Gracious Mother in our Israel, Madam Elizabeth Hutchinson, Late Vertuous Consort of our Hon. Judge, Col. Elisha Hutchinson," Broadside, Boston, 1713.
16. A comprehensive analysis of the participation of women in these evangelical sects is Deborah M. Valenze, *Prophetic Sons and Daughters, Female Preaching and Popular Religion in Industrial England* (Princeton, N. J.: Princeton University Press, 1985).
17. Ibid., p. 30.
18. Ibid., p. 7.
19. Ibid., p. 40.
20. Ibid., p. 72.
21. Joseph Smith, *Teachings of the Prophet Joseph Smith*, sel. Joseph Fielding Smith (Salt Lake City: Deseret News Press, 1938), pp. 38–39.
22. Wilford Woodruff Diary, 23 Aug. 1844, in *Wilford Woodruff's Journal, 1833–1898*, Typescript, ed. Scott G. Kenney, 9 vols. (Salt Lake City: Signature Books, 1983), 3:451–52.
23. B. H. Roberts, *A Comprehensive History of the Church of Jesus Christ of Latter-day Saints, Century I*, 6 vols. (Provo, Utah: Brigham Young University Press, 1965), 2:538–39.
24. Minutes of the Nauvoo Female Relief Society, 17 Mar. 1842, pp. 3–4, LDS Church Archives, Salt Lake City, Utah.
25. Edward R. Tullidge, *The Women of Mormondom* (New York: Tullidge and Crandall, 1877), p. 534.
26. Tullidge, p. 485.
27. Blessing given to Esther Russell by William Smith, n.d., Nauvoo, Illinois; blessing given to Anna Landers by William Smith, 23 June 1845, Nauvoo, Illinois. According to President Joseph Fielding Smith, " . . . while yet in pre-existence, many of the faithful and devoted spirit children were set apart and chosen to come to earth through the lineage of Abraham, Isaac, and Jacob," which means "that the house of Israel was foreknown as a distinct group in the pre-mortal life." (See "Mothers in Israel," *The Branch*

Magazine of Christ's Church, Aug. 1979, 10–12.) All copies of blessings not otherwise designated are in possession of author.

28. Blessing given to Lovinia Dame by William Smith, n.d., Nauvoo, Illinois.
29. Blessing given to Louise Y. Robison, no other data given, Louise Y. Robison Papers, LDS Church Archives.
30. Blessing given to Angelina Avilda Packer by William Smith, 6 June 1845, Nauvoo, Illinois.
31. Special blessing given to Zina D. H. Young by Elder Francis M. Lyman, 1901, Salt Lake City, Utah.
32. Tullidge, p. 4.
33. Blessing given to Pamela Elizabeth Barlow Thompson by Israel Barlow, no other data given, LDS Church Archives.
34. Blessing given to Pamela Elizabeth Barlow Thompson, 27 May 1875, Panaca, Nevada, LDS Church Archives.
35. Blessing given to Martha A. Riggs by Zebedee Coltrin, 11 Nov. 1876, LDS Church Archives.
36. Blessing given to Lucy Meserve Smith by John L. Smith, 30 Sept. 1880, St. George, Utah.
37. Blessing given to Lucy Emily Smith by Patriarch Silas S. Smith, 1897.
38. Wilford Woodruff Diary, 13 Apr. 1848, in Kenney, 3:343.
39. During the settling of Cache Valley, for example, disease was rampant, and in a Relief Society meeting, stake president Ezra T. Benson reminded "the sisters who had been ordained" that they had "power to rebuke diseases and that we [women] could all have the same power if we would exercise faith." At a later meeting he raised the subject again, saying that "every Mother in Israel should be the Physician of her family, and it was her privilege to administer to her children when no Elders were present." (Cache Valley Stake Relief Society Minute Book A, 18 June 1868, and 8 Feb. 1869, LDS Church Archives)
40. Blessing given to Margaret Eliza Clement by John Smith, 1 Feb. 1869, Plain City, Weber County, Utah; blessing given to Catharine Thatcher by John E. Carlisle, 2 Apr. 1923, Logan, Utah.
41. Blessing given to Louise Yates Robison, no other data given, Louise Y. Robison Papers, LDS Church Archives.
42. Blessing given to Charlotte Cornwall by John Smith, 27 Oct. 1882, Salt Lake City, Utah.
43. See specifically the blessing of Abigail Hall by Isaac Morley, 21 Mar. 1846, Nauvoo, Illinois; reprinted in George R. Partridge, ed., "The Death of a Mormon Dictator, Letters of a Massachusetts Mormon, 1843–1848" *New England Quarterly* 9 (December 1936): 608–9. See also blessing given to Margaret M. Martin by James Adams, 7 July 18— (not clear), Bancroft Library, University of California at Berkeley.
44. "Elizabeth Ann Whitney," *Woman's Exponent* 10 (15 March 1882): 153–54.

45. *Relief Society Magazine,* Feb. 1916, p. 68.
46. "In Memoriam," *Woman's Exponent* 22 (1 October 1893): 44.
47. Lucy Woodruff Smith, "Past Three Score Years and Ten," *Young Woman's Journal,* Oct. 1901, p. 440.
48. "Affectionately," *Woman's Exponent* 12 (15 July 1883): 25.
49. Joseph F. Smith, *Gospel Doctrine* (Salt Lake City, Utah: Deseret Book Co., 1978), p. 460.
50. Apostle John Taylor in Orson F. Whitney, *The Life and Labors of Eliza R. Snow Smith* (Salt Lake City: Juvenile Instructor Office, 1888), pp. 24–25.
51. Joseph Fielding Smith, "Mothers in Israel," pp. 10–12.
52. Blessing given to Louise Y. Robison by John B. Whitaker, Louise Y. Robison Papers, LDS Church Archives.
53. "Position and Duties," *Woman's Exponent* 3 (15 July 1874): 28.
54. Ibid.
55. Elizabeth Little, "A Welcome," *Woman's Exponent* 9 (1 April 1881): 165.
56. Blessing given to Louise Y. Robison by John B. Whitaker, Louise Y. Robison papers, LDS Church Archives.

The Writings of Paul about Women

KEITH NORMAN

*P*aul's attitude about women is a question much debated among biblical scholars and concerned Christians. There are several reasons for this, not least of which is Paul's importance in laying the foundations of Christianity. Not only are his writings the earliest in the New Testament, and thus the closest — in time, at least — to Jesus, but they also form the largest single body of work by one author in the canon. Paul's enormous influence on Christianity has, if anything, expanded over the years.

A further complication is determining just what Paul actually said or wrote. When I refer to Paul in this paper, I am confining myself to the epistles generally agreed by scholars to have actually been written or dictated by the apostle. This methodology excludes Acts, which is largely about Paul but which was written some decades after his death and can give at best only indirect information about his thought and words. It also excludes several New Testament writings commonly attributed to Paul but probably written later, perhaps by devoted disciples who meant such attribution as a tribute. The seven undoubted Pauline Epistles are 1 Thessalonians, 1 and 2 Corinthians, Galatians, Philippians, Philemon, and Romans. Scholars still debate the authenticity of the remaining epistles. A comfortable majority credits 2 Thessalonians as genuine, whereas the view on Colossians is about evenly divided. Most

Keith Norman works for BP Research in Cleveland, Ohio. He earned a master's degree from Harvard and a doctor of philosophy degree from Duke University in early Christian studies. He has published in BYU Studies, Sunstone, *and* Dialogue. *His fictional work,* B.I.C.: A Boy among the Saints, *is an orphan book in search of adoption by a publisher. Brother Norman has served as scoutmaster, taught seminary and led hymn practice in the Solon Ward of the Kirtland Ohio Stake. He and his wife, Kerry, are the parents of four children.*

now reject the authenticity of Ephesians, and almost all agree that Paul did not write the Pastoral Epistles—1 and 2 Timothy and Titus. The view that Paul is not the author of Hebrews is virtually unanimous. All of this is not to say that these writings are of questionable value or that we should revise the canon to exclude any of them from scripture, only that we may have been wrong in attributing them to Paul. And this, after all, is a study of Paul's views on women, not a comprehensive survey of the broader category of Pauline literature. To be on the safe side, therefore, I am excluding the secondary epistles from consideration, despite any remaining uncertainty about authorship.

Unfortunately, the apostle never sat down and wrote, "Now, concerning women, here's what I think of them." When he mentions women, it is usually in the context of another subject: proper decorum, marriage, or simply a personal greeting. Since Paul didn't set down his views methodically, simply to look up the isolated texts from a concordance and pretend that we can paste them together to form a definitive whole is deceiving ourselves. We will have to take the clues he gives us and analyze them in context before we can relate them to each other. Only when that context has been established can we start on the task of what biblical scholars call *exegesis,* which means to draw out the meaning from the text, rather than read something extraneous into it. Exegesis demands that we know something about the culture and prejudices of the writer, so that we can differentiate them from our own.

The warning of 2 Peter 3:16 that Paul is something of a slippery character, easily misunderstand, applies to his writings about women. Just when you think you've got the Apostle pegged, he turns around and says something clearly contradictory. If Emerson was right that a stubborn insistence on consistency is the hobgoblin of little minds, then Paul's place among the larger intellects of Western thought must be reckoned as secure.

On the one hand, Paul has been hailed as a champion of women's liberation who advocated the complete abolishment of distinction between the sexes. In one of his earliest epistles,

Galatians, he wrote of those who had been baptized, "there is neither male nor female: for ye are all one in Christ Jesus." (Galatians 3:28.) At the other extreme he is credited with one of the most blatantly sexist put-downs in the Bible: "Let the woman learn in silence with all subjection. But I suffer not a woman to teach, nor to usurp authority over the man, but to be in silence. For Adam was first formed, then Eve." (1 Timothy 2:11–13.) But, as we noted, 1 Timothy cannot be ascribed to Paul, however sincere the disciple was who "dedicated" it in his honor. First Timothy comes several decades later in the development of the church, when things were settling down into a more regularized, conventional pattern, with a set hierarchical organization. The passage in question is evidence of the shift to conform more closely with Jewish and Roman social mores, in contrast to the almost freewheeling attitudes to be found in Paul's own writings.

Nevertheless, Paul is not so easily exonerated from the charge of sexism. In fact, the excerpt from 1 Timothy 2 was probably based on, or inspired by, a passage from one of the genuine epistles: "Let your women keep silence in the churches: for it is not permitted unto them to speak, but they are commanded to be under obedience, as also saith the law. And if they will learn anything, let them ask their husbands at home: for it is a shame for women to speak in the church." (1 Corinthians 14:34–35.) It has been argued[1] that these two verses are not from Paul but were inserted by a later editor, perhaps the same disciple who wrote 1 Timothy. Unfortunately, because there is absolutely no manuscript evidence to support this theory of a later interpolation, most scholars accept the verses as genuine. Earlier in the same epistle, Paul had pointed out that "the head of the woman is the man" (that is, her husband) and then exhorted women to cover their heads when praying or prophesying in church, because woman was made from man and created for his glory, not the other way around. (1 Corinthians 11:3–10.) Apart from the obvious contradiction of Paul's approving of prayer and prophecy by women in church as long as they are dressed for it, and then telling them

204

to keep quiet until they get home, one can hardly credit Paul with advocating full equality of the sexes in church life.

Although Paul was not a feminist in the modern sense, his attitude toward women was remarkably progressive in the context of his time and culture. To take isolated passages from his writings in support of sexist doctrine is to distort his views unjustly. Before we examine his writings in further detail, it will be well for us to consider the prevailing attitudes toward gender in his world.

With Paul, one almost has to speak of two worlds or cultures: that of Judaism, in which his values were instilled "as a Pharisee" (Philippians 3:5; cf. Acts 23:6; 26:5), and the Greco-Roman world in which he grew up and carried out his commission to the Gentiles.

Despite such notable exceptions as Sarah, Ruth, and Deborah, women were usually considered more possessions than persons in the Old Testament. Women had few legal rights in marriage (Deuteronomy 25:5ff), and even the Ten Commandments bid everyone rest on the Sabbath—except the mother. (Exodus 20:9–10.) Alas, there is nothing new under the sun. By Paul's time, the situation had changed only for the worse. Women were openly despised, described as "greedy, inquisitive, lazy, vain and frivolous."[2] Women could not read the scriptures in public, nor could they bear witness, instruct children in religion, or even pray at table. They were to stay out of sight of the men in the synagogue, hidden behind a screen, and it was considered shocking even to speak to a woman, as Jesus was wont to do. (John 4:27.) According to the followers of Hillel, a prominent Pharisee contemporary with Jesus, a man could divorce his wife if she put too much salt in his food, or even if he found someone more beautiful.[3] Josephus, a few years after Paul's death, reflected the rabbinic attitude of male superiority: "The woman, says the Law, is in all things inferior to the man. Let her accordingly be submissive."[4]

In this respect, Greco-Roman society was more liberal. A Roman matron could initiate divorce, although she would then have to support herself. Rome remained very much a patriarchal culture, however, and females were expected to stay at home for domestic chores, to be modest and submissive, and to refrain from embarrassing their fathers or husbands.

Set against this background, Paul stands out as much more than a moderate. His advice on marital relations in 1 Corinthians 7 tends to focus on equal rights and duties to a surprising degree. Chapter 7 begins a section in which Paul is responding to questions or assertions put to him by the Corinthian church—the original "I Have a Question" format now used in our modern Church publications. Here we should note that the Greek word most commonly translated as "woman" in Paul's writings, *gunē*, can mean either "wife" or "woman," and the context here seems to indicate the former connotation. Paraphrasing their proposal, the Corinthians were asking, "It is better for a man to abstain from sex with his wife, isn't it?"

Why such a question? Paul's views on the imminence of the end of the world (1 Thessalonians 4:15; 1 Corinthians 7:29; 15:51–52) and the transformation of life in Christ were taken up enthusiastically by some of the Corinthian Saints, particularly women, who wanted to live the life of the Spirit here and now. From Paul's comments, we can infer that these earnest disciples understood they had already attained the angelic state that would supersede marriage (Luke 20:35), and make sex obsolete.[5] That women were the most prominent and probably also the most numerous among this group of enthusiasts seems apparent from the discussion of problems in Corinthians 7, 11 and 14.[6] If, as Paul said, there is neither male nor female in Christ (Galatians 3:28), why, these women were apparently asking, should we be required to submit to our husbands' carnal demands? Anyone who is or has ever been married will easily imagine the level of tension that seems to have existed in the church at Corinth, particularly in view of the other extreme evident in chapters 5 and 6, where Paul refutes some — perhaps the frustrated husbands of these same women—who were arguing that since all things are lawful to the Christian, there was nothing wrong with visiting prostitutes.

Paul writes that each husband (1 Corinthians 7:2f, supplying the alternative reading of *andros*) should stay with his own wife, and vice versa; otherwise, the temptation to immorality will be too strong. Note in the verses that follow how carefully Paul balanced the duties between the husband and the wife. The King James Version is pretty hopeless here in verse 3, translating *opheilēn* as "due benevolence." Literally, the word means a debt, what is owed; in this context, to give or to render the spouse's conjugal rights, that is, sex. Both partners owe this debt; neither has exclusive control over his or her own body. Verse 5 specifies the only exception to normative sexual union within marriage allowed by Paul, when both agree to devote themselves to prayer for a short time. This concession was apparently to those who could not get over the idea that sexual intercourse involved Jewish cultic impurity (Leviticus 15:18) and would therefore hinder prayer. Paul, who resisted applying the strictures of the cultic law to Gentile converts, refused (v. 6) to make such abstention mandatory and further warned couples not to prolong their celibate prayer vigils to the point that they became self-defeating.[7]

Paul's evenhanded advice on mutual obligations and rights within marriage was certainly at odds with his male-oriented Jewish heritage, and this balanced tone continues when he speaks of divorce in verses 10 and 11: in accordance with what Jesus ("the Lord") had taught, the husband had no more right to initiate divorce than did the wife.

But what of part-member families? Here (vv. 12–16), in the absence of explicit guidance handed down from Jesus, Paul must give his own opinion ("to the rest speak I, not the Lord"): the believer, whether it happens to be the husband or the wife, should not dissolve the marriage just because the spouse is not a believer. "For the unbelieving husband is sanctified by the wife, and the unbelieving wife is sanctified by the husband." (V. 14.) We can only marvel at the liberality shown here by Paul, who mentions not a word about the disadvantage such women were under from the lack of priesthood in their homes. The efficacy of the faith and the faithfulness of a wife in sanctifying her unbelieving husband was just as great as that of a believing husband with regard to his wife who had not seen the light. Similarly, in verse 15, the husband in such a marriage should no more force his spouse to remain, if she wished to end the marriage, than should a wife expect to control her husband so inclined; neither is bound. Such equal consideration was hardly the norm in Paul's culture,[8] and that this counsel comes from his own authority, rather than from scripture or from the brethren in Jerusalem, is all the more telling.

Sister missionaries will be pleased to note in verses 32–35 that Paul seems to value their service equally with that of his own sex, when he commends the unmarried who are devoted to the Lord's work. Unmarried disciples are undistracted from holy endeavors by the worry of pleasing a spouse. While Hellenistic philosophers of Paul's era often decried the burdens of marriage, they usually pinpointed women as the disturbers of intellectual tranquility. Paul's concern, by contrast, is to free believers, male or female, to wholeheartedly fulfill their missions.[9]

If we could end 1 Corinthians right here, and add only Galatians to the books of Saint Paul, we might portray Paul as the apostle who was a straightforward advocate of equal status for women and men. But Paul then lapses into talking about marriageable women as though they were the property of their fathers (or fiances—it is not entirely clear whom he is addressing). He can marry her off or not, as he chooses, Paul says. (Vv. 36–38.) Of course, the subject here is what to do with the little time remaining before the End, not how to achieve social justice. Verse 39 addresses the widow no longer bound to her late husband—she at least does have control over whether or not she will remarry. Neither here nor in Romans 7:2–3, where Paul repeats the principle in the context of explaining the limits of the law of Moses, does he mention a reciprocal relation or obligation on the part of the male. The subordination of the wife is taken for granted, as we would expect given Paul's Jewish background.

Similarly, in 1 Thessalonians 4:4, Paul speaks to the brethren of "possessing a vessel"—by which he means a wife. This phrase was "a common idiom in both Hebrew and Greek usage, reflecting the view of both cultures that the wife passed into her husband's possession at marriage."[10] Again, we should not make too much of this in light of the context, which is sexual morality, not patriarchy or the equality of women. But it is precisely the unconscious attitudes revealed at the periphery of an argument that betray cultural biases. Paul had to work at overcoming his upbringing.

Although Paul's advice on marital relationships overall advocates more balance, we note in 1 Corinthians 7:1*b* that the starting point is from a male perspective: whether or not it is good for a man to touch his wife. Furthermore, his insistence that only the unbelieving partner could exercise the divorce option presented greater difficulties for women than men, since the legal prerogative to control the religious practices of members of the household remained the man's. Thus, in a pattern still familiar today, a female believer from a part-member family could be seriously hampered in her religious and social freedom.[11]

Further along in 1 Corinthians we seem to confront even clearer indications that Paul had not cast off the sexism of his culture to the extent that his ideals as expressed earlier in this epistle would apparently warrant. It is difficult to read chapter 11 without seeing an underlying commitment to the patriarchal subjection of women. Verse 3 begins an argument for women to keep their heads covered when they pray or prophesy in church. Now this argument cuts both ways. It clearly shows that women participated in the worship of the Corinthian church, and Paul does not, at least not yet, voice any objection to their doing so. Rather, his concern is only that they dress appropriately, with a head covering of some sort, to distinguish them clearly from the men. What is the context of this rather curious argument?

The traditional view of 1 Corinthians 11 is that women were being insubordinate to their husbands on account of their understanding of freedom in Christ. Thus Paul was putting them in their place with the head covering as a symbol of their subordination. But Gordon Fee, in his exhaustive commentary on 1 Corinthians, argues that, as with 1 Corinthians 7, Paul is confronting a group of women who feel they are ready to live the higher law and who want to abolish all distinctions between the sexes.[12] If there is neither male nor female in Christ, we imagine them saying, why should we be required to dress differently? Paul's answer indicates that they were looking beyond the mark, and the indications are that he was motivated by missionary concerns. Unkempt hair in women was a sign of religious frenzy among Greco-Romans and could mark an adulteress in Jewish culture.[13] To behave in the present reality as though gender no longer mattered could be seen as disgraceful or scandalous by potential converts, and Paul's concern above all was to avoid offending anyone unnecessarily. (1 Corinthians 9:19–22; 10:32–33.) He sums up his rather convoluted argument for modest female head attire by asserting in 1 Corinthians 11:14 and 15 that even nature (read "custom") itself teaches us that men should have short hair and women long. Flaunting your freedom in Christ to the point of scandal is to pervert it. "If any man seem to be [is disposed to be] contentious, we have [or recognize] no such custom [or practice], neither [do] [any of] the [other] churches of God." (1 Corinthians 11:16).

If this analysis is correct—that Paul was not in fundamental disagreement with these free spirits but just wanted them to be more conscious of the effect they were having on others—why does the apostle go to such lengths to shore up his instruction with such sexist-sounding arguments?

At first reading, it does seem that a Jewish belief in the inferiority of women, adduced from the Genesis 2 creation account that Paul cites, underlies the whole discussion.[14] But that interpretation reads modern cultural and linguistic assumptions into the text. Take the word *head* in 1 Corinthians 11:3. Obviously, a double meaning is intended here, but it is not the same pun we might assume in English. The Greek *kephalē* does not connote the idea of authority or rulership so much as the idea of source; in this context, the source of life, as verses 8 and 12 indicate. "Thus," according to Fee, "Paul's concern is not hierarchical (who has authority over whom), but relational. . . . Indeed, he says nothing about man's authority; his concern is with the woman being the man's glory, the one without whom he is not complete (verses 7–9). To blur that relationship is to bring shame on her 'head,' [her husband]."[15]

In Paul's understanding, a man, as the image and glory of God, ought to leave his head uncovered. (1 Corinthians 11:7.) Just why disregarding this stricture would dishonor God is unclear; perhaps it was a cultural bias. We are reminded that men today remove their hats as a token of reverence during prayer or the Pledge of Allegiance, but that is hardly the same thing. The crucial question, however, is why Paul thought it was important to maintain the visible distinction between the sexes in worship. Paul does not mean to imply, when he alludes in 1 Corinthians 11:7 to the creation of man in the image of God (Genesis 1:26–28), that woman is not included in that divine image, but he does seem to blend the first account of the Creation with that in Genesis 2, where the man is created first and the woman taken out of his side afterward. Nevertheless, Paul's focus is on man's relationship to his creator: man brings out the glory of God. Likewise, woman, created from and for man as the only living being suitable to be his companion, is his glory. Since man is the source (head) of woman and she is his glory, to disregard this visible mark of distinction, the head covering, when praying and prophesying, is to bring shame on him by negating the appropriate male-female relationship still a reality in the present age.[16] Thus, when Paul reminds us in 1 Corinthians 11:11 and 12 that men and women are interdependent, he is not switching gears but rather expanding on the meaning of the relationship he has been talking about all along. These verses show that verses 8 and 9 are not arguments for the subjection of women: that woman was created "for man's sake" does not entail male dominion but signifies that man without woman is incomplete, missing something vital. "She is not thereby subordinate to him, but necessary for him."[17]

It is interesting to note that Latter-day Saints have used 1 Corinthians 11:11 to support the contention that eternal marriage is a prerequisite for celestial exaltation. The man and woman, we read, must be "with" each other, together, to be in the Lord's program. Unfortunately, the King James translation of *chōris* as "without" in this case is misleading. More frequently, *chōris* is used in the sense of "different from," "unlike," "of another kind." Thus, Elizabeth Schussler Fiorenza translates verse 11: "In the Lord, woman is not different from man nor man from woman."[18] This variation of Paul's "there is neither male nor female in Christ" certainly fits the context better, leading more logically into verse 12: since both are from God, neither man nor woman has ultimate priority. The point that men and women are "of the same kind" also fits nicely with the reference to Genesis 2. Of all created beings, woman is the only suitable companion to man. (Genesis 2:18–24.)

Verse 10 contains perhaps the most puzzling statement in 1 Corinthians 11 and deserves somewhat closer scrutiny. The King James Version has Paul telling women they should have "power on their heads"; literally, "authority" is a better rendering of *exousia*. Generally, this word has been taken to refer to the head covering of which Paul has been speaking, and some later manuscripts amend the word to *kalumma*, "a veil." More likely, *exousia* should be taken in a more literal fashion as the freedom or the right to choose. In other words, women, particularly those in Corinth, should indeed take authority upon themselves, but responsibly, by covering their heads with decorum, so as to honor their relationship to their husbands and to God.

How, then, does the phrase "because of the angels" fit in? Possibly it is some reference to tempting or offending angelic beings who watch over them,[19] but it seems more likely that Paul is alluding to the Saints' eagerness to live "as the angels" here and now.[20] Note how smoothly this reading leads us into 1 Corinthians 11:11. Yes, Paul concedes, you should exercise your freedom as the angels, but that should not make you independent of your husbands. All things are from God, and that includes your relationship as men and women. In the final analysis, certainty about the meaning of verse 10 eludes us, but the idea of exercising angelic or spiritual freedom responsibly seems to fit Paul's overall argument best.

We turn now to 1 Corinthians 14, the notorious "silence in church" passage. As we noted, a number of scholars have argued, on the basis of its inconsistency with most—or the best—of the rest of Paul's writings, that verses 34 and 35 are not genuine—they were added by a later editor. But every early manuscript includes these verses, and such arguments look suspiciously like those who object are picking what they like, what they want Paul to say, and throwing out the rest. The command to silence on the part of women is undeniably inconsistent with 1 Corinthians 11, where Paul makes absolutely no suggestion that women who pray or prophesy in church should stop; but inconsistency in itself does not rule out a single author.

Yet why would Paul tell the Corinthians something so obviously at odds with his earlier counsel, and we may venture, rather out of character for him? He even appeals to the law of Moses, which elsewhere he dismisses as irrelevant to the believer "in Christ." Here again, the context goes a long way toward explaining this seeming anomaly. Chapters 12 through 14 in 1 Corinthians are concerned with a situation in which certain of the Saints are flaunting their spiritual gifts and thereby claiming superiority to those less demonstrably spiritual. Chapter 14 addresses those who are speaking in tongues, a form of ecstatic utterance in an unknown language, which impressed its hearers as a most dramatic manifestation of the Spirit. But Paul decries such activity as meaningless babbling meant only to impress, not to edify. In the absence of an interpreter, he admonishes, those possessed with such a spirit should restrain themselves. God is the author, not of confusion, he contends in verse 33, but of peace.

We can easily picture Paul as being quite upset over these vainglorious Saints. If we can conjecture that the persons involved included the same group of overly eager women in Corinth who considered themselves beyond the legalisms and strictures of conventional society, then the following outburst on Paul's part is quite understandable. To paraphrase, "If that's the way these women are going to act, let them just keep quiet altogether in church. They can stay subordinate to their husbands, just as the law says they should. If they must talk, let them do it at home; their husbands can tell them what is going on. The way these women carry on in church is shameful!" Let us admit that the sentiment seems extreme; Paul may have overreacted, falling back on the marital ethos of his Jewish-rabbinic upbringing and the Greco-Roman sentiment against public demonstrations and speeches by matrons.[21] Our conjecture is strengthened by 1 Corinthians 12:13, which essentially repeats the baptismal formula of Galatians 3:28: in (the body of) Christ we are neither Jew nor Gentile, bond nor free. But the "male nor female" pair is conspicuously omitted in this context.

While we cannot be sure just who Paul had in mind in the 1 Corinthians 14 passage, it is clear he is addressing an unusual situation in Corinth. Just as competitive prophets and those who claimed the gift of tongues were told to control themselves, certain married women — perhaps those same ones who wished to negate their marriages and dress like men — were told to keep quiet in the public assembly. As verse 40 shows, Paul's main concern was that "all things should be done in decency and order." Again, Paul's missionary zeal probably underlies this passage. He may well have been upset with the prospect of alienating "investigators" or giving ammunition to critics, who were prone to confuse Christians with one or another of the licentious mystery cults of the time. Such fanatical groups were viewed as foreign and subversive of public order and morality, in part because they blurred sex roles.

So far, we have reviewed what Paul said about women, but what can we learn of how he interacted with them? Here again, we don't have a lot from the authentic epistles, but what we have is quite tantalizing. In Philippians 4, Paul mentions two women, Euodias and Syntyche, whom he describes in verses 2–3 as having labored side by side with him and his companion Clement. Apparently these women had a falling out with each other, and the apostle entreats an unnamed intercessor to try to reconcile them. Since Paul's labors were focused so much on missionary work, we can fairly surmise that these two were fellow laborers in the field — the first known sister missionaries. Paul speaks of them with no hint that their service was any less valuable than that of Clement and himself; they are among those whose names are inscribed in the book of life. Certainly, as his experience with Barnabas shows (Acts 15:36–40), Paul could understand a serious disagreement between missionary companions.

As he does to Euodias and Syntyche, Paul refers to Priscilla, along with her husband, as "my helpers in Christ Jesus." (Romans 16:3–4.) But Romans 16 contains even more striking references to women's roles in the church, and they are mentioned by Paul with obvious approval. He describes Phoebe as a *diakonos*, literally, a "deaconess," as he urges the Christians in Rome to assist in whatever effort she engages, implying that she had been given an official capacity, and a rather wide-ranging one at that. (Vv. 1–2.) Then in verse 7, in a list of notable and beloved people in Rome deserving special salutation, Paul includes Junia as someone "of note among the apostles," who had also been imprisoned with him.[22] Before we get too excited about this situation, we need to remind ourselves that Paul's writings are the very earliest we have from the new Christian movement, and they reflect an organization in which hierarchy, titles, and priesthood offices were not yet formalized. *Apostle,* in its root meaning from the Greek verb *apostellō,* denotes someone who is sent out in a representative capacity, as an ambassador. *Diakonos* is literally one who ministers to the needs of others; thus the King James Version rendering of "servant." It is not hard to see how these descriptive words took on the status of specialized titles, but with Paul, we are still in the formative period, when status in the ministry was likely more on the basis of manifestations of the Spirit than on hierarchical appointment. The context of Paul's usage of these terms makes it clear, however, that women could be important functionaries in the early Church. As one prominent scholar has pointed out, referring to Romans 16:1, since Phoebe apparently had a permanent and recognized ministry, "one may at least see an early stage of what later became the ecclesiastical office."[23]

Having now surveyed the passages referring to women which can be confidently ascribed to Paul, what are we to conclude about his attitude toward women? The apparent discrepancy in his remarks has resulted in the standard view that Paul's nonsexist ideals, represented in Galatians 3:28 ("there is neither male nor female in Christ"), were focused on the future kingdom of God, when sex would be abolished and his own preference for celibacy made the norm. But for the present, in the real world, the sexual or gender roles of the culture prevailed and should be obeyed. According to this view, Galatians 3:28 is an aberration, not representative of Paul's day-to-day dealings with women or his real attitude toward them. Our analysis indicates that such a reading of Paul is seriously flawed; on the contrary, closely considered in context, the epistles indicate that Paul went to considerable lengths to introduce the ideal stated in Galatians into church life and that it is the statement at the other extreme—"women should keep silent in church" (1 Corinthians 14:34–35)—that is the aberration.

But the one passage we still need to subject to careful scrutiny is, in fact, Galatians 3:28. Just what did Paul mean by his assertion that male and female become one in Christ? The standard view is that Paul anticipated a sexless condition in heaven, based on a similar interpretation of Jesus' statement that there will be no marriage in the resurrection. (Luke 20:35–36.)[24] Obviously, for Latter-day Saints, such an interpretation is highly questionable, but whether Paul was familiar with the saying at all is equally debatable. After all, it would be some decades before Luke wrote it down in his gospel. What we have is a classic instance, in both passages, of *eisegesis,* reading preformed notions into the text. Our goal, as you will recall, is *exegesis,* drawing the meaning out of what is in the text within its own context. Let's try a little of this technique on Galatians 3:28.

Galatians is a tract justifying the universal applicability of the gospel, the power of God unto salvation (Romans 1:16), against the "Judaizers," those who insisted that no one could be saved who did not first become a Jew and submit to the demands of the law of Moses. Paul's argument is that the distinctions made under the law are no longer applicable; through faith and baptism, Christ has freed us from the bonds of the law and made us his. The old divisions don't matter any more;

they have ceased to count. Unlike circumcision, the former sign of the covenant, which was for Jewish males only, the new sign, baptism and the clothing donned afterwards as a token of putting on Christ, is for all.[25] Race is irrelevant to salvation, as is social standing, as is gender: all are equally the children of God by virtue of their faith in Christ Jesus.

Correctly understood, Paul is not hinting here that we will all be neuter in the resurrection. What he is saying is that you don't have to be male or Jewish or a free person to be saved. We have seen that working out the practical applications of this theological equality presented challenges to Paul, particularly by the Corinthian Saints, some of whom took it very seriously indeed and wanted to abolish gender distinctions entirely. In response, Paul delineated the roles and relationships between women and men appropriate to his time and culture, specifying behavior that would not give needless offense to others. In that context, Paul's attitude toward women is remarkably liberal. Only by isolating selected pronouncements from their cultural setting and missionary motivation can he be cast as a misogynist.

What do Paul's pronouncements on women mean to us? Because of his position as founder, mentor, apostle, and traveling shepherd over so many congregations, Paul found himself called upon repeatedly for advice and assistance. It is primarily for this reason that we have his epistles — they were written to address the immediate needs of his congregations. Paul was responding to specific situations when he wrote to the Saints, not sitting down to compose theological treatises. His off-the-cuff responses to ad hoc problems often come across with a disarming personal touch, along with his characteristic emotionalism. He likely had no idea that his letters would be collected and someday added to the sacred text of the Law and the Prophets. The New Testament wasn't even a gleam in the scribe's eye at that point.

But by now, a couple of thousand years later, we have had a lot of time to repeat to ourselves the mantra that scripture equals transcribed revelation. This belief allows us to ignore context, to read by the letter, which is much less bother than struggling to understand the Spirit. Joseph Smith's attempt to teach us about the limitations of the scriptural tradition and the fact that prophets are quite capable of acting on their own has not, it seems, made much of an impression on us. Surprisingly, we can find a similar disconcerting disclaimer in Paul. We have already cited 1 Corinthians 7:12, where Paul specifies that it is "I, not the Lord" who speaks. In the same chapter he prefaces his remarks on the unmarried ("virgins," v. 25), with a similar caveat: "I have no commandment of the Lord, yet I give my judgment"—in other words, his opinion. He then expounds in verses 29 through 34 on his personal preference for remaining single, so as to be undistracted in the service of the Lord, advice which, we note, applies equally to men and women. After telling widows and widowers they are better off not to remarry, he sums up by reiterating in verse 40 that this statement is after his own judgment, "and I think also that I have the Spirit of God," he ventures. His "I think" does not exactly carry the same weight of authority as "Thus saith the Lord" might.

So we have two forms of contextual abuse here. On the one hand, a simplistic view of scripture has caused Christians, including Latter-day Saints, to fail to recognize the ad hoc nature of Paul's pastoral advice. On the other hand, inadequate translations and proof-texting—quoting verses in isolation from their context to score doctrinal points—have distorted our understanding of what Paul said. Add to that the secondary Pauline writings reinforcing a sexist misreading of the authentic Paul, and Paul comes out sounding like a chauvinist. I believe such a view of Paul says more about us than it does about him.

Nevertheless, Paul was demonstrably influenced by the sexism of his time and culture and cannot therefore be taken as a definitive guide for our time in the matter of gender roles. A little reflection would make the absurdity of doing so obvious. If Paul were the last word, our attitude about sex would certainly be different. Though I don't suppose we Mormons would require priesthood holders to be celibate, as the Roman Catholics do, we would at least frown on marriage for full-time Church workers. On the other hand, it would probably be good for men to run the Primary, which is what we would need to do if we banned women from speaking in church. (It would be rather a different experience for the kids.) We could still permit the sisters to pray in church, and perhaps prophesy (which we would undoubtedly interpret as "testimony bearing"—prophesy is a bit strong), provided they wore a head covering. Such wholehearted submission to Paul's counsel would certainly demonstrate just how liberal even Catholics have become—they no longer require women to cover their heads in church.

In fact, despite the thirteenth article of faith, we Latter-day Saints have not followed every admonition of Paul. We have already exercised a particle of doubt in applying these scriptures to our situation. Indeed, the principle of discernment recommended in Doctrine and Covenants 91 may be applied to the received canon as well as to the Apocrypha: there are many parts that are good and some that are flawed, and we have to call on the Holy Spirit to aid our common sense in distinguishing between the two. As proponents of progressive revelation, we need make no apology in doing so. What is valid and even inspired for Paul's day is not automatically binding on us. It is inviting trouble to make temporary expedients into eternal principles. We need only recall the Mormons' prolonged suspension of black members from priesthood ordination in response to antiabolitionist sentiment in Missouri in the 1830s to see the folly of that.

To reassure those who may be disturbed by the hint of feminism behind all this scholarly rumination, I am not campaigning for a gender-neutral church. I do think, however, we can contain patriarchy within the bounds the Lord has set and thus free ourselves from its abuse. A proper understanding of the *spirit* of Paul's epistles can be of just as much help in this endeavour as Doctrine and Covenants 121. For Paul is the apostle of freedom. He proclaimed the liberating effect of the gospel from every kind of bondage, and our analysis shows that he also wanted to make his vision a reality with respect to women. In some ways, we have yet to catch up to him.

Notes

1. See Hans Conzelmann, *Der erste Brief an die Korinther* (Gottingen: Vandenhoeck and Ruprecht, 1969), p. 290. See also Gordon D. Fee, *The First Epistle to the Corinthians* (Grand Rapids, Michigan: W.B. Eerdmans, 1987), p. 699; similarly, Murphy-O'Connor, Jerome, *I Corinthians* (Wilmington: Michael Glaxier, 1979), p. 133.

2. Oepke, Albrecht, "*gunē*," in *Theological Dictionary of the New Testament*, Ed. Gerhard Kittle, trans. Geoffrey W. Bromiley (Grand Rapids, Michigan: W.B. Eerdmans, 1964), pp. 776–89.

3. Ibid., p. 782, and Wayne A. Meeks, "The Image of the Androgyne: Some Uses of a Symbol in Earliest Christianity," *History of Religions*, Vol. 13 (1974), pp. 165–208. It should be noted that there was a kinder, gentler strain in early first-century Judaism with regard to women, but it was decidedly a minority view. See Elaine Pagels, *Adam, Eve, and the Serpent* (New York: Random House, 1988), p. 14.

4. Quoted in Fee, p. 707.

5. A similar mindset, though with quite different results, may have been operative among nineteenth-century Mormons who lived polygamy as an expression of the heavenly kingdom already fulfilled. See Jan Shipps, *Mormonism: The Story of a New Religious Tradition* (Urbana and Chicago: University of Illinois Press, 1985), pp. 125f.

6. See Robin Scroggs, "Paul and the Eschatological Women," *Journal of the American Academy of Religion*, vol. 40 (1972), pp. 283–303; Fee, p. 269.

7. O. Larry Yarbrough, *Not Like the Gentiles: Marriage Rules in the Letters of Paul* (Atlanta, Ga.: Scholars Press, 1985), pp. 99–101.

8. Wayne A. Meeks, *The First Urban Christians: The Social World of the Apostle Paul* (New Haven: Yale University Press, 1983), pp. 199f.

9. Yarbrough, p. 106. We might note that many commentators have taken Paul's advice here as the voice of experience, inferring that Paul had been previously married, although apparently he now enjoyed celibacy as a kind of spiritual gift. See also Charles Kingsley Barrett, *The First Epistle to the Corinthians*, 2d ed. (New York: Harper, 1988). Barrett, p. 158, argues that 1 Corinthians 7:7a refers not to Paul's celibacy but to his avoidance of sexual immorality. This view, however, robs the contrast of verses 7b and 8 of their force. See Yarbrough, p. 99.

10. Yarbrough, p. 70. See also Meeks, pp. 23–25. The usage is similar to that in 1 Corinthians 7:2.

11. Elisabeth Schussler Fiorenza, "I Corinthians," in *Harper's Bible Commentary*, ed. James L. Mays (San Francisco: Harper, 1988), p. 1177.

12. Fee, pp. 497f.

13. Schussler Fiorenza, p. 1183.

14. Price, James L., "The First Letter of Paul to the Corinthians," in *Acts and*

Paul's Letters, ed. Charles M. Layman (Nashville: Abingdon Press, 1983), p. 214.

15. Fee, pp. 503–4.
16. Ibid., p. 518.
17. Ibid., p. 517.
18. Quoted by Yarbrough, p. 116.
19. Genesis 6:2–4 is often cited as a reference point; see also Joseph A. Fitzmyer, "A Feature of Qumran Angelology and the Angels of 1 Corinthians 11:10," in *Essays on the Semitic Background of the New Testament* (Missoula, Mont.: Scholars Press, 1974), pp. 187–204.
20. Fee, p. 522.
21. Schussler Fiorenza, p. 1186.
22. Some manuscripts read "Junias," the masculine form of the name, but this is most likely an emendation by a scribe who was bothered by the idea of a female apostle.
23. Kasemann, Ernst, *Commentary on Romans*, trans. Geoffrey W. Bromiley (Grand Rapids, Mich.: Eerdmans, 1980), p. 411.
24. On the historical development of celibacy as the ideal spiritual state, see Pagels, especially pp. 13–21, 28–31, 78–97, 140–44.
25. William Baird, "Galatians," in *Harper's Bible Commentary*, p. 1208.

Women Writers

If someone cares enough to write, she must value writing. And in some way she must know that her language is a deeply personal attribute and that in learning the possibilities of her language, she is learning about herself.

—SUSAN HOWE

The Madonna Oma

LOUISE PLUMMER

The following are excerpts from Louise Plummer's prize-winning novel, The Romantic Obsessions and Humiliations of Annie Sehlmeier *(Delacorte Press, 1987).*

*J*n some other world, not the one I lived in, beautiful people gathered in the evening, sat on their satin-covered bottoms at a table decked out in Lenox china, and ate a civilized meal of exotic dishes like breast of unicorn. Their eyes feasted on unpronounceable flowers — anemones and forsythia — bunched artfully in silver urns. I knew it existed. I saw it in a glossy magazine, and I wanted a perfect life like that. Photographs don't lie. Do they?

We ate in the kitchen on a table spread with a vinyl cloth that Henny and I wiped down with a damp sponge after the dishes were cleared. Our eyes feasted on linoleum. Yet our kitchen had a glittering cleanness about it that I appreciated, and Mother hid the dirty pots and pans in the oven while we ate dinner. That *was* civilized. It was the dinner conversation, or rather the lack of it — the spats — that depressed me, and they were Oma's fault. She was the cause of our mealtime fights. Like the dinner when Jack Wakefield called me on the telephone for the very first time.

Oma was refusing to eat, her lips held shut in a stubborn, tight line, and Mother simply wouldn't let it be. She was afraid

Louise Plummer has written two novels, The Romantic Obsessions and Humiliations of Annie Sehlmeier *(Delacorte Press, 1987) and* My Name is Sus5an Smith. The 5 Is Silent *(in press). She has also published stories and articles with* Young Miss, Lake Street Review, New Era, *and* Ensign. *She received her master of arts degree from the University of Minnesota and teaches critical and creative writing at Brigham Young University. She has served in all the auxiliaries and has taught seminary. She and her husband, Tom, are the parents of four boys.*

Oma might starve herself. Fat chance. Oma ate Oreos on the sly.

"Please have some soup now," my mother pleaded, soup spoon poised in the air in front of Oma's clamped lips.

Oma, her arms folded across her chest, turned her head away from Mother. Her hair fell loose from the knot in back of her head. She looked unkempt, like pictures of old people in rest homes I had seen. Sometimes, I thought she smelled different, too—not a good smell either.

"Open up wide," Mother said. You'd have thought she was talking to a one-year-old.

Oma shut her eyes, wrinkled her nose, and did not open her mouth wide.

"Eat your dinner now, Riet," Father said, buttering a roll. "She'll eat when she wants to."

"She never eats," my mother said.

"She eats all day," said Henny. "She's in the refrigerator whenever she thinks no one's looking. She ate all the Twinkies last week."

"She's not going to get better if she doesn't eat properly," Mother insisted, implying that Twinkies kept one senile and the minute Oma changed her diet she would be herself again. I couldn't believe it.

"Eating is not going to make her better," Henny said. "Nothing is."

Mother offered Oma a buttered roll.

"I hate it," said Oma in Dutch, through her teeth.

"Then *I'll* eat it," said Henny, snatching the roll from Mother's hand. "I love them."

As soon as Henny bit into the roll, Oma wanted it back. If she was not interested in eating, she was interested in possession, and it was *her* roll.

"Give it back," she shouted. "It's mine."

That was when the telephone rang. "Give it to me," Oma cried.

I got up and answered the phone, which sat on a small table in the hall adjacent to the kitchen.

"You don't want it, so I'm going to eat it," said Henny.

226

"Hello," I said into the receiver.

"Tell her to give it back!" Oma yelled. She began wailing.

"Hi, this is Jack."

"Jack." Unbelievable. Old Spice aftershave seemed to waft through the telephone receiver. Jack Wakefield was calling me.

"Henny, stop teasing your grandmother," Mother said.

"Can we eat in peace, for once?" Father asked Henny.

"How are you?" asked Jack.

Not fine. Not fine at all. And marvelous. Never felt better. All of the above.

"Fine," I said. The kitchen was exploding with noise.

"What's going on?" he continued. He could hear everything, I was sure of it.

"Oh nothing," my voice was serenely casual. "My grandmother sometimes gets upset at dinner." I put one finger in my free ear.

"Your grandmother?" he asked. I could hardly hear his voice.

"People who don't eat don't get anything," Henny taunted Oma. She picked up the entire basket of rolls and held them above her head.

Oma, frantic, howled like an animal.

"Henny!" My father's balled-up fist smashed the table surface. Dishes clattered.

"Are you eating dinner?" Jack asked.

"No. I mean, yes. Can I call you back in a few minutes?" I couldn't believe I was making this request, but Oma was bawling so loudly, I couldn't concentrate on his voice. I didn't want him to hear her. I didn't want him to hear my whole crazy family.

"Okay, I'll talk to you in a few minutes then. Bye." I was sure he had heard everything. Good-bye, my love. Jack Wakefield had called me, and I couldn't talk to him.

"Why should the rest of us have to listen to her whining all through dinner?" Henny shouted at Father.

"You make it worse when you tease her." Father's hands were still fists. It occurred to me that he wanted to punch Henny, and even though I was mad at her too, the thought

made me sad. We were so far from those Lenox china advertisements.

"I can't stand it," Henny screeched. "Every night Mother
begs her to eat. Just let her alone!" She had turned to Mother.

Oma had parts of three rolls stuffed into her mouth, chew-
ing on the dry bread and watching Henny to make sure she
wouldn't get them back. Fat crumbs fell from her mouth onto
the table.

"See, *now* she's eating. Are you satisfied?" Henny pushed
her chair back and stood up. "You don't have to beg her." She
sneered at Mother. "You just have to steal it from her."

"Henny, sit down!" Father's face was white.

"I will not sit down. I hate this family. Hate it, hate it." She
knocked her glass of milk over, swerved around to the back
door, and was gone. The walls shook with the door's bang.

For a second we all watched the milk spread across the
vinyl cloth and drip into Oma's lap. Oma began crying all over
again. The rest of the bread fell from her mouth.

"I'd like to kill her," Father said. I believed it.

"Let her be," Mother said. Her head nested in her hand.
"It's not her fault." She shaded her eyes with her fingers.

"Then tell me whose fault is it?" exclaimed my father. No
one answered. I had never seen him so mad. This was dangerous. I felt it.

It is Oma's fault, I thought. I wiped the table and Oma with
a dishtowel and told her to hush. She continued weeping
noisily. I wish you would die now. A part of me—the good
part—was shocked and sorry I had thought such a thing; but
another part agreed that it was Oma, as she was now, who was
the center of these all too-frequent fights. I tried hard to remember the Oma of before, her hair thick, humming morning
hums that nurtured a small girl. Oma, picking asters out of her
garden on Poortstraat and arranging them perfectly in a blue
delft vase. Oma, my link to the civilized world of the glossy
magazines. There was a light about her then, like Madonna
paintings; or was that my imagination? This woman, the present
Oma, weeping and choking on her bread, her nose running—
she wasn't the same person even. There was no resemblance

between the two. This person was the one I wanted to die. Not really, of course. Not really. I hope I didn't mean it. Mother's head was bent over the table. I didn't mean it, Mother. Erase. Erase.

Erase it with Jack Wakefield. I pictured Jack's family dining in formal clothing, drinking wine from Waterford crystal. I returned to my place and ate my soup in silence.

After dinner, I sat with Oma out on the front porch while Father and Mother attended English lessons at the junior high across the street. Henny had not returned. I was sure she was hiding out at Farrah's until she cooled off. Henny almost lived over there lately. I had tried to call Jack once, but the line was busy. Now I was stuck with Oma. We couldn't leave her alone. She either grew frightened like a child, calling loudly for my mother, or she wandered off down the block, forgetting the way home. Often she sat on Mr. Eberley's porch repeating my grandfather's name. Once Mrs. Spivack, our neighbor, had called to say that Oma had walked into her house and was napping on her bed.

We sat in the green, painted metal chairs behind the porch railing and the climbing roses. The neighborhood smelled clean, green. *The Thorn Birds*, the book Maggie had lent me, rested in my lap. I hoped to read it while we sat. Already I wanted the handsome priest, Ralph de Bricassart, and the young Meggie Cleary to become one flesh, as it said in the Bible. At least I thought that's what it said in the Bible. Colleen McCullough was not going to gratify me too quickly on this score. Oma was humming softly. I picked up the book. She stopped humming.

"Do you remember me—what I was like—before the car accident?" I was startled by this completely lucid question from her. She was so crazy most of the time. I laid the book down again.

"I used to read a lot too," she mused.

"I remember," I said. It was only a vague memory.

"You are a lot like me," she continued. I wanted to disagree, and perhaps she saw that in my expression because she added, "The way I used to be. You are like I used to be." I thought again of the asters in the delft vase, but I couldn't think of anything to say. She wanted a response from me, but I couldn't make one.

"You even look like me." She stroked my cheek briefly and then looked out to the street. A blue Ford truck burning a lot of oil sputtered its way up the steep hill.

"I was young once," she repeated. "Like you."

"Annie, hi!" Jack Wakefield's red scooter jerked to a stop at the curb in front of our house. He wore white shorts and a tee-shirt and held a tennis racket. He parked the scooter and walked to the porch.

Oma's face hardened immediately at the sound of his voice.

"Jack!" My voice didn't sound like my own. "I tried to call you, but the line was busy." I pulled my feet down from the porch railing and tucked my skirt modestly under my legs.

"I know. My brother Milton was on the phone. I decided to stop by on the way to the courts." He glanced at Oma.

"I'm Jack Wakefield." He extended his hand for Oma to shake. Oma sat tight-lipped and stared straight ahead.

"She's senile," I whispered. "And she doesn't understand English." I didn't want him talking to her. I just never knew how she would react. It was bad enough having her sit there like a stone. My face felt about two hundred degrees, and I was sure my neck was developing those ugly red splotches. Soon he would know that I was a person susceptible to rashes. Unclean.

"Oh, I'm sorry," Jack whispered back. He smiled at Oma and nodded to her. He was irritatingly polite.

"You're going to play tennis," I said, trying to veer his attention away from Oma.

"Yes, I'm meeting Tom Woolley." That was the first time I heard Tom Woolley's name. Jack's tall frame leaned against the porch. "I was wondering if you'd like to . . . "

"*Geef hem niets te eten ook al bedeld hy er voor!*" interrupted my grandmother. I felt my neck definitely redden. No question about it.

"What did she say?" Jack asked.

"She said not to give you anything to eat, even if you beg

230

for it," I said. I would have made something else up if I could have thought of anything.

"Tell her I just stopped by to say hello," he said.

"Let's just ignore her," I said quickly. "She'll stop if we ignore her."

"Annie, she's your grandmother." Jack had a wretched respect for the elderly. "Tell her," he insisted. He made a gesture with his hand that indicated I should get on with it.

I told Oma that Jack had come by to visit us both and that he didn't want anything to eat. Jack seemed pleased to hear me speak Dutch.

Oma jumped to her feet with surprising vitality and waved her fist fiercely at Jack, who drew back involuntarily. "Liar," she yelled at him in Dutch. "You've come to steal the potatoes and leave us here to starve. Get out. Get out of here." She leaped forward to the stairs. Jack backed down the front walk. Oma grasped the garden hose, turned the spigot and aimed the spray directly at him, catching him full in the face. Jack dropped his racket and spluttered, "But I'm not even hungry." He started the scooter and sped awkwardly away.

"She thought you were stealing potatoes," I called out after him, but he was gone.

"You stupid woman!" I turned on Oma. "You stupid, stupid woman." I yanked the hose from her hands and wrapped it imperfectly around the spout next to the porch. "How could you do such a thing?" I yelled. Her disheveled head was bowed, her shoulders sagged. She reminded me of an abused dog. I wanted to hit her.

"Go in the house," I said, picking up Jack's tennis racket off the lawn. I wiped it with my skirt.

Oma stood inside the screen door looking out at me. "He'll come back to get it," she said plainly and disappeared into the house.

I hoped it was true.

Across the street, on the playing field next to the school, a man in white pants and shirt guided a model airplane by remote control. It buzzed in the air like a tin insect. I wanted to fly too—spell Jack's name with my white breath across the sky. I wanted to be transformed into some magnificent glittering creature in a silver, sequined gown by Bob Mackie, who designs dresses for movie stars, and gauzy wings designed by God, and hover over the neighborhood while ordinary mortals like Farrah Spivack stared at me in awe, calling my name, pleading for my autograph from the sidewalk below.

I walked into the house. Oma sat asleep in the recliner, her jaw hanging slack, arms folded across her stomach. The skin on her hands was loose and translucent, the blue veins bulging in a way that made me shrink back. My own hands were smooth as porcelain, the veins only pale blue lines mapping the surface. Then I noticed it. The veins in my hands were the same configuration as Oma's. Exactly. I held my hand, fingers spread, close to hers. Exactly the same. "You are a lot like me." Oma's words boomed in my head. "The way I used to be." I fought the idea that her hands were ever as smooth as mine. I fought the possibility that someday I might be old and forgetful and that someone young and smooth and pretty as Meryl Streep would yell at me and call me "stupid."

Quietly, so as not to awaken her, I covered her with a knitted afghan. I covered the hands that were like mine and remembered the other Oma, the Madonna Oma, holding me on her lap. I leaned forward and kissed her face. "I still love you, Oma," I said.

On Friday night Henny and I just about died when Mother and Father said they were going to a wedding reception in Provo, an hour away, and we wouldn't be able to use the car.

"We need it," Henny demanded.

Father informed her that the tail did not wag the dog in this family.

"Can we take the truck?" Henny asked anxiously. "I have to go see *Amadeus,* this movie about Mozart. I have to write a report on it for Monday. It's downtown," she said.

"You can go tomorrow," Mother said.

"No, I can't. I have to go tonight. There's going to be a lecture after the movie. Some professor from the university is giving it. I have to be there." Henny was a terrific liar. I admired her quickness.

"Maybe you can go with Farrah," Mother suggested. "You can't both go, in any case, because somebody has to stay with Oma."

Henny groaned out loud. I groaned inwardly. Oma again. Always Oma.

While Henny and I were still washing dishes, Mother and Father left for Provo. Mother had helped Oma into her nightgown so Henny and I wouldn't have to do it. Oma sat at the kitchen table watching us. "You don't do the dishes as well as your mother," she observed icily.

"Thanks," Henny said.

I was disappointed about postponing our plan to decorate Woolley's car. I had secretly looked up his address. He lived in the same neighborhood as Maggie, on Macalester Street.

"We can start next week," I said to Henny, who was practically throwing dishes into the drainer.

"No, we'll go tonight. It's always going to be complicated," she said. "You can drive the truck."

"It has SEHLMEIER printed all over it," I said.

"So what? We'll park it a block away."

"What about Oma? We can't leave her alone," I reminded her.

"We'll take her with us." She dumped the dirty dishwater into the sink.

"We can't!" I protested. "She could yell or do something crazy."

"No, she won't." She opened the refrigerator door and pulled out a package of Twinkies. "You can feed her these while I do the toilet-papering." She grinned at me. "Good idea, no?"

"No."

The drive in the truck to Woolley's house took only about five minutes. Henny knew exactly where it was. I killed the engine only a couple of times, usually at stoplights. I wasn't real good with the clutch yet. Woolley's white VW was parked in front of his house under a street light.

"It's too dangerous with that light right there," I whispered to Henny as we cruised past the car.

"I'll work fast," said Henny. "Do you see him?" She was looking up at the house. I lowered my head. The windows of his house were all lit up, but I didn't see any people and said so.

"Let me out here," Henny said at the corner, a roll of toilet paper in her grasp. "Go around the block and stop about a half block from the house." She unraveled the toilet paper.

I parked far enough away to feel somewhat safe but at a distance near enough to watch Henny and Woolley's house. I crouched down behind the steering wheel.

"What are you doing?" Oma asked in Dutch. To anyone looking in, she was sitting alone in the cab of the truck.

"I'm hiding from Henny," I said. I pulled a Twinkie out of my coat pocket. "Would you like this?" She grabbed at it. "Eat it slowly," I said.

I was crunched down for several minutes and had to go to the bathroom something awful. One leg was asleep. After a while I poked my head up to see how Henny was doing. The car was already covered. Henny was tying long pieces of toilet paper to the antenna.

Then I saw him. Even from a distance, I knew it was him. He was standing at a side window at what seemed to be the kitchen sink. My mouth grew dry. If he turned his head, he would be able to see Henny. I wanted to honk, but that would get Woolley's attention too. It's finished, Henny, I thought. Come back now. Henny began wrapping the windshield wipers carefully. I dug in my pocket for the other Twinkie, my palms sticky. "Here, Oma," I said. I handed it to her. "Eat this and stay here," I commanded. "Stay!"

I opened the door softly and moved around the back of the truck and onto the sidewalk. I ran on tiptoes to a cluster of fir trees on the lawn next door to Woolley's house.

"Pssst," I called from the trees.

Henny looked down the street at the truck. Oma sat in it alone, eating a Twinkie.

"Here," I whispered as loud as I dared. "Come here. Over here in the trees." Her eyes searched in the direction of my voice. I stepped out briefly and frantically waved my arms. She rolled the remaining toilet paper under the car and ran over to me.

"He's standing right by the window. If he turned his head, he'd see you for sure," I whispered. I had to go to the bathroom so badly. Henny stepped out of the trees and hid behind the bushes that separated Woolley's yard from the one we were in.

"Oh my gosh," she said, and squealed.

"Let's go," I whispered. My bladder was bursting.

Henny led out to the sidewalk and then pushed me back into the trees. "There's a car coming." She motioned down to the truck. We waited for a moment, and then both of us leaned cautiously out of the trees. The car, its headlights shining in our direction, had stopped adjacent to Father's truck.

"Is it the police?" I whispered. Henny had her neck craned further than mine.

She pulled back. "Worse," she whispered. "It's Maggie and her parents."

I immediately wet my pants. "Oh jeez," I breathed.

"Shhh." She waved her hand at me.

I heard Maggie's voice. "She's all alone in here," she was saying to her parents.

"Mr. Sehlmeier must be close by," Dr. Connors said.

"She's not supposed to be alone," Maggie said. "She walks away sometimes."

"It's odd they left her in the truck by herself—in her night-gown, even." This was Mrs. Connors's voice.

"Daddy, let's go home and call the Sehlmeiers. It will only take a minute." She got back into the car.

"The girls are hiding in the trees!" Oma shouted suddenly. "They're in the trees!" She pointed in our direction. Henny and I crouched into what we hoped was an invisible heap. Then I realized that they couldn't understand Oma's Dutch.

235

She was speaking Dutch. My heart was beating like a budgie in a box.

The Connors' car made a U-turn back in the direction of Maggie's house.

"Let's go," ordered Henny. We scampered to the truck. It took three tries to start the engine. The seat of my pants was cold with urine.

"Go, go, go!" commanded Henny, nervously.

I let my foot off the clutch as carefully as I could, but the truck leaped and bumped forward like a bucking bronco.

"I'm going to tell your mother on you, about hiding in the bushes," Oma said as we were safely cruising down 8th South.

Henny and I burst into a loud, nervous guffaw.

"I am," said Oma. "You girls are nothing but hoodlums."

We both knew that by morning she would have forgotten all about it.

ZZZZZucchini

This essay was originally published in Network *magazine and is reprinted by permission.*

t's amazing how often the simple truth in a cause-and-effect relationship is missed by an otherwise intelligent observer. For instance, a few years ago, the makers of Postum and Sanka looked into their sales reports and found an amazing peak in the Utah area. Excited by how well their products were doing, they sent a research analyst with a well-cushioned expense account to Utah with instructions to put in six weeks' research time in order to discover why the Beehivers bought so much Postum and Sanka. I've always been curious as to what the analyst did for the five weeks and six days after finding the answer. Maybe fortune smiled, and the assignment came during ski season.

All this is by way of admitting that I have just recently come to understand why there are so many zucchini recipes in the world, and especially in this part of the world. Just the other day I saw a pamphlet claiming to offer one hundred recipes for zucchini. Now, we don't have green bean cookbooks, do we? Or *One Hundred Wonderful Ways with Watermelon?* We don't have recipes for radish bread, or celery cake, or cucumber

Elouise Bell is professor of English at Brigham Young University, where she has taught since 1963. A 1988 recipient of the Karl G. Maeser Distinguished Teaching Award, Sister Bell also lectures widely throughout the Intermountain region on subjects as diverse as poetry, creative writing, journal writing, and women's issues. In the summer of 1989, she toured five Western states doing dramatic monologue performances as nineteenth-century Mormon midwife Patty Bartlett Sessions. She has served on the General Board of the Young Women, has taught in all the auxiliaries, and has taught her ward's Gospel Doctrine class.

soup. (Yes, I believe there is such a thing, but no one carries on about it.)

You see, that was what stumped me — the way people carried on about the recipes. I have friends who greet the announcement of a new zucchini recipe with a great deal more excitement than they gave to the discovery of cold fusion. What am I saying? I know newborn babies who don't get the welcome a new zucchini recipe gets!

And, until recently, this reception always puzzled me. Did other people really find this nondescript little vegetable all that delicious that they were ever on the watch for new and better ways to serve it? Was it really such ambrosia to them that they couldn't get enough of the stuff and vied with each other for more and more imaginative concoctions? ("Look, Madge: zucchini waffles! Hey, Harriet — have you tried home-made zucchini ice cream yet? Listen, Louise, take my word for it: zucchini-oyster dip is terrific!")

In a way, it was like being color-blind. Apparently, everybody else in the world was seeing, or in this case tasting, something that just didn't come through to me. I didn't especially dislike the stuff, but I was not about to vote for it to replace chocolate chocolate-chip as the All-American dish.

And then, as I was sitting in my office one day, gazing pensively (or perhaps just groggily) out the window at majestic Timpanogos, the whole Truth came into my mind, all of one piece, as the Theory of Gravity came to Newton.

Eureka! There are so many zucchini recipes because . . . there is so much zucchini!

And why is there so much zucchini? Because apparently, zucchini crops never fail. I hear tales of people running out on frosty nights to cover up their tomatoes, tales of fruit farmers burning smudge pots to protect the apricots or peaches. I see people planting marigold borders around the vegetable garden to ward off the corn borer. But nobody seems to lose a wink of sleep over the zucchini: it seems to be the weed of the vegetable world.

I may have told you about my nongardening but devout Mormon friend who finally decided she should follow the counsel of Church leaders and put in a garden. She tore up a portion of her plush backyard, tilled and harrowed, and then put in four rows of zucchini. Four rows. Long ones. Of zucchini. When, in the fall, she began showing up at our meetings with dark circles under her eyes, I asked about it. Seems she had been getting very little sleep since harvest time. Instead, she was making nightly forays, out in ever-widening circles, to deposit bushel baskets of zucchini (with a few tomatoes on top as window dressing) on doorsteps of neighbors, ward members, stake members, neighbors of relatives, relatives of neighbors.... Last thing I heard, she was doing a midnight shuttle out Wendover way.

Why do people climb mountains? Because they are there, we're told. And why do people plant zucchini? Because it grows. And because it grows so abundantly, people in this region will sell the family water rights to find yet one more way to use the darn stuff up!

But I've heard of a group of women in east Salt Lake who may have licked the whole problem once and for all. It seems they have discovered a method of laminating zucchini. Do the possibilities ripple out before you? Zucchini coasters? Zucchini napkin rings? Zucchini playing cards? (That'd solve the face-card dilemma permanently for card-loving Mormons and bring an end to the nuisance of playing pinochle with Rook cards.) Zucchini earrings? Bracelets? Zucchini campaign buttons? Zucchini picture frames?

Why, we haven't even tapped the possibilities yet! Don't give up the zucchini!

Calling Myself a Poet

SUSAN HOWE

*I*t is amazing how many people write poetry. Individuals you would never suspect, of both sexes and all occupations—homemakers, accountants, attorneys, truck drivers, sales clerks, and athletes—record their thoughts, feelings, and experiences in verse form, but many then hide their poems in a drawer or a notebook and never show them to anyone else. Perhaps the reason for their reticence is that they feel their work isn't any good or isn't really "poetic"; after all, they haven't been educated in the writing of poetry.

It is unfortunate that so much poetry is hidden. If someone cares enough to write poetry, she must value it. Her writing must fulfill a need for creativity and self-expression. She must understand that the rhythms and sounds of words themselves can be a joy. And in some way she must know that her language is a deeply personal attribute and that in learning the possibilities of her language, she is learning about herself. Poetry is a pleasure, and the writing of poetry is a talent, and both talents and pleasures should be shared.

I do not mean to say that the quality of one's poems does not matter or that any poem is as good as any other. The best poets tell you that they have given their whole life to learning to write and that they still have much to learn. Someone who wants to improve as a poet must write and write and write—and read and read and read. But poems don't have to be perfect

Susan Howe is an assistant professor of English at Brigham Young University. She received her doctor of philosophy degree in English and creative writing from the University of Denver in 1989. She is the author of Burdens of Earth, *a play depicting Joseph Smith's experience in Liberty Jail. Her poems have appeared in* Shenandoah, Kansas Quarterly, Literary Review, *and* BYU Studies. *She is currently the poetry and fiction editor of* Exponent II *and won the 1988* Sunstone *D. K. and Bookie Brown Memorial Fiction Prize for short stories.*

to be worth sharing. They don't even have to be good. One of my best poetry teachers once said in class, "Anything worth doing is worth doing poorly." Until something is done poorly — and shared — it cannot be improved. A poem often becomes better when the poet revises it with the benefit of the suggestions of other readers. Understanding the value of feedback can take a lot of the fear out of offering your work to other people. And even if a particular poem doesn't turn out to be good, the next one might be extraordinary.

I found that one of the things that helped me have the courage and confidence to share my poetry was simply that I began to call myself a poet. The change in attitude that that naming brought about allowed me to do several things I had previously been unable to do. It stimulated me to write more (after all, a poet is someone who *writes poems*) and to read more (I needed to understand what other contemporary poets were doing). It gave me permission to share my work because I needed advice, comments, suggestions. It gave me the freedom to experiment, to try new and more difficult forms and techniques, even if I might fail. Most important, it gave me the right and even the responsibility to let other people read my poems, to try to use them in church callings and for special occasions, and finally, to have them published in ward newsletters, in Mormon periodicals, and eventually in literary journals.

So. Calling myself a poet, I want to share with other poets (*you!*) five of my poems and explain at least part of the process I went through when composing them. I hope that by doing this I might encourage you to write your own poetry or to share the poetry you have already written.

The Death of a Guppy

It was all,
all of it,
edible,
suspended
before my
round fish mouth,
open and
opening,
taking in
all of the
floating food.

I ate it,
ingested
it, inhaled
it, absorbed
all the food
through my mouth,
my round fish
mouth for food
and for gorg-
ing, gorging
on floating
fat morsels.

I ate, not
in hunger,
but because
all the food,
untasted,
was there at
my round mouth
that opened
and opened
to let it
all enter.

Now bloated
and heavy,
I lie on
my side and
I flounder
out, bulging,
weak in the
weight of all
edible,
burdening,
oppressive
food I have,
yes, eaten.

For me a poem is the result of an experience that works on my imagination till I have to try to record it, to find the language that will express it to myself and — hopefully — to others. "The Death of a Guppy" is about my developing a neurosis — the habit of nervous eating, which I learned from a roommate. Before living with her, I had been more prone to stop eating than to start when I was nervous, depressed, or under pressure. But nervous eating was my roommate's major means of coping with disappointment or disaster. In her worst moments she would use a kitchen chair to prop open the refrigerator door and then sit in front of the racks, letting the cold air chill her face so she could reach the food faster. She would buy frosted animal cookies or chocolate licorice and

eat the whole package in a sitting. I liked chocolate licorice
and frosted animal cookies myself—to say nothing of Mystic
Mints!—and soon I joined her, greedy to get some of the
goodies before they were gone. Thus I learned about food as
solace, companionship, and comfort. And—little by little—I
began to put on weight. I wrote this poem as a sort of therapeutic expression of my anxieties about what such eating might
lead to.

I don't remember coming up with the poem's metaphor—
the guppy that eats until it bloats and turns over on its side to
die. The metaphor seemed to surface as part of my neurosis.
While I was eating, I felt like a fish in a tank, not even hungry
but opening and closing its mouth anyway with mindless reg-
ularity. In the poem, I become that fish, lost in its own fishbowl
to the inexhaustible supply of food floating around it. For the
structure of the poem, I chose syllabics—three syllables per
line—because that rhythm seemed to me to approximate the
rhythm of a fish mouth opening and closing. Each line offers
just a little meaning, just a little food, but together they finally
lead to fatness—and my inevitable personal responsibility
for it.

To My Great-Great Grandmother,
Written on a Flight to Salt Lake City

Caught here, in an arc
Between the sea coast where your ocean
Voyage left you, and the mountains
Where you walked to make your home,
I see, at last, grandmother
Of my grandmother, you whom I have never known.

It is the light. Flying westward
In a craft of air holds darkness off.
It has been sunset for a long time.
Hours stretch in a thin curve, arcing
Back before flight, before the sun
Caught vapor trails across the sky.

You were the one who walked this route
Seven miles below, stone-cut

243

Feet seeking sand or turf to ease
The stiffness—and your arms, thin,
Spare from pulling all your earthly
Goods behind. You were almost lost

Within those miles where the earth curves
Away from me, but a stream of light
Burned—and when I looked away, there
You were. Perhaps because the legacy
You offered me finds symbol in the place
To which I journey as deliberately

As you walked. Or because at the end
Of every seven-, ten-, or fifteen-mile day,
You stood, just at sunset, squinting at the golden
Dust of those who walked ahead, sure that your journey
Would endure. You saw then the burning
Through which I see you. Sunlight where we both dwell.

Sometimes in the course of my everyday experience, a moment will come of insight, clarity, or understanding, when I know that what I am learning, thinking, and feeling should be a poem. Such a moment was the genesis of this poem. I was flying from Boston, where I was then living, to Utah, where I had been raised and where my pioneer ancestors had come. And suddenly it occurred to me that my great-great grandmother had followed exactly the same route I was taking across the continent. Having taken passage from England on a ship, she landed in Boston, traveled westward, eventually joined a handcart company, and walked to Utah. The ease of my passage through the sky made me think of what a different experience her trip had been and brought her imaginatively before me—the agony of the journey and the physical strain she must have endured. And most important, I imagined the faith and dedication that made such a journey possible, worthwhile. I tried to use the specifics of my experience—the curve of the earth so far below, the setting sun as we flew toward it—to create a poem that would help me know my great-great grandmother and would join me to her in some tangible, human way.

Freak Accident Claims Rhino

> The female rhino and her mate
> were playing in the open pen at
> the zoo when the female fell and
> caught her nose under a rock
> ledge and suffocated.

She blundered to her death, like a woman running
into her husband and his lover in a dusky restaurant
downtown. "David," the woman says, "I thought
you were going to Boulder." She stumbles
to their table and the truth and the air
escapes her so that she has to fall.
The rhino's name was Minette. In her brute
innocence she came out to lumber around
in the sun. But her bulk and her tiny brain
behind the one horn and pig eyes couldn't grasp
the possibilities—the crack, the ledge,
if it is there, is hidden and is always
a surprise. She bumped against her mate;
she stumbled about. Ignorant, she made the stupid
mistake and rock closed over her, wedging her down.
Extremity claimed her: how knowledge comes
To the body—heave and throe, heave and throe.

I often find poems in things I read, particularly in the newspaper, which is full of struggle. The title of this poem was the title of a small article I clipped from *The Daily Universe* several years ago, the epigraph to the poem the caption under a picture of a rhinoceros that had just died at the Hogle Zoo. I saved the clipping for years, and when I finally was ready to write the poem, I was also thinking of a friend—a sensitive, intelligent, compassionate woman. I had just learned, although she had not, that her husband was having an affair, and I was imagining the disillusionment she might have before her. (I also knew her husband, a man I considered arrogant, aggressive, and selfish, not sensitive or compassionate at all.) However farfetched it might seem, I perceived a relationship between the death of the rhinoceros and the pain this woman might soon feel. I tried to join the two incidents in my poem, which is, in its own way, a protest against marital infidelity and an expression of the pain women suffer because of it.

The Stolen Television Set

At the Seaview Retirement Home, the elderly
Came to believe life would come
Through the screen. Like light on waves,
It reflected their faces, blue-green in bright
Shifting patterns, reflected their eyes
As now and later passed. So in the night
When someone cut the cord, lifted the Wheel
Of Fortune, Jeopardy, and all the stars, stole
The show, they lost their umbilical, outside connection,
And light drained off, leaving them exposed like
Fetuses suspended in glass jars.
These elderly are facing the crisis.
They sit in the televisionless lounge, cough,
Stare at the harsh blank walls, shrivel
Slightly, wonder where they are now.
No one can say how they yearn
For the liquid, blue-green light only yesterday
Filling the room, flickering waves
Stretching and wobbling time, the steady
Throb of comfort like a dark, first home.

This is another poem that had its source in the news, this time, a story on the ten o'clock news about the theft of a television set from the lounge of a retirement home. The story made the air waves, I think, because the theft was a particularly mean-spirited gesture: the elderly residents of the retirement home had no surplus funds and no hope of obtaining another set. But what was interesting to me was the slight note of hysteria I heard in the voices of the residents who were interviewed for the news. It seemed to me that the television had become their connection to the world as well as their comfort, and that its loss threatened them with the exposure both of themselves and of the emptiness of their lives. I imagined the television lounge as womb-like, the set itself as the umbilical connection that kept these people alive, the liquid light of the screen as a comforting and enthralling fluid. It was disturbing to me how much my own television-viewing habits forced me to identify with these images. If my television set were stolen, I, too, would feel exposed.

Summer Days, A Painting by Georgia O'Keeffe

The skull of an elk is the center—parched, cleaned
Of flesh, whorls of brown and white space
Where eyes and nostrils used to be.
Three-pronged antlers curl out of the head
Like our best thoughts, pointing out
Where things are and what we do
And do not know. The skull floats in the vacant
Sky, a mirage as deep as life, antlers
Earth-brown, darker along the curves.

The skull broods over the living
Flowers, the rest of the mirage, bright desert
Blossoms of yellow, red, mauve. Sturdy and
Delicate, they pull us in like a heart
Beat, like love. Pull us as far as we can go.

Behind the skull and the flowers, the horizon
Marks the limits. Hot sandstone mountains
Range under a sea of clouds as here and there the sky
Pools. We want to see forever into
Summer, but boundaries hold.
Brought back to the center, we belong
To the mirage: Above a brief flowering
Heart, behind our own faces, we feel
Eyeless sockets and the silent, imminent skull.

One much-repeated tradition in poetry is to write a poem about another work of art—a musical composition, a sculpture, a painting. I have long admired Georgia O'Keeffe, the great American artist who died in 1986 at the age of ninety-eight. What most impressed me about her was her knowledge of herself and her faithfulness to her own vision. (I keep something she wrote on the bulletin board above my computer at home: "To create one's own world in any of the arts takes courage."[1])

Because I have such admiration for her, I wanted to try to write a poem about one of her paintings. I chose *Summer Days,* the painting she selected for the cover of a book of reproductions of her work, and I hope you can imagine the painting from its description in my poem. O'Keeffe had an amazing ability to create lines and forms that seem simple and yet curve in such provocative patterns that one's eye is drawn by their beauty. The colors she uses are rich and full, and they blend remarkably. There seems to be something particularly female about her colors, lines, and forms, even when her subject is, as it often is, bones from the desert. In the caption that appears opposite *Summer Days* in her book, she writes, "I have picked flowers where I found them. . . . When I found the beautiful white bones on the desert I picked them up and took them home too. I have used these things to say what is to me the wideness and wonder of the world as I live in it."[2] The painting *Summer Days* seems to me to be about life and how life is experienced more fully as it is juxtaposed with death. In my poem I attempted to capture the contrast I see in her painting between life and death, in order to connect us with the mortal, with what finally meets its limits.

I hope that knowing how these five poems of mine originated might help you to identify the poetry in your own life. A poem is deeply personal. It comes from being connected to one's own experiences and attempting to make sense of them. It is born of a specific event and the attempt to convey that event imaginatively. It is rooted in language and involves the poet in discovering her original language and thus herself. Call yourself a poet; find the part of you where poetry resides. The more sensitive you are to poetry, the more poems you will see — both in others and in yourself. Then share what you discover, both to make yourself grow and to enrich the other people in your life.

Notes

1. Georgia O'Keeffe, *Georgia O'Keeffe* (New York: Viking, 1976), text opposite plate 11.
2. Ibid., text opposite plate 1.

Women in Society

Women in every era have expressed themselves on a wide variety of topics, including the nature of their being and experience; but few expressions made it into print, fewer have been preserved to this day, and even fewer are taught side by side with the opinions of Aristotle, Aquinas, Locke, and the other great shapers of our culture.

— KATHLEEN BENNION BARRETT

Still Pending: Legal Justice for Women

KATHLEEN BENNION BARRETT

*N*utritionists tell us that we are what we eat. In the law, we are who we've been. That is, a person's legal status today is the result of centuries of legal history. In the common law system we inherited from England, judges interpret the law and reach decisions in new cases by relying on the reasoning in and results of older cases. This doctrine, called *stare decisis*, ensures stability in the law and protects the law from periodic fads or the whims of individual judges. The doctrine also ensures stability in deeply rooted assumptions and attitudes. Change occurs slowly and then only after the old ideas are repeatedly challenged and discussed. Thus, a short survey of some cases regarding the legal status of women reveals centuries-old attitudes about women that have survived into modern times.

Myra Bradwell passed the bar exam in Illinois, but the bar refused to admit her. In 1873, in *Bradwell v. Illinois*,[1] the United States Supreme Court upheld the State of Illinois, finding that because she was a married woman (she was married to a judge), Myra Bradwell was not competent to perform the duties required of an attorney. In an opinion that has become notorious, the Court declared: "The natural and proper timidity and delicacy which belongs to the female sex evidently unfits it for many of the occupations of civil life." The judge noted in passing that although some women are not married, they are exceptions, and the law can't be based on exceptions.

Kathleen Bennion Barrett received her juris doctor degree from the University of Utah College of Law in 1980. Active in many community organizations, she has served as chair of the Utah State Bar Committee on Needs of Women and Minorities and was president of Women Lawyers of Utah. She has three children and has been a choir director and teacher in her ward. Recently she moved to Tacoma, Washington, where she practices law with a private firm.

Question: What is the nature of the incapacity which over-
comes a woman upon marriage? What is it about marriage that
makes a woman incompetent?

In the case of *Minor v. Happersett,*[2] decided in 1875, Virginia
Minor tried to register to vote and sued the registrar when he
refused. The United States Supreme Court held that it was not
the "intent" of the framers of the Constitution to enfranchise
women. The Fourteenth Amendment, ratified just seven years
earlier, stated "no state shall make or enforce any law which
shall abridge the privileges or immunities of citizens of the
United States." Nevertheless, the Court upheld the Missouri
statute prohibiting women from voting. Citizenship does not
mean suffrage, said the Court. Women are citizens but a special
category of citizens whose inability to vote does not infringe
upon their rights as citizens or persons, and therefore the
Fourteenth Amendment does not apply.

Question: If being unable to vote doesn't infringe upon
one's rights as a citizen, what does?

In 1908, in *Muller v. Oregon,*[3] the United States Supreme
Court upheld an Oregon statute that limited the work day of
a woman in a laundry to ten hours. The laundry in question
promptly gave up hiring women. Other protective legislation
followed, which protected thousands of women out of their
only means of support.

Question: Are women unable to decide for themselves
whether to starve or to work in harsh circumstances? If the
circumstances are harsh for women, aren't they harsh for men,
too? Cannot women organize and press for limited working
hours, minimum wages, and safer work places, just as men do?

In the case of *Hoyt v. Florida,*[4] the Supreme Court of the
United States upheld the constitutionality of a Florida statute
that required jury duty of all citizens but excused all females
unless they individually registered as willing to serve. The Court
acknowledged that that meant very few women served on juries
but found it reasonable that Florida could conclude that "a
woman should be relieved from the civic duty of jury service
unless she herself determines that such service is consistent
with her own special responsibilities."

252

Question: What "special responsibilities"? No particular woman is discussed; do all women by reason of their gender, alone, have special responsibilities? Don't men have responsibilities that make jury duty inconvenient? What is so special about a woman's responsibilities that she should be excused from a basic duty of a citizen? And what about the defendant in this case, who was convicted of the second-degree murder of her husband, who had abused her; did she receive her right to a jury of peers impartially selected? This case was not decided a century ago; it was decided in 1961.

In *Brown v. Board of Education,*[5] decided in 1954, the United States Supreme Court held that separate was not equal and ordered the racial desegregation of the public schools. James Meredith was finally registered at the University of Mississippi in 1962. It was not until 1970, however, in *Kirstein v. Rector and Visitors of the University of Virginia,*[6] that a federal district court held that four women applicants were entitled to attend the University of Virginia, a state-supported university that previously had not admitted women. The court refused to extend its ruling beyond the facts of the case and would not order the State of Virginia to admit all applicants, without regard for gender, to all the state-supported schools.

Question: Is there something peculiar about a woman's mind that her education should be different from or separate from a man's?

In *General Electric Co. v. Gilbert,*[7] the United States Supreme Court decided in 1976 that an employer need not compensate women for maternity-related disabilities. The insurance plan in question covered absences due to sports injuries, attempted suicide, venereal disease, elective cosmetic surgery, disabilities incurred while committing a crime, prostate disease, circumcision, hair transplants and vasectomies, but not absences associated with pregnancy. The Supreme Court stated that the plan did not violate the equal protection clause of the Fourteenth Amendment because no one was excluded on the basis of gender: the insurance plan just excluded a certain physical condition from coverage.

Question: Is there something intrinsically less important

about women's physical problems? Was there an underlying assumption that women just don't belong in the work place and shouldn't be encouraged to have that choice? Was there an assumption that there was no need for coverage because a pregnant woman must be married to a man whose insurance would cover her?

In *Nelson v. Jacobsen,*[8] the Utah Supreme Court upheld the right of a husband to sue a third party for damages for the alienation of the affections of his wife. The dissenting opinion pointed out that this cause of action, formerly called seduction or abduction, was based on the old notion that a wife was a man's property and that the woman had no capacity to give her consent to her own seduction. The wife in this case had not been abducted but rather had voluntarily left her husband for another man after her husband had repeatedly subjected her to physical abuse. Nevertheless, the court held that the husband had the right to get damages from the other man for alienating her affections.

Question: Is marriage a voluntary, consensual association? Is a woman the property of her husband so that he should get damages if someone steals her? If a person is taken against her will, we call that kidnaping and prosecute it as a crime. Why wasn't this woman's capacity to consent recognized? This case is even more recent; it was decided in 1983.

Two disturbing questions are prompted by this review: what is the origin of the ideas about women on which these decisions were based, and why are these ideas so persistent?

American lawyers and judges did not invent the recurring themes of weakness of mind and body, the inability to consent, and the need to "protect" a woman from the duties and privileges of citizenship. These ideas come down to us from antiquity and pervade all of Western civilization. Aristotle described woman as a mutilated or incomplete man, a concept proposed in modern times by Freud. Aristotle taught that the male's contribution to conception was more valuable than the female's because he supplied the form and soul for the child whereas the female provided mere nutrients, an idea that persisted until the invention of the microscope. Females have less soul, Aristotle claimed, and are therefore less rational. "The male is by nature fitter for command than the female," he declared. Arguing by analogy from the family to society, Aristotle found women subordinate to men socially and politically.[9] It is hardly possible to overestimate the influence of Aristotle's writings on the development of Western thought.

Paul the apostle recorded disparaging words about marriage and women in his letters to the Corinthians. Although the Joseph Smith Translation explains that he was addressing missionaries when he advised that it was better not to marry, Paul's opinions about women are solidly within the Jewish tradition of the day, which held women to be subordinate and separate. "Let your women keep silence in the churches," wrote Paul, "and if they will learn anything, let them ask their husbands at home." (1 Corinthians 14:34–35.) These attitudes and assumptions, rather than the example of Christ, set the pattern for how women were viewed by the early Christian church.

Thomas Aquinas finished his *Summa Theologica* in 1272. His summation of theological doctrines relied heavily on philosophical tradition. Aquinas adopted Aristotle's idea that women are less rational than men and combined that idea with the early Judeo-Christian idea that women are subordinate to men because women were created for the benefit of men and are less morally discerning than men. These opinions became the official dogma of the Roman Catholic Church for centuries and thus had a pervasive influence on Western civilization, including the law.[10] The ecclesiastical courts developed a body of law called canon law, much of which influenced or was incorporated into the formation of both civil and common law in Europe and England.

These doctrines produced and supported the attitude that women — less rational and morally flawed — are a necessary evil, to be kept under control and in check for their own sakes and for the sake of society. Many thinkers concluded, with Paul, that the safest route was celibacy. For example, Francis Bacon, in 1612, wrote in his essay *Of Marriage and Single Life:* "He that hath wife and children hath given hostages to fortune; for they are impediments to great enterprises.... Certainly the best works, and of the greatest merit for the public, have proceeded from the unmarried or childless men."[11]

As feudalism waned and the power of parliaments grew, political philosophers searched for some alternative to the divine right of kings. Foremost among the social contract theorists was John Locke, who lived and wrote at the close of the seventeenth century. He proposed that although men have individual differences, those differences do not give one man the right to domination over another without his consent: each has a right to autonomy, or self-rule. The right to govern is derived from the consent of the governed; however, women, as a class, are naturally disabled because their reproductive functions make them weak and dependent. Therefore, rule "naturally falls to the man's share, as the abler and stronger."[12] Locke explained that men are therefore the natural owners of all property, with the sole right to dispose of the property and to determine heirs.

Jean Jacques Rousseau, whose radical ideas about universal citizenship for all men burst upon the political scene in the middle of the eighteenth century, went even further. He also found women to be naturally weak and dependent by their very nature, and he argued that this dependence precludes the autonomy of judgment that is necessary for the citizen to participate in society. "Woman is made to submit to man and to endure even injustice at his hands," he wrote. "You will never bring young lads to this: their feelings rise in revolt against injustice; nature has not fitted them to put up with it."[13] Rousseau, sometimes credited with inventing the modern romantic idea of the male-dominated nuclear family with children cared for by the constant devotion of a biological mother, drew a sharp distinction between the private life of the family and the public life of the citizen. The family was the sphere of appetite, emotion, and sentiment (the body), whereas the sphere of the citizen was that of reason, discourse, and judgment (the mind).[14] This view of women seems to rest not on the assumption that women are specifically well-suited to family life but rather that they are specifically unsuited for public life.

It was in this context that the Declaration of Independence

and the Constitution of the United States were written. Thomas Jefferson was especially influenced by the writings of John Locke. When the Founding Fathers wrote, "All men are created equal," they meant "all males." The Supreme Court, in *Minor v. Happersett*, was quite right in 1875 when it said that it was not the intent of the framers of the Constitution to enfranchise women.

All of these ideas about women came together in the common law doctrine of coverture, which emerged in England during the feudal era. This doctrine stated that upon marriage, a woman's legal existence was suspended and merged into her husband's identity. A married woman could not sue or be sued. If she was injured, her husband could sue for damages to his property, or if she injured someone else or even committed a crime, her husband could be held responsible because it was assumed that everything a wife did was under the direction of her husband. She could not own property and could not make a contract, because that would have required her individual consent, something that she was not thought capable of giving.[15] This doctrine did not mean that women could not work outside the home as well as in the home. It meant only that a woman could not enforce an employment contract against her employer. She could not vote, serve on juries, or hold public office, but that did not mean that women were not charged with crimes. It meant only that they were not tried by juries of their peers. It did not mean that they were excused from paying taxes. It meant that they paid taxes but were not entitled to the use of public institutions, such as schools, that were supported by taxes. As we have seen, aspects of the doctrine of coverture have persisted well into the twentieth century.

In a technical sense, the old doctrine of coverture is gone now. Women vote and hold public office, and in 1975, the Supreme Court finally ruled that women cannot be excluded from serving on juries.[16] In 1978, Congress overturned *General Electric v. Gilbert* by making it illegal to exclude benefits for maternity-related problems where other benefits are provided. Almost all the old "protective" legislation is gone, too. Instead, minimum wage laws and laws regulating safety conditions and

257

the length of the working day apply to all workers. Nevertheless, the old attitudes and assumptions about the nature of women that created and perpetuated the doctrine of coverture for so long stubbornly endure. Many still see women as naturally weak in judgment and intellect and more emotional, impulsive, frivolous, and less disciplined than men. These attitudes are reflected in the law.

Women are still not considered entirely capable of forming independent contracts when they are married. Although it is illegal in many contexts, a woman is frequently asked by a lending institution to obtain her husband's signature even though she qualifies for the loan independently. Our society still assumes that a woman exchanges her labor in the home for support and protection by her husband, but it is true now — as it has always been — that if he does not provide support and protection, she has no remedy except divorce. When a marriage ends in divorce, a woman is at a grave disadvantage economically, because it is then assumed that her labor has provided nothing of lasting value for the family unit. In contrast to her husband, she has no equity that she can take with her out of the marriage that is of any value in the marketplace to provide for herself or her children. This attitude toward traditional "women's work" is reflected in inadequate awards of alimony and child support and the subsequent failure to provide accessible means of enforcement. By ignoring or denigrating the economic value of a woman's work in the home, our society has fostered the feminization of poverty.

Many employers still assume that women are weak and emotional and consequently will have higher rates of absenteeism and will change jobs more frequently, although research has shown otherwise. Women continue to be hired primarily in low-paying, tedious jobs, and are paid less than 70 percent of what men are paid for comparable work. Laws against discrimination and sexual harassment on the job do exist but are very difficult to enforce. To complain is to risk losing your job.

In most states it is still true that a man cannot be prosecuted for raping or sexually assaulting his wife. Her consent is assumed, no matter what the act. Although some progress has been made, domestic violence is still not prosecuted with the same seriousness as identical acts of violence in other settings. Police do not respond, prosecutors do not charge, and judges do not sentence as they do when the context is not domestic. In civil suits, women generally receive less money for personal injury or wrongful death than do men. Lower values are awarded to women by the courts for the loss of arms, legs, or lives than for comparable injuries to men.

Finally, in the jurisprudence of the United States, the most telling reminder of the old devaluing attitudes toward women is the refusal of the United States Supreme Court to subject discriminatory classifications based on gender to "strict scrutiny," its highest level of examination. In *Frontiero v. Richardson*,[17] the Supreme Court reviewed several statutes affecting members of the uniformed services. Under these statutes, a serviceman could claim his wife as a "dependent" for the purpose of obtaining increased quarters allowance and medical and dental benefits. A servicewoman, however, could not claim her husband as a "dependent" unless she could prove that he was actually dependent upon her for more than one-half of his support. No proof of spousal dependency was required of a serviceman and, in fact, benefits were provided regardless of the actual dependency of the wife. Four of the justices reviewed the legal status of women in the United States:

"There can be no doubt that our Nation has had a long and unfortunate history of sex discrimination. Traditionally, such discrimination was rationalized by an attitude of 'romantic paternalism' which, in practical effect, put women, not on a pedestal, but in a cage. . . . Indeed, throughout much of the 19th century the position of women in our society was, in many respects, comparable to that of blacks under the pre-Civil War slave codes. Neither slaves nor women could hold office, serve on juries, or bring suit in their own names, and married women traditionally were denied the legal capacity to hold or convey property or to serve as legal guardians of their own children. And although blacks were guaranteed the right to vote in 1870, women were denied that right—which is itself 'preservative

259

of other basic civil and political rights' — until adoption of the Nineteenth Amendment half a century later."[18]

Although some progress has been made, the justices continued, "women still face pervasive, although at times more subtle, discrimination in our educational institutions, in the job market and, perhaps most conspicuously, in the political arena."[19] The justices concluded:

"With these considerations in mind, we can only conclude that classifications based upon sex, like classifications based upon race, alienage, or national origin, are inherently suspect, and must therefore be subjected to strict judicial scrutiny. Applying the analysis mandated by that stricter standard of review, it is clear that the statutory scheme now before us is constitutionally invalid."[20]

Four of the other five justices concurred in the conclusion that the statutes were unconstitutional,[21] but they were not willing to find gender a suspect classification. In a separate opinion, three of the justices noted the current Equal Rights Amendment debate and claimed that judicial action to declare gender a suspect classification would have indicated a lack of respect for the democratic, political process of ratification.

Thus, by one vote, the nine-member Court failed to find that classifications based on gender are suspect. Therefore, such classifications need not pass "strict scrutiny" by the Court, but rather are reviewed by a lower, less demanding standard. Neither then nor since has the Court explained why the legal status of women should be left to the political process while the legal status of racial or ethnic groups may be decided by the courts as a matter of law. If the legal status of black citizens had been left to the popular vote, black women and men might still be standing in the backs of buses.

Why are the old attitudes toward women so persistent and so resistant to change? Ideas that devalue women and the legal disabilities those ideas have created and perpetuated directly affect more than half of the population, but those ideas are not seriously discussed. Indeed, they are not even recognized by most people. In contrast, even though racial bias still pervades our society, racism is a topic addressed seriously by scholars and jurists. Legislators, educators, and employers know that they cannot treat racial issues lightly. Gender bias, however, is a topic still struggling for credibility. History books now teach our children about the infamous *Dred Scott* decision, in which the United States Supreme Court declared that even freed slaves were not citizens, and about the Thirteenth, Fourteenth and Fifteenth Amendments which enfranchised and protected the rights of the former slaves. But why aren't our children taught, as well, about the *Minor* decision and the Nineteenth Amendment, which, only sixty-nine years ago, gave the citizen's basic right—the right to vote—to our great-grandmothers?

A concept called "gate-keeping" suggests both why the old attitudes are so persistent and why we are so slow to recognize and discuss them. According to this theory, persons in decision-making positions in any institution or system set the definitions of what is excellent, noteworthy, valuable, and important.[22] The definitions naturally reflect the experiences and assumptions of the decision-makers. In our society, almost all the individuals who select the information and ideas that will pass through the "gates" to be incorporated into our culture are men. Because these decision makers—powerful legislators, judges, and corporate officers—assume that their male experiences and assumptions are valid for all of humanity, women's differing perceptions and experiences are automatically excluded as less important, less valid, and even trivial. Neither malice nor conspiracy is needed to bring about this result. For example, in the print industry and in other media, corporate officers decide what issues are important enough or interesting enough to discuss publicly. Because changes in our most significant legal concepts and traditions generally occur only after much public debate and discussion, these policy makers and opinion makers hold great power either to effect change or to maintain the status quo. How important or interesting are women's issues to these male gate-keepers?

It is not true that women through the ages have silently acquiesced in the disabling and demeaning ideas about them. Women in every era have expressed themselves on a wide variety of topics, including the nature of their being and experience; but few expressions made it into print, fewer have been preserved to this day, and even fewer are taught side by side with the opinions of Aristotle, Aquinas, Locke, and the other great shapers of our culture.[23] It has been claimed that the writings of women are not taught because their ideas are inferior or are less well expressed than those of men; but who set the criteria for importance and excellence? Textbooks, journals, and other instruments of media are compiled by gate-keepers who share the viewpoints and assumptions of Aristotle, Aquinas, and their descendants.

In our society the law continues to give less regard to women and their work and to show a lack of faith in the capacity of women to make wise choices. If the legal disabilities affecting women are to be removed from the law, women must be their own gate-keepers. If society's attitudes and the laws based on those attitudes are to change, women must decide for themselves what issues are important and what ideas need to be discussed and then have the courage to discuss them seriously. Women must seek out their foremothers—both recent and long past—and learn from them so that their experiences can be built upon rather than repeated. These foremothers have written on every topic that concerns women now: safety for our families, economic security, education, freedom of choice, equality before the law for women and for others, peace in our communities and in the world. Our courageous foremothers can give us and our daughters the dignity, pride, and strength we need to press for change. We don't need to be strident; we do need to be quick to identify archaic ideas about women when they occur in the law and be persistent in pointing them out. Only then will we find legal justice for women.

Notes

1. *Bradwell v. Illinois*, 83 U.S. 130 (1873).
2. *Minor v. Happersett*, 88 U.S. 162 (1875).
3. *Muller v. Oregon*, 208 U.S. 412 (1908).
4. *Hoyt v. Florida*, 368 U.S. 57 (1961).

5. *Brown v. Board of Education,* 344 U.S. 1 (1954).

6. *Kirstein v. Rector and Visitors of the University of Virginia,* 309 F. Supp. 184 (E.D. Va. 1970).

7. *General Electric Co., v. Gilbert,* 429 U.S. 125 (1976).

8. *Nelson v. Jacobsen,* 669 P. 2d 1207 (Ut. 1983).

9. Rosemary Agonito, *History of Ideas on Woman: A Source Book* (New York: Putnam, 1977), pp. 41–54.

10. Ibid., pp. 81–90.

11. Ibid., pp. 91–94.

12. Ibid., pp. 103–13.

13. Jean Jacques Rousseau, as quoted in Lynda Lange, "Rousseau: Women and the General Will" in *The Sexism of Social and Political Theory: Women and Reproduction from Plato to Nietzsche,* ed. Lorenne M.G. Clark and Lynda Lange (Toronto: University of Toronto Press, 1979), p. 49.

14. Ibid., p. 49, 50.

15. Frances Gies and Joseph Gies, *Women in the Middle Ages* (New York: Crowell, 1978).

16. *Taylor v. Louisiana,* 419 U.S. 522 (1975). In his dissent, Justice Rehnquist argued that there was no Constitutional basis for the decision because the systematic exclusion of women from juries does not necessarily result in biased or partial juries.

17. *Frontiero v. Richardson,* 411 U.S. 677 (1973).

18. Ibid., 684, 685 (citations and footnotes omitted).

19. Ibid., 686.

20. Ibid., 688.

21. Only one member of the Court, now Chief Justice Rehnquist, voted to uphold the constitutionality of the statutes.

22. Lynne Spender, *Intruders on the Rights of Men: Women's Unpublished Heritage* (London: Pandora Press, Routledge and Regan Paul, 1983), p. 5ff.

23. Katharine M. Rogers, *Feminism in Eighteenth-Century England* (Urbana, University of Illinois Press, 1982); see especially appendix of women writers 1660–1800.

Index